House of Fun

20 **Glorious** Years in Parliament

House of Fun

20 **Glorious** Years in Parliament

SIMON HOGGART

guardianbooks

Published by Guardian Books 2012

2 4 6 8 10 9 7 5 3 1

First published in Great Britain in 2012 by
Guardian Books
Kings Place, 90 York Way
London N1 9GU

www.guardianbooks.co.uk

A CIP catalogue record for this book is
available from the British Library

ISBN 978-0852-65381-4

Text design by seagulls.net
Cover illustration by Steve Bell
Cover design by Two Associates
Printed and bound in Great Britain by CPI Group (UK) Ltd,
Croydon CR0 4YY

Mixed Sources
Product group from well-managed
forests and other controlled sources
www.fsc.org Cert no. TT-COC-2139
© 1996 Forest Stewardship Council
FSC

Guardian Books supports The Forest Stewardship Council (FSC),
the leading international forest certification organisation.
All our titles that are printed on Greenpeace approved
FSC certified paper carry the FSC logo.

Contents

Introduction

As the title of this book implies, sketchwriting is huge fun and for some mysterious reason it counts as work, so you get paid for it too. I've actually been doing it for more than 20 years – as a young political correspondent I sometimes filled in for the late Norman Shrapnel, whose elegant and pointed essays are still remembered with huge affection by older Guardian readers. In those days, back in the mid-1970s, I would knock off a quick sketch of prime minister's questions – twice a week then, but only 15 minutes a time – then do my real job of digging up political news, which often involved staying in the House until 2am or so, much the best time to get MPs, ministers and so forth to reveal their secrets.

A 5am session in the Tory whips' office, along with half a dozen MPs and a similar number of hacks, ended when blue Curaçao was the only fluid left in the drinks cabinet. I gave up smoking as soon as I woke up, which was some time the following afternoon, feeling that death would be preferable to the way I felt then.

Often I would hang around Annie's Bar, then the exchange and mart for political information, where journalists drank on equal terms with MPs. It was a strange place, sometimes similar to the bar in Star Wars, full of grotesques. I recall a terminally drunk Labour whip telling a dirty joke, then telling it again immediately afterwards, at which he fell on the bar, fast asleep. There was the second most boring man in the world (we felt that to be the most boring man in the world would be, in its way, quite interesting). He invariably arrived brandishing some extraordinarily dull document, and insisted that we read it all. Willie Whitelaw, by now deputy prime minister, would occasionally turn up. We would inquire what he wanted to drink, and he would reply, 'A little whisky, please.' Asked if that meant a small whisky, he would reply, 'No, when I say a little whisky, I mean a large whisky. Thank you very much!' Ten minutes later he would buy large scotches for everyone in the bar. We were a happy band in Annie's – drunk but happy. And we didn't miss deadlines either. Well, not very often.

In 1982 I left the Guardian to join the Observer. One of my first jobs there was sketching the only Saturday debate to take place in the Commons in living memory, just after Argentina had invaded the Falklands. Then in 1993 the Guardian bought the Observer and I was transferred back to my old paper. The sketchwriter's job was vacant at the time; I applied for it and got it against, it must be said, no competition.

Most of the sketches in this book have appeared in earlier collections, so if you have any of those there will be some repetitions, except for pieces that have appeared since the summer of 2011. I have tried to balance the historic events – general elections, campaigns for party leader, the Iraq war, the creation of the coalition – with the more trivial matters which sometimes occupy the time of parliamentarians: Norman St John-Stevas complaining about the House of Lords Christmas card, a junior minister sailing smoothly along until he inserted the extraneous letter N into a condemnation of defence cuts. And some which fall in between, such as the House of Lords contemplating the hunting bill, or Gordon Brown's desperate attempts to resemble a normal human being.

Parliament has not had a good press lately, what with the expenses scandal, and a general perception that it actually doesn't matter very much any more. Governments decide what they want to do then dragoon the foot soldiers to follow their banners. But there is a story I have told before, and which I think sums up the whole business. It involves a very bad word, but since I have told the story – unbowdlerised – at the tennis club in Frinton-on-Sea, ground zero for British gentility, and nobody walked out, I think I can risk it here.

Bill Stone was a northern Labour MP for a mining seat. He had miner's lung, and spent his days drinking pints of Federation ale in the Strangers' Bar. He almost never spoke in the Commons, or tabled questions, but he always voted as he was bidden. Once he was earwigging a conversation at the bar. Someone said, referring to the Commons, 'The trouble with this place is that it's full of *cunts!*'

Bill took a swig of his beer, put the glass down, wiped the froth from his lip and said, 'They's plenty of cunts in t'country. And they deserve some representation.'

I cannot imagine a better definition of a parliamentary democracy.

John Major

21 September 1993

The political year begins in September, with the anti-climax that is the Liberal Democrat conference. Actually, I've always been rather fond of the party. Deprived of power for so long, they became rather like lonely schoolboys sitting in their bedrooms, working out how they would rule an imaginary nation, in this case Britain. The awful reality is that many of their best-loved policies, such as the campaign against 'secondary drinking', have had to be abandoned thanks to the often gruesome realities of coalition.

Little changes at the Liberal conference except, periodically, the name of the party. They assembled at Torquay, all those half-remembered bald men with beards and ecologically sound shoes, the herbivorous women offering passers-by leaflets on site value rating and all those gentle middle-class people laughing hilariously at unfunny jokes. Custom cannot stale their infinite sameness. And all those Liberal motions, describing in anally retentive detail how to save rural bus services or the British economy, every one partitioned into several sections so they could be voted on through exhaustive ballots. It was only the presence of Lord Jenkins that prevented the Lib Dems from being the political equivalent of a train spotters' convention.

The most controversial debate of the day was on ethnic minorities, a source of considerable embarrassment to the party since the allegations of racism among the Liberals who run Tower Hamlets. Finding racism in the Lib Dems clearly came as a gruesome surprise to the delegates, like finding an anaconda in your anorak.

So of course the debate wasn't actually controversial at all. The only argument was about who could be even less racist than the last speaker. They arrived at the podium quivering with anti-racism. The Lib Dems are so anti-racist that, as the main speaker, Ramesh Dewan, pointed out, white people were welcome – even encouraged – to join the party's ethnic minorities group. This was fortunate, since as one looked around the hall it was pretty obvious that this would otherwise be a very small organisation.

The best speech of the day was from Charles Kennedy, who, like Lord Jenkins, used to be a member of the SDP, a party you may vaguely remember. Behind him was a young woman who was signing for the deaf. But of course Roy was signing too, with a selection of his own favourite gestures.

Mr Kennedy attacked the Labour party and Lord Jenkins started strangling someone. Mr Kennedy moved on to Norman Lamont and Lord Jenkins began washing his hands. John Major was roundly scorned and Mr Jenkins prepared to play the piano. Mr Kennedy was vituperative about the rot in British politics and Lord Jenkins started chopping wood.

The real signer got tired and paused, concentrating all attention on Lord Jenkins. How one yearned to see the famous cupped scooping motion with which he enlivened so many of his fine speeches. All it needed was for Mr Kennedy to announce: 'Fellow Liberals, we must replace burnt-out light bulbs!' Or even, 'We must caress the bosoms of young women!'

28 September 1993

The Labour party, like so many idealistic organisations, has always been ruthless in its desire to quash dissent. It's a party in which anyone can believe or say what they like, provided it has been approved by the leadership.

The room was packed, waiting for what everyone really knew already. It had been predicted for months but the shock – that jolting sense of an era finishing – was no less for that. Comedienne Hattie Hayward, in the Women Only revue at the conference, told a heterosexist joke based on the idea that a woman might actually enjoy sleeping with a man. It was a very funny joke which I sadly cannot repeat here, except to say that it involved a Greek waiter and a box of Tampax. But it indicated a huge seismic shift. The audience roared.

Marjorie Mowlam, the frontbencher who had organised the evening, beamed with relief. 'That could never have happened 10 years ago,' she said. 'The party really has changed.'

Oh, and Tony Benn lost his seat on the national executive after 34 years. Regrettably I have to report that this caused glee among most other Labour MPs. I have often wondered why this courteous, faintly dotty old gentleman causes such hatred among his colleagues, and conclude that it is his good nature which riles them most – it's like being given a stern moral lecture by M. Hulot while he simultaneously picks your pocket.

Mr Benn took his defeat with good humour and grace, waving to the applause. An MP near me said he wanted to spit.

The Labour party these days really is different. It is painfully earnest. It spends endless hours working on strategy with high-powered advisers. Even people who have no special interest in the subject admire it as a plucky British battler, though there the resemblance ends.

You can see how much the conference has changed. These days MPs are allowed to speak without being booed. There were even attacks on the Conservatives, which not long ago would have been thought an irrelevant frivolity by many of the comrades.

There were some reminders of the past. I heard the word 'socialism' at least twice. A woman in the health debate declared 'Reality is not working!', a slogan which served the hard left well for many years.

But the success of the new regime was clear from the start, with the vote on smoking in the hall. This was ruthlessly determined on the principles of OMOV, with no block vote. The chairman then decreed, 'I don't think we'll bother with those against.' For one moment Mr Smith must have thought he had died and gone to party leaders' paradise.

6 October 1993

The Tory conference that year was remarkable for two events. Margaret Thatcher's memoirs had been leaked to the Daily Mirror, and the Sun published a list of four women who, allegedly, had been enamoured of the transport minister, Steven Norris.

Lady Thatcher arrived in Blackpool like a character from Oscar Wilde. Not Lady Bracknell – far too mild mannered – but Gwendoline, who also wrote memoirs in order to have something sensational to read on the train.

Yesterday the hunt was on for the source of the leaks which revealed her contempt for John Major. Clearly it must be someone with intimate knowledge of the memoirs, someone who covertly despises Major and wanted this to be known.

One imagines the phone ringing in the Daily Mirror office. A curiously muffled voice comes on the line. 'Now pin back yer lugholes and cop this, me old china, me old mate!'

'Ah, good morning Lady Thatcher.'

Mr Major is coming to resemble another well-loved British character who has taken enough punishment and ought to consider retirement. Like Frank Bruno, he could go into pantomime. One could catch him in, say, Harrogate, along with other half-remembered figures such as Billy Dainty, Helen Shapiro and 'John Major as Buttons'.

But the saddest figure on the platform yesterday was Steven Norris, the transport minister. The Sun had pictures of no fewer than four of his mistresses on its front page yesterday. His head must whirl with double meanings – underpasses and box junctions, contraflows and gyratory systems. Mr Norris looked steeped in misery throughout. One longed for him to hear from a cheerful cockney clippie: 'Never mind dear, room for one more on top.'

9 October 1993

Poor John Major was evidently a decent man who gave the appearance of being constantly out of his depth as prime minister. Twenty years later, as an ex-prime minister, he appeared to be poised, reflective, experienced and generous, whereas Gordon Brown, who also found the premiership harder than he had expected, was grumpy and vengeful. In the speech described here, Major used a phrase which would come back to plague him. 'Back to basics' was supposed to refer to timeless Conservative values, on education and justice, for example. But one of Major's aides, Tim Collins, briefed the press that it also referred to moral values, so giving the papers limitless opportunity to investigate the private lives of Tory MPs.

Later Mr Major had the intense embarrassment of hearing Edwina Currie describe an affair they had had, before he became prime minister. This caused astonishment among Tory MPs who asked themselves two questions: 'What, him?' and 'With her?'

The event was the result of an accident. The co-author (not the ghost) of Major's memoirs was Julian Glover. Between them they wrote far more than the publishers could print, so they were asked for massive cuts, which Glover obligingly made. The excisions included a kindly reference to Edwina and her travails over the safety of eggs. When she saw that she was not even mentioned in the index, she was furious and made her revelation. It didn't hurt that she was publishing her own memoirs at the time, though these did not name Major as her lover.

John Major's speech yesterday at least did the business. It wasn't a great speech – it never is – but it was rousingly adequate, even thrillingly average. The jokes are almost funny, the tone almost assured, the peroration almost moving.

Afterwards a colleague said to me, 'It's not every day you learn the solution to one of life's *great* mysteries: how do horses get up?' But that was unfair. It was better than that. At the risk of damning with faint praise, it may have been the best speech he has ever made.

Of course the delegates were desperate to applaud him after the past year. They would have cheered him crazily even if he had read a John Prescott speech.

As it happens the Conservatives have now seized on Mr Prescott as the official socialist bogeyman, replacing Tony Benn, who you may be sure will soon re-emerge as a symbol of the decency now lost by the Labour party. In fact, just before the prime minister began, they ran a jokey video of Mr Prescott's celebrated speech in Brighton last week, backwards. And yes, you still knew exactly what he was talking about.

Major has the opposite problem. The speech is coherent and grammatical, the individual words make sense, but at the end you're still not clear what it was all about.

But the biggest cheers were for the greatest truisms. Lady Thatcher is alleged to say in her memoirs that Major is 'frightened by platitudes'. No he isn't. He loves them. They inspire him. He pronounces them with the wondering certainty of someone who has just learned the secret of life from a Tibetan monk with three eyes.

'Crime cannot be excused and, I give you my word' – the voice drops confidentially – 'never will be.' What does this mean? Did anyone imagine that the Tories were going to send ramraiders on Club 18-30 holidays? As platitudes go, this is just duck-billed.

Of course, Major was facing the problem which all speakers have had to cope with this week: how is it that the country is in such a mess when our lot have been running it for the past decade and a half? Major had two different means of coping with this difficulty. Firstly he blamed the 60s – that devil's decade when fashionable orthodoxies destroyed schools, family life and respect for law and order. Abbie Hoffman or some other bearded American once said that if you could remember the 60s you couldn't have been there. That, for John Major, is their great attraction. He wasn't there and so can't be blamed.

The second technique is to say that after 14 years of Tory misrule, it's time for a change. He talks about crime as if they had just inherited the problem from the last bunch of incompetents who were in office, which, of course, is exactly what happened. The same went for education, the Health Service and the budget deficit. The Tories, he promised, were going to clean up the mess left to them by the Conservative party. After the speech some MPs were even thinking the unthinkable: that he might be leader at the same time next year.

So, as the delegates trooped home, they were at last united in unstinting praise for the man whose performance has dominated the party and the headlines all week, Transport Minister Steven Norris. As one of his colleagues said to me, 'To have one mistress is a peccadillo. To have two is a scandal. But to have five is a matter for the profoundest admiration.'

I had long held my own theory about Major's curious use of language:

I have come up with radical new theory, which occurred to me while listening to Major's speech last weekend. A propos unemployment he declared, puzzlingly, 'Fine words butter no parsnips!' Later in his text he was to say 'Drat it!', though he changed this to 'Damn it!'

These antiquated proverbs and phrases will be familiar to anyone who has spent time in any of our former colonies. The British Council library always contains, along with rows of Dickens and Shakespeare, masses of well-thumbed detective stories plus dusty books with titles such as Speak English the English Way. These elderly works generally contain lines like, 'If you wish to tell your British friend that what you do is more important than what you say, tell him: "Fine words butter no parsnips." Someone who is very angry indeed may exclaim "Drat it!"'

My theory is that our prime minister is actually Nigerian. According to his biographies he went to Nigeria in 1966 to work in the northern town of Jos. I surmise that he was actually born and raised there. The nearest British Council library was in Kaduna, 100 miles away over the mountains – nothing to a barefoot boy with a yearning for knowledge. Here, through the stilted prose of Agatha Christie, he would have learned his famous circumlocutions, such as 'plied his trade in the environs of' for 'worked near'.

This would account for the surprising vagueness about his early life: where he actually lived, how many O-levels he gained, the variable family surname. It would also explain his pronunciation of 'wunt' for 'want' – unknown in Brixton but, I gather, frequent among the Hausa people.

It might be pointed out that for a person of African ethnic origin, Mr Major is the wrong colour. To which I reply, look at Michael Jackson.

18 January 1994

It is a fond myth in Britain that, while our politics may be venal, greedy and mendacious, they are not actually corrupt. For example, there is no gerrymandering. Think again.

It was exactly 4.29pm yesterday when Ian Lang, the Scottish Secretary, said it. At the end of a long, much-interrupted and necessarily defensive speech about Scottish local government, he decided to close with a stirring peroration – a battle cry for his backbenchers to stitch into their banners, something to put a bit of lead in their cabers.

'We want', he declared, 'to get back to basics!'

There was a brief silence, perhaps a nanosecond (defined as the period between the light turning green and the idiot in the Escort GTi behind you blowing his horn) while the Labour benches absorbed this. Then they erupted in a single, gigantic, gleeful, delirious shout. The rafters shook and the welkin rang. It was, for Labour, a moment of pure distilled joy.

Labour's pleasure at the mistake was heightened by the fact that the bill in question goes back to the basics of the 18th century. It is probably the most ambitious piece of gerrymandering attempted by a British government since the Reform Act.

It appears to have an ecological function, being designed to preserve the few remaining examples of a breed as seriously threatened as the golden eagle.

The bill replaces the old two-tier system with a single layer of 28 new councils. When these are likely to be Labour controlled they are vast and sprawling; where there is a small breeding colony of Tories they are small, delicately preserved and carefully defined.

Take West Renfrew – population 265,000 – which is to be separated from Tory East Renfrew, which has but 88,000 citizens. Whereas the boundaries of some new councils are described in a single phrase, East Renfrew requires some 49 lines. It's worth quoting at length because it is a rare chance to see what that fabled creature, the gerrymander, actually looks like close up:

> ... *including those parts of polling districts PS28 in Paisley Abercorn and PS14 (in Strathclyde electoral division 77 (Paisley Central)) lying to the south and east of a line beginning on the White Cart water and running southwards along the Oldbar Burn to the eastern cartilages [cartilages are grounds, not what foot-ballers tear] of Nos 39-41 Ben More Drive... passing to the east of the property known as The Bungalow, then south-westwards and westwards along the eastern and southern perimeter of Hawkhead House Farm to No 43 Ben Lui Drive, Nos 52 to 50 Ben Wyvis Drive ... then crossing the dismantled railway line ... along the road to its junction with the path leading to Glenapp Road...*

The effect of this absurd list is richly comic, which is why Mr George Robertson, the shadow Scottish secretary, was able to suggest that Mr Lang 'should ring up the inhabitants of numbers 52 and 50 Ben Wyvis Drive to make sure they vote the right way, so that if necessary the appropriate amendment can be made'.

1 February 1994

At this stage, we did not know about Edwina Currie's exciting love life. We did know that she had published a novel (later revealed to be the story of her relationship with John Major) and that the cover of this book had been embellished with the House of Commons portcullis logo.

The Speaker, Betty Boothroyd, rose to address parliament on a matter of grave importance. It concerned the emblem of the House of Commons, which might look like an exploding waffle iron to you but, in fact, is a crown portcullis. The symbol embodies the dignity of parliament and perhaps of democracy itself, which is why Ms Boothroyd was so cross to see it displayed on the cover of Edwina Currie's naughty novel about the cut and thrust of politics, A Parliamentary Affair.

The sacred symbol – parliament's equivalent of Mickey Mouse's ears – is depicted on the heel of a stocking which encases a long female leg. The Speaker was so angry that the other day, I am told, she privately gave Mrs Currie a heated telling-off.

But yesterday Edwina was not to be seen. 'Where is she?' MPs growled. As it happens she was signing books in Birmingham, but those who have read her oeuvre tend to be suspicious of what she might be up to when she is not in view (though I should point out that Commons offices have no locks, which must have given her characters an extra frisson).

I rushed out to buy a copy but the booksellers told me that it is so popular they cannot obtain supplies. So I did what any hack worth his salt would do and made it up:

Edwina gazed at herself in the mirror, admiring the pert nose and the moist, red receptive mouth. 'Not bad for 47,' she thought, 'Not bad at all.' It was lucky the camera adored her because she loved publicity – needed it, could never get enough of it. And she did not mind who gave it to her, just as long as they kept it coming, strong and hard.

The phone rang. A seductive, lilting voice was on the other end.

'It's Colwyn Bay Hospital Radio here, Mrs Currie. We wondered whether you could take part in a three-minute discussion...'

Her lips parted and her voice was husky, distant, barely in control. 'Yes, yes, yes!' she managed to say. 'How will you get here?' the man asked. 'You will have to take me, take me!' she cried, as rhythmic, uncontrollable emotions pulsed through her arching body.

Then she balanced the smallest strawberry gently on his very bobbit tip where it wobbled dangerously. After a thoughtful pause, she covered it with a whirl of cream. 'I have always wanted to eat you, Roger Dickson,' she said.

'Elaine, careful with your teeth – I cannot get a replacement,' he said.

Oops – sorry: a colleague tells me that the last two paragraphs are actually from the book, except that Edwina does not use the word 'bobbit'.

Ms Boothroyd did not mention the book, though she left no doubt about who she meant. 'It is one of the principal duties of the Speaker to uphold the dignity of the House. I hope I have made it abundantly clear the importance I attach to this matter.'

No doubt Edwina, whose career in the Commons is now wobbling as dangerously as her hero's strawberry, will be quietly delighted by this publicity, insofar as she is quietly delighted by anything.

8 March 1994

Like cartoonists, we sketchwriters have to invent characteristics for our subjects. Just as Steve Bell always draws Tony Blair with one mad staring eye, and David Cameron with a condom on his head, we need to highlight and, if necessary, exaggerate the physical appearance and the foibles of those we write about. And we need to create new people to populate our columns. We don't actually invent them; we simply bring them to public attention.

One of the first backbench MPs I spotted was Michael Fabricant, who sat for mid-Staffordshire, now Lichfield. He hated my attentions and would demand to know how I could be stopped. Then in 1997, he held his seat against the Labour landslide by just 238 votes, which I persuaded him was the total number of Guardian readers in Lichfield. They had all voted for him, I claimed, in order to keep me writing about him. He seemed to accept this, and we have been good friends ever since. Here is the first piece in which I wrote about him.

My attention was riveted by Michael Fabricant's hair. Mr Fabricant is the Conservative MP for Mid-Staffs and his hair creates something of metaphysical problem (rather like the old conundrum: is the statement 'this is a lie' itself a lie?). His hair looks so peculiar that everyone assumes that it is a wig. On the other hand, nobody would conceivably buy a wig which looked like that.

It is strawberry blonde and has a shiny plastic sheen. The lower part stands off the face, which implies that it is indeed a syrup (lovable cockney rhyming slang: syrup of figs) yet, as one views it from above, it appears to be firmly anchored to the scalp. Overall it looks as if My Little Pony had been in a terrible accident and its tail had been draped over Mr Fabricant's head.

The owner of the glistening tresses was in an agitated state yesterday afternoon. He had a question for Mr Waldegrave, the open government minister. Mr Waldegrave is the nominated fall guy, all ready to resign when the Scott Inquiry reports a turkey being slimmed for Christmas. This will be easy because, unlike most of his cabinet colleagues, he is a man of honour and has no apparent wish to become prime minister.

As Mr Waldegrave answered earlier questions his impending fate seemed to make him poised and confident. Mr Fabricant tapped his feet nervously. He kept consulting notes scrawled on his order paper. Now and again he looked anxiously at the Speaker, fearful that she might not realise he was there.

Finally Mr Fabricant rose. Was not Megalab (this is some government wheeze to make children more interested in science and technology) a *marvellous* idea? Wasn't it wonderful, he inquired, that the BBC and the newspapers were promoting it to young people and children?

He sat down, exhausted. Now and again he stiffened his back, as if to let his body recover from the tension. He crossed and uncrossed his legs and looked round the Chamber as if to drink in the triumph of his daring question.

My guess is that his father, Isaac, was originally called Oldcastle. Then one day he invented a new miracle hair-substitute – possibly a coal-tar byproduct. The only way it could be fixed was by sewing it into the skull. What better way to demonstrate the new textile, now named Miracle Fabricant, than by sewing it on to his son and changing his name as the ultimate advertising gimmick? 'No, no, Isaac, you cannot do this to your own son!' pleaded Mrs Oldcastle, but in vain. The boy's head was implanted. But the new fibre was a terrible disappointment and made only one sale: to Michael Heseltine.

21 June 1994

Now and again, we take ourselves down the corridor to what is referred to in the Commons as 'the other place' and in some quarters as 'the Upper House'. There is a great charm to the Lords. Because – apart from a few frontbenchers – they have no need to smarm up to their party leaderships, they often speak more candidly, engagingly and sometimes more ludicrously than anyone in the Commons.

Debates on sex tend to be worthy and responsible, so I went to the Lords yesterday with something to read – the official German guide to the Chamber. As I took my place overlooking the *Sitzungssaal*, the *Tagesordnung* were about to begin. The topic was the age of consent for homosexuals.

Lord McIntosh (Lab) began with calm sort of speech saying the Lords would be well advised to agree with the Commons and lower the age to 18. At one point he made a sly reference to Tory peers who had been to public schools, with the faint implication that the playing fields of Eton resembled the Dionysian bath houses of San Francisco.

Lords' *Sitzungsprotokolle* prevents barracking but the almost imperceptible rumblings, like thunder beyond distant mountains, were the equivalent of a full-scale Commons shouting match.

Next was Lord Simon of Glaisdale, once a Conservative minister, now a crossbencher. I was delighted to learn that cross benches in German is *Querbanke*. I flipped to the French guide to check the Woolsack, It is, disappointingly, *Sac de Laine* and not *pouffe*. From the Queer Banks, Lord Simon contrived to somehow suggest that taking the age of consent to below 18 would be harmful to the feminist cause.

The Archbishop of York gave a first-rate impression of the Rev Flannel. The churches faced an agonising issue. He would not endorse the hatred and contempt felt for homosexuals. 'But we cannot say that homosexuals and heterosexuals are in all respects equivalent, because they are not.'

He concluded with a masterpiece of even-handedness: the age of 18 – two years higher than for heterosexuals – was right 'because it says something about society's acceptance of heterosexuality as the norm'. By this time the Archbish was so firmly impaled on the fence he was in danger of perforating himself along his own *Sitzungsplatz*. Next came remarks by the Earl of Arundel, the Earl of Surrey, Baron Beaumont, Baron Maltravers, Baron FitzAlan, Baron Clun, Baron Oswaldestre, and Baron Howard of Glossop.

This could have taken ages but since they were all the same man – the Duke of Norfolk – and since he spoke for only 90 seconds it was over very quickly. Homosexual acts were morally wrong and this was made clear in the Bible. Kinsey had claimed that 10 per cent of men were homosexual, but the true figure in this country was 0.9 per cent. The homosexual lifestyle reduced life expectancy from 75 years to 42. Then they all sat down.

Lord Skidelsky thought that a Roman Catholic like the Duke ought to understand about unfair discrimination, though it

21

must be long time since gangs of hooligans went out Duke of Norfolk-bashing.

Lord Longford rose. 'As my dear old friend Rowse said, the trouble with me is that I lack homosexual experience... I wonder how many other noble lords lack homosexual experience? I do not see many hands going up. I regard all human beings as equal in the sight of God but I cannot say I am sorry that none of my children, my grandchildren or my great-grandchildren, so far as I can see, are homosexuals. It's a terrible handicap in life...'

Packenham burbled gently onward as we floated down to the sea, borne upon his stream of consciousness.

Then things got nastier. Lord Ashbourne said that homosexuality was 'unnatural and a perversion and, according to the Book of Leviticus, an abomination unto the Lord'. And sat down.

The trouble with quoting the Book of Leviticus, is that it does cast its net rather wide. For example, the same text forbids us from eating lamb or beef fat, and recommends that we sacrifice turtle doves as a means of expiating our sins. Even Mr Howard, in his quest to go back to basics, has not yet recommended: 'Let 'em sacrifice a few turtle doves! That'll teach these youngsters what's what!'

In the end, some 71 peers went into the *Abstimmungswandelgang*, or division lobby, to vote for the age of 16. But 245 voted against. The *Querbanke* were defeated. (Later, after a speech by Earl Ferrers, who has said privately that he would like to see the gay age of consent raised to 94, but who supported the government view that 18 would have to do, the peers did vote to join the Commons and settle on 18.)

22 July 1994

John Smith, leader of the Labour party, died unexpectedly in 1994, and was greatly missed on all sides. I was especially fond of him, following a sleeper trip down from Glasgow one night in which he, and a Scottish Nationalist MP, joined me in my cabin for a serious whisky-drinking session that didn't end till Rugby. What made it especially amusing was the flow of malicious gossip about other Scottish politicians. The Labour party north of the border is a particular snake-pit. At university, people often say they make friends whom they cherish for life. In the Scottish Labour party they make enemies they cherish for life.

The plotting to succeed Smith began long before he was buried. Peter Mandelson abandoned his old chum Gordon Brown and backed Tony Blair. It soon became clear that Blair was overwhelmingly the popular choice. At the celebrated meeting in the Granita restaurant, Islington, Blair and Brown appear to have carved up the next Labour government between them – Blair would be prime minister (foreign affairs) and Brown, nominally the chancellor, would be prime minister (domestic matters).

It must have been a terrible wrench for Brown. In the Blair–Brown team he had always been the senior partner, more intellectual, far better versed in the ways of the Labour party. Imagine the eldest son of a duke being visited, on the old man's death, by the family lawyer. He says he realises that the heir expected the title, the house, the land and the money. But, regrettably, his little brother looks much better on television... You would never quite get over such a snub, and Brown never did.

As we say these days, Tony Blair got it sorted. David Blunkett introduced him as the new leader of the Labour party, and for

...ment we feared it might be a case of the blind leading ...e bland.

But the speech was much better than that: it was tough, angry, but also optimistic. It spoke to the party's heart as well as its head. This, one felt, was a speech that would not only bring in the voters but also bring out the party workers.

Not that many of them were around for yesterday's coronation. Glossy suits, silk ties, expensive haircuts… that was just the trade union leaders, and they were banished to the back of the hall behind the TV cameras (the modern equivalent of below the salt). No one wanted the day to be spoiled by an unexpected glimpse of Jimmy Knapp.

It was a day for the new Labour aristocracy: successful lawyers such as Helena Kennedy and Geoffrey Bindman; women in suits tugging heavy briefcases; chaps with pony tails; rich men such as David Puttnam and Clive Hollick. Held in a small, dark basement, the meeting had the air of a trendy London nightclub; one suspected there were frightfully civilised bouncers on the door to keep the ugly people out. The chatter was of the Dordogne and when the delegates were going to arrive. John Prescott was possibly the only son of toil there, and even he ended the meeting blowing out kisses.

I don't want to be alarmist, but the middle classes are back in charge of Labour. They will celebrate Blair by listening to The Archers on Radio 4 longwave or by fitting new doors to their French farmhouses – louvres for Labour.

The lights went down for the announcement of the results. The winner was Tony Blair. The lights stayed down for a while, encouraging us to believe that the new Labour party wasn't quite as efficient as we'd come to believe. But it is.

As Mr Blair began speaking, the giant white rose behind him was touched by a spotlight with the faintest blush of pink. The shade grew sharper and more scarlet... at the end the stage was bathed in the red flag's hue. The speech worked because he presents Labour as a national party facing a national crisis, not merely a collection of factions: 'I shall not rest until once again the destinies of our people and our party are joined together in victory.'

But he is also anxious to allay the expected horrors of the left. He rejected 'dry academic theory and the student gospel of Marxism'. At one point he said, 'There is a place for anger and a place for passion, but ours is a passion allied to reason' – code for 'don't expect any revolutions'.

The most effective part of the speech came early on, when he used what is clearly going to be a standard rhetorical device: the rolling sentence. This continues, clause after clause, mounting up to in one case 56 words, in another 61, as if the monstrosities of Conservative rule are too great to leave time for breathing or punctuation.

The middle of the speech began to sag, but then recovered with a furious, John Smith-style assault on Tory sleaze. When he said, 'I would expect ministers in a government I lead to resign if they lied to parliament,' he got cheers as loud as any of the day.

Towards the end he talked about a revolution, but one which could not come overnight but would only arrive through hard work, guts and persistence. He gave the example of South Africa.

By chance, my next appointment was at the first cricket Test between England and South Africa for 30 years. I sat amid a group of white South Africans who were cheering the white

South African team while waving the brand new, black South African flag.

The privileged holding the banner of the dispossessed may prove to be a symbol for the new Labour party.

5 October 1994

Tony Blair made his first conference speech as Labour leader. He began by sacrificing one of the party's sacred cows, but in secret.

Tony Blair scooped the Labour party up in his strong arms yesterday, gazed long into its eyes, like amber pools of light, and told it how deeply he cared. Then, almost before the party knew what was happening, he led it softly yet insistently towards the bedroom door.

The speech was as artful a seduction as I've seen. He left the party quivering with anticipation, helpless in the face of his throbbing desire for office. Which leaves the question of whether, like Princess Diana's lover James Hewitt, Mr Blair will turn out to be a Love Rat.

This is, of course, the view of the left, and specifically Arthur Scargill, who sat scowling during what was probably the longest standing ovation a Labour leader has received. But he was virtually alone. Around him people cheered and bayed their support.

Mr Blair reminded me of Anna Pasternak's novel about Princess Diana. 'At last they were properly united... she lost her intolerable sense of isolation...' Her lover sounds more like Tony Blair all the time, 'bringing joy to those who have suffered too long the anguish of rejection'. The speech included some dazzling sleight of hand.

The ending of Clause Four was never even mentioned, being murmured in the party ear as 'it is time we had a clear, up-to-date statement of the object and objectives of our party' and cunningly linked to the name of John Prescott, who has in this business the same role as the Princess's detective: aware of what is going on but powerless to prevent it.

It took the delegates quite some time to realise what Mr Blair meant. We journalists, however, were luckier, since we had the benefit of Mr Blair's spin doctors. This profession, which was once thought unnecessary – Gaitskell's 'Fight, fight and fight again' required no spinning – has now become a massive youth employment scheme, as Mr Blair's Myrmidons fan out to explain precisely the significance of the text, like flying rabbis interpreting the Talmud. Many of these physicians are unnervingly young, having just left Balliol with starred firsts in oscillatory medicine. They line the aisle in the press room, which has become a Gyratory Gynaecologists' Gulch.

This is necessary, since quite lot of Mr Blair's speech did require at least a gentle twirl. For instance, a boilerplate attack on the home secretary ended with a passage that could have come from a Daily Express leader. Michael Howard said he was building six tough new prisons. Butlins wouldn't win the contract, he said. He was right. The Savoy got it.

His style, like all the most cunning seducers, is to pass swiftly over the reality and get on to the dream. The passage which said that the free market alone could not rescue the economy began: 'It won't be done by state control.' After that, he was free to rouse the party's fantasies. And the special achievement of the spin doctor is to furnish innumerable explanations of each passage so that a single oration becomes a blend of several different speeches, the underlying pattern emerging as in those Magic Eye books – only after you squint at it for hours.

Yesterday morning, to prepare for the speech, I rode on Blackpool's new rollercoaster, The Big One. It is terrifying. After an unnervingly long climb, you suddenly dip into the longest and fastest drop anywhere in the world. What makes it even more gut-wrenching is that the train is turning round 90 degrees on its own axis, so that you resume at right-angles to where you began the vertiginous descent.

But that's enough Labour party metaphors for one day. It now remains to be seen whether they still respect Tony Blair in the morning. They certainly adored him last night.

12 October 1994

There was a strange ghost who attended almost all Tory conferences from 1991 onwards, sometimes corporeally, sometimes only as a phantom presence. This time she turned up in order to haunt her successors in person.

She looked absolutely dreadful. We haven't seen Lady Thatcher this way since she was last worried in public about her son. That was when he was lost in the North African desert during a car rally. How wonderful, one might think, if he had stayed lost and now lived in a tent learning the simple wisdom of the nomadic peoples, swigging the odd goat's milk and tonic.

She arrived at the conference hotel on the clifftops early yesterday, rising up from sea level like a drowned sailor, if without the healthy glow. Her face was unnervingly white and tense, the hooded eyes drawn together like the curtains in a crematorium. She resembled, said a colleague of mine, 'a slightly confused elderly lady being led into a home'.

Someone shouted, 'Are you embarrassed by the revelations about your son?' (Her son Mark had been accused of involvement in an arms trading scandal.) The eyes narrowed even more for a brief moment. Nobody asked her if she was going to resign as Mark's mum. Behind the silk dresses and the beautifully coiffured hair, there was always the gleam of a drunken navvy looking round a bar for the chance of a fight. That had gone.

An hour later she turned up on the platform at the Tory conference. The delegates rose to applaud for about 20 seconds, but that was a mere blip compared to the receptions she has had in the past. She looked like a rock star greeted at the end of a gig with cries of 'Less! Less!'

I don't think they were being cruel or using some internal stopwatch to comment on the allegations against her son. She has become something of an irrelevance, her crusading leadership half forgotten by this ragtag army in retreat.

Later, John Major strode out from the conference centre and marched purposefully up the hill to lunch. A few minutes later she emerged, more pallid and frail than ever. She climbed slowly into a limousine for the 100-yard drive up the hill. Her police escort car had to honk to persuade chattering bystanders to get out of the way. There was a time when they would have been glad to scatter from the knives on her hubcaps.

19 October 1994

The new Labour leader faced the prime minister for the first time. It was to be the first of nearly three years of jousting, which ended with total victory for one man, humiliation for the other.

Tony Blair seemed nervous. He arrived to a massive cheer from his own side, but he sat tautly on the front bench, knotting and unknotting his fingers. The famous teeth 'n' rictus smile flashed briefly, to be replaced by an expression of thin-lipped neutrality.

By contrast, John Prescott was relaxed and at ease. He grinned warmly across at the cabinet, eased back in his seat and blew out his cheeks once or twice. I remembered where I'd seen that watchful insouciance before: he looked like a detective guarding the Prince of Wales. And, apart from the big flappy ears, Mr Blair has the same air of conscience-wracked earnestness. On the rare occasions I have met Prince Charles, I have been struck by his almost anguished desire to say the right thing to avoid giving offence to any of his subjects, just like Tony Blair.

As the new team arrived, Ann Widdecombe, the surprisingly effective employment minister, was laying waste to various Labour MPs who made the foolish mistake of opening their traps. The first question to the prime minister came from the admirable Anne Campbell of Cambridge, who resembles her boss Mr Blair in that she asks rude questions in a sweet, ingenuous fashion. Had Lady Thatcher broken the code of conduct for ministers when Mark Thatcher made £12 million from the Saudi arms deal? As it happens, this was the first of three questions dealing with matters of immense constitutional importance.

The others were the royal soap opera (the show where anything can happen and probably will, as the Radio Times used to say) and the question of a single European currency.

Mr Major's tactic is to imply that even to raise the first topic is to commit moral solecism on a level at least with that great dinner party scene in The War of the Roses, when Michael Douglas pees in the entrée. He sniffed at Mrs Campbell, 'I have no doubt that Lady Thatcher acted with complete propriety; if you have any evidence to the contrary, I hope you will produce it rather than peddling remarks like that.'

Finally Mr Blair got up. After a courtesy gesture towards peace in Northern Ireland, he asked about Kenneth Clarke's announcement that we wouldn't get a referendum on a single European currency. I cannot believe that in the pubs of Sedgefield they speak of little else. However, it laid the way for his soundbite: 'The chancellor takes one view on Europe, Mr Portillo takes another view and you hover in between.' In reply Mr Major accused Mr Blair of wanting to follow slavishly whatever Europe says.

The soundbite duly appeared on television; the issue has been taken up by the more earnest Prince of Walian type of newspaper, so the question did the business.

If I were Mr Blair, though, I would stop waving my arms around in an illustrative kind of way. He is not presenting Blue Peter. And he should not allow himself to be shouted down. At one point Betty Boothroyd had to rescue him from the horrid rough boys, and that looks feeble. He should simply shout above them.

Finally the prime minister, asked to declare his government a sleaze-free zone, announced his intention to root out wrongdoing wherever it might be found. But the point about this government is not that its members, supporters and families break the law. What they do is perfectly legal, and that is the terrible scandal.

27 October 1994

There were many scandals at around this time, several involving the then owner of Harrods, Mohamed Al Fayed. Mr Geoffrey Dickens brought an unusual new twist. He claimed that he had once been followed round a Conservative fete by a very ugly woman who smiled at him, but seemed too nervous to approach. A few days later he received a letter from her, explaining who she was, and asking for an autographed picture. She gave her name, and added underneath, 'Horseface'.

He was so impressed by this candour that he bought a frame, signed a picture of himself with a greeting: 'Best wishes, Horseface!' After he had posted it, his secretary asked, 'Did you get the letter from that frightfully ugly woman? I wrote "Horseface" after her name, so you'd know who it was...'

MPs returned to Westminster agog with the most sensational political news of the past few months. The Times newspaper has revealed that Mr Geoffrey Dickens (Littleborough) was the only MP who had actually given presents to Mr Mohamed Al Fayed. Humbugs. House of Commons after-dinner mints; that sort of thing. Someone should take Mr Dickens, who is currently fighting a courageous battle against cancer, on one side and explain, slowly and carefully, the way these things work.

I have an awful feeling that he might have got other things wrong as well. For example, if some sleazy consultant were to suggest he ask a parliamentary question, adding that the fee would be a grand, the portly MP would be down at the Table Office in a trice and would send off his cheque for £1,000 immediately afterwards.

One of the most curious arguments we've heard lately concerns the idea of the full-time MP, or what the prime minister called earlier this week the concept of the 'wholly professional politician', which will only isolate politicians. When I meet a Tory MP who is broadening his knowledge by working as a hospital porter or supply teacher, I shall feel more confident about his links to the life of the common people.

The problem could get worse. Someone, to use the politically correct term, as differently sleazed as Mr Dickens might find a colleague murmuring in his ear: 'If you want a spot of boodle, old chap, you need to link up with Greer,' and find himself on the books not of Ian Greer Associates, but Germaine Greer Associates.

Under this arrangement, MPs and their wives get to spend a week, free, at Ms Greer's house in Essex (total value at least £17.65).

There, along with various Big Issue salesmen, they are harangued about their sexual inadequacies.

7 December 1994

One thing I learned over the years is that being intelligent, even brilliant, is no guarantee of success in politics. Indeed, it can often be a disadvantage. Perhaps the cleverest MP I have ever met was George Walden, who used to be our ambassador in Moscow. Being a brainbox did him little good.

There is an ancient Chinese proverb (actually there isn't, I've just made that up) that in the Land of the Lunatics, only the sane are nuts.

The one sane man around Commons yesterday was George Walden, the Tory MP for Buckingham. Mr Walden has had an instructive career. Until 1983 he was one of the most important and influential chaps in the Foreign Office, no mere mandarin, but a Grand Satsuma among civil servants.

Then he resigned and became an MP. Apart from one very junior government job, which he held for just two years, he disappeared from sight. He has been taught the terrible lesson learned by wise backbenchers: they do not prowl the corridors of power, so much as skulk down the alleyways of impotence. But Mr Walden has not wasted his time. Almost alone among his colleagues he ponders such questions as our national future, our need to address reality rather than a mythological version of the past – in short the things which matter rather than the trivial ephemera most MPs bother about.

Which is why they think he's mad, bonkers, too few anchovies in his Gentleman's Relish. 'As much use as a cat flap on a submarine,' I heard one of his colleagues say last year.

And yesterday he did it again. He stood up in prime minister's questions and began: 'Do you think, when a member of this House makes proposals concerning the constitution...'

Labour MPs sensed an attack on Jack Straw and his remarks about the Royal Family. They took in deep gulps of air, preparing for a long, pipe-clearing boo and a hiss. Tory MPs wiggled with pleasant anticipation.

Mr Walden continued: '... that it is grown-up politics or, for that matter, intelligent politics...'

Some of the stupider Labour MPs exhaled, causing various rude noises. Some of the smarter Tories began to look worried.

'… for ministers to hunt him like a pack of demented *corgis*? Do you think that we, as a party, can hope to reconcile the encouragement of indiscriminate deference towards *well-born nonentities*…'

Suddenly Labour twigged. A Tory MP was actually making an attack on the Royal Family, and a fairly offensive attack at that. You could almost hear their brains whirling round, like police cars on a skid pan. They began to shout in agreement.

'… with the policy of encouraging the promotion of social parity in this country?'

Labour MPs cheered like mad. Tories sat there looking glum. It is an article of faith with them, one held in spite of every opinion poll and every shred of anecdotal evidence, that the British people revere the Royal Family and will be prepared to vote against anyone who would reduce their rank or standing. It is also an article of faith that they can win bucketsful of votes by accusing Labour of being against the Royal Family. Tony Newton, deputising for the prime minister, said that Mr Walden had 'underestimated the support for the monarchy' among the British people.

But of course Mr Newton has made the same mistake as other Conservatives who have been hiding behind the throne this week. It's not that the British people have anything against the ideal of a Royal Family; they just don't like this Royal Family.

1 February 1995

John Major, faced with a persistent and growing band of Euro-rebels,
found himself having to create minor, often meaningless victories for
himself, in order to persuade his party that he was not in the thrall of
the EU. Sometimes it worked; more often it did not.

Let's get it straight: John Major and Jacques Santer are in total
disagreement about the future of Europe. On the only issues
that matter – the single European currency and the voting
power of the bigger states – they are at loggerheads.

(Not many people know that there is a real place called
Loggerheads, in Staffordshire; England's best-ever goal-
keeper, Gordon Banks, made it his home. Presumably all the
other inhabitants are very fractious and live permanently at
Loggerheads.)

Santer is the president of the commission only because John
Major put him there. Mr Major had single-handedly vetoed
the other, Jean-Luc Dehaene, and welcomed his replacement
as 'the right man in the right place at the right time'. Since
then, Santer has lost no opportunity to rubbish his patron.
He has bitten the hand that fed him with the same relish as if
it were a tranche of pâté de foie gras, or whatever European
commissioners have for elevenses.

Last week, Santer called for early progress towards a single
currency. He also feels strongly that the bigger states such as
Britain – especially Britain – should have less power. At the
risk of sounding less than *communitaire*, may I say how annoying it is that someone from a country as small as Luxembourg,
which has approximately the same population as Croydon,
has any authority over our lives?

If somewhere with a similar population, were to declare itself an independent Duchy, would the people of France dream of being ordered around by its *functionaries*, whether the Mayor or even the Grand Duchess Fergie?

So when Peter Shore at prime minister's question time raised the question of Santer – 'Is he not, in fact, the wrong man in the wrong place at the wrong time?' – Mr Major might have been stumped. Could he disown his child? Of course not. He launched into an encomium of Santer. 'It would be extremely difficult to find a commission president who upon those two points would not take that position,' he said cheerily, as if the single currency and voting strength were minor marginalia. Then he began a list of all the points on which he and Santer agreed. Increased competitiveness! Free trade! A common security policy! He went on and on. 'Each and every one of those is a British priority endorsed by the President of the Commission!'

My mind wandered back nearly 500 years, to papal question time in the Vatican. Pope Sixtus IV was explaining that he was entirely at one with Martin Luther. 'In his fascinating 49 Articles, Dr Luther endorses the need for abolishing sin on a phased basis and for the on-going glorification of our Lord; points which I have always stressed. As for the sale of relics and indulgences, I suppose honourable members opposite would return to a nationalised, centralised system of sales, by which only people who were absolved and shriven could go to Heaven. We on this side of the aisle believe in freedom of choice.'

You can tell when Mr Major is getting rattled when he produces more Majorisms. Yesterday's crop included a slip of the tongue; talking about the railways he accused Mr Blair of spreading 'scare services' – one pictured a phosphorescent ghost service steaming through Nuneaton at midnight. He said it would be impossible to sterilise the British railway system in all its complexity.

As with former President Bush, you know what he means but can't quite work out why he says it.

14 February 1995

Twice David Davis ran for the leadership of the Conservative party and twice he failed – perhaps because he is to speechmaking what Edward Scissorhands was to balloon animals.

David Davis, MP for Boothferry and Foreign Office minister, is sometimes spoken of as the next prime minister but one. He certainly has one important qualification: he is a terrible speaker.

His speech yesterday on the topic of a referendum on Europe wasn't a disaster. It would have been more fun if it had been. It was just goose-pimply embarrassing, like one of those best man's speeches one sometimes hears which is so inappropriate and so long that you yearn for him to sit down and leave the bride and groom their happy memories.

The debate had been chosen by the Liberal Democrats, so Labour decided to more or less ignore it. Bringing down the government is one thing, but handing any credit to the Lib Dems quite another. When the debate began there were eight people on the Labour backbenches. Mr Ashdown made a dull but workmanlike speech. Then Mr Davis the Dauphin rose. He was clearly nervous, since at curious moments he interjected a short high-pitched laugh: 'Much of what I have heard was political opportunism. Ha, ha!' Next he failed the critical Skinner test. Inward investment, he said, was bringing 'hundreds of thousands of jobs to Britain. Even in Derbyshire,' he added.

'Name one,' Mr Skinner growled. 'Toyota,' said the minister brightly. Mr Skinner rose authoritatively and, with a flick of his wrist, waved the minister down. And down he sat, as meek as a chastised schoolboy. And they say that deference is dead.

To be fair, Mr Skinner rather lost the House by saying that he, for one, did not welcome Toyota's jobs. Nevertheless, he had clearly defeated Mr Davis. He celebrated his triumph by pushing a Curiously Strong Mint into his face and sucking it menacingly.

Tony Marlow, one of the nine whipless rebels, rose with a trick question which he signalled by saying, 'I am told that my Honourable Friend is on the threshold of the cabinet.' Mr Davis fell for it anyway. 'I am trying to work out whether he is complimenting me by saying that I am on the threshold of the cabinet,' he cooed. By this time, the handful of Labour ruffians present (their numbers had rocketed from eight to nine) realised that they had a victim and kept up a stream of unnerving insults.

Mr Davis then produced an alarming mixed metaphor of which John Major himself would have been proud: 'When the fog clears, we will see that most of the political landmarks of our age have our fingerprints upon them.'

Then Tory MPs even, including Sir Norman Fowler, began to stick out their legs and trip him up. One asked the prime minister's view. 'It's a pretty easy question when you ask the minister of state if he reads the prime minister and – hee, hee! – that is, I think, the case still.' The man's syntax was in meltdown.

Hugh Dykes rose. He is a Euro-fanatic with a broken nose who looks as if he has just been fighting Chris Eubank, or at least Nick Budgen. 'Sit down – he's in enough trouble,' shouted Gwyneth Dunwoody with mock solicitude. Mr Dykes had a question, but Mr Davis did not have the answer. He ended with less an answer than gurgle of despair: 'The proposition… er… that… er… that proposition that the…' Even when he had finished he had lost his place. A Major for the new millennium.

21 March 1995

The hangers and floggers seem to have more or less abandoned the Conservative party as a lost cause these days, though some no doubt have wistful thoughts of places such as Iran and Saudi Arabia, where soggy liberals have failed to gain much traction in the judicial system.

Few MPs bother turning up on Monday now, so I looked in vain for Elizabeth Peacock of Batley, who at the weekend called for criminals to be flogged on TV before or just after the National Lottery draw. Until now, Mrs Peacock has not been particularly well known. Perhaps her best-loved remark was recorded during a parliamentary tour of Japan during which there was a small earthquake. Next morning, she asked her breakfast companion, 'Did you feel the earth move last night, too?'

Her suggested penal reform is a good idea, especially as the two events could be combined for added excitement. You could have six yobs every week. After each ball drops from the machine, they could be thrashed that number of times, with a special beating at the end. It would make for heated arguments on Saturday evening: 'We're a Blind Date family, at least when it's on, though obviously we wouldn't want our children to miss the flogging. It would be a valuable formative experience. You've got to give them some idea of what happens to the kind of people who dawdle when they should be getting ready for school.'

On the other hand, they might perversely continue to prefer Cilla's winsome *double entendres* to the sight of young men screaming in agony as the skin is flayed from their naked buttocks: 'Argghhhhh! I have certainly learned my lesson and will get a job at £1.75 an hour cleaning the toilets in a fast food outlet rather than mug any more old ladies. Aieeeeeee!'

Actually, I detected a certain impatience among Conservatives yesterday. I sense that Mrs Peacock might have gone too far. An idea so hideous, so brutal, so hopelessly impractical and ineffective would have made a perfect centrepiece for the home secretary's speech at the next Tory conference. As it is, he is stuck with boot camps. These have nothing to do with Michael Foot, or KGB Agent Boot, as one paper claimed he was known. I have this image of his KGB controller tapping out coded messages to Moscow: 'Agent Boot reported that Dean Swift's doctrine of rational freedom was not incompatible with his Whig background.'

Boot camps are places where US army recruits are given their harsh initial training. By extension they have come to mean unpleasant institutions for the reform of criminally minded young men. The home secretary wishes to introduce them here, where they can be used for the chastisement of hooligans who have escaped being thrashed on TV by Noel Edmonds.

Mr Howard's shadow, Jack Straw, was cross yesterday because, having tabled a question asking for studies on the boot camp system to be placed in the Commons library, he had

had to wait a month for the reply. What's more, the documents the minister had provided did not include a report by his own advisers. This report said that the system didn't work. Naturally, the home secretary will have the camps built anyway. Britain and the United States now seem to be among the few western countries where penal policy is based almost entirely on revenge rather than reform.

Over in the Lords, the Home Office minister, Baroness Blatch, was admitting – with a measure of regret – that Labour's home secretary would be able to release prisoners who, under the Conservatives, could expect to stay locked up for life. She thought the public would be outraged if people who had committed the worst crimes were released. According to Lord Monkswell, Britain is the only country in the world, outside the former Soviet Union, which locks people up for life.

We could, of course, end the whole controversy by hanging the lot during the Antiques Roadshow. They could run the flogging in the corner of the screen, in the same way as they show the winning lottery numbers. Or just have a soundtrack of the screams: 'Now tell us, pet, was there jollity in the Jacuzzi?'

23 June 1995

In June 1995, John Major, weary of all the carping and disloyalty on his own benches, took an extraordinary decision. He resigned, not as prime minister, but as leader of the Conservative party, and challenged his critics to stand against him. MPs were astonished. Nobody had ever done such a thing before.

At last we have the name of the stalking horse… and it's John Major. He arrived in the Downing Street garden late, having had the pleasure of leaving the hacks to broil in the sun for half an hour. Over in the lobbies, the news was already spreading like an oil slick in the North Sea. 'I have good news and bad news,' said a Labour MP. 'John Major has resigned!' Cheers. 'The bad news is, he's still prime minister.' Booo!

We should have guessed. Earlier, at prime minister's questions, he had been poised and confident, like someone who has had the weight of a difficult decision taken from him. He even offered one, perhaps final, Majorism: 'Terrorism', he ringingly declared, 'is unpleasant and should be resisted.' He spoke elegiacally about Sir Patrick Mayhew, the Northern Ireland secretary, who had taken the extraordinary step of writing to the newspapers in his support. 'My right honourable friend is an honourable friend in every sense of the word,' he said. 'Few men have been blessed with better friends.' It was sounding like a funeral oration, but we'd got the wrong funeral.

Finally, there was a rare sighting of a John Major joke, about nepotism in Monklands council. Their personnel department was 'more like a family planning department'. Fake hilarity swept the Tory benches.

He drove back to Downing Street to polish up not so much a suicide note as his cry-for-help memo. In the Chamber, Labour was covering itself with rage, like a plastic veneer. You know the lads are making it up when they go on about the royal family. John Austin-Walker (Woolwich) demanded, 'This is an important constitutional matter. Has Her Majesty the Queen been informed?' As if he cared. Stephen Dorrell answered for the government (he just happened to be there). He slipped easily into the pompous 'march of history' mode:

'This does not affect my Right Honourable Friend's status as the Queen's First Minister, and all Members of the Treasury Bench will continue to serve in Her Majesty's Government,' the heritage secretary intoned. Mr Major is certainly a fine old edifice badly in need of restorative work; perhaps the National Lottery could be tapped to help.

The Chamber was full of survivors of scandals – Jonathan Aitken, Graham Riddick, Steve Norris, Alan Duncan – suddenly looking like figures from the distant past, their faces beginning to blur as if on the pages of yellowing newspapers. Someone tried to keep the mood of excitement by crying 'I Spy Strangers!' – the traditional way of clearing the galleries and obliging the House to sit *in camera*. The vote was lost by 216 votes to 10. It made little difference.

MPs poured out to the real centres of power. On College Green (the scrap of lawn opposite the House) I counted 108 people milling about, conducting or granting interviews. Back in the corridors of impotence, one of the grandest of the Grandees admitted, 'I wouldn't be surprised if nobody ran against him.' Twenty yards away, on the Terrace, Norman Lamont was drinking wine, alone but not unaccompanied. Plotters hovered around him like plump dragonflies. Others were lurking in the corridors and crannies.

'Lurk before you leap' has always been the motto of serious Tory conspirators.

27 June 1995

As it happened there was a challenger. After a few days, John Redwood, a right-wing Eurosceptic, known to his colleagues as 'the

Vulcan', as in Star Trek, announced his candidacy. Now Major had a problem; he had not only to win, but had to win so convincingly that all talk of a leadership crisis would end. As so often, the actuality fell somewhere in the middle.

The word was first whispered, then shouted: 'He's coming.' The foetid human mass in the Jubilee Room pulsated with excitement, like some mutant organism about to devour itself. At last we could answer the question that has been on everyone's lips since the weekend: what on earth does John Redwood look like?

It was hard to tell. Thanks to the information revolution, in which yet more news is balanced by still less enlightenment, Britain now has what the Americans call 'goat-fucks' – those swaying edifices of cameramen, snappers, sound recorders and hacks which lurch perilously round press conferences like the towers used to besiege medieval cities. You couldn't see through them, either. In fact, in the past few days Westminster has been a Glastonbury for the political classes. They will endure any privation, any discomfort and loss of sleep, just to say they were there.

Out on College Green, there were nine camera crews milling about, waiting for someone – anyone – to interview. To be the one Tory MP not invited there suggests terminal social oblivion, like being crossed off the Readers' Digest mailing list.

Mr Redwood arrived, accompanied by his clique. He looked quite normal, which is more than can be said for the others. Teresa Gorman was in her usual primary colours. Tony Von Marlow wore a multi-coloured, striped blazer, like a chair from the passenger deck of the Hindenburg.

From Mr Major's point of view, there were more bastards than the day the US army left Saigon. I suspect this didn't help the cause. The message to Tory MPs was 'Vote Redwood and this lot will be running things'. Nor did it help that they cheered their new leader almost every time he spoke, like so many Young Conservatives. But Redwood was good; very good. It helps to have created no expectations. Anything was better than his public image so far.

He started peevishly (a team of Sorbonne analysts have deconstructed his opening): 'The rotten swine didn't tell me he was resigning, oh no, not even after I had been to see him. Not good enough. I'm outside the loop, I suppose.' Well, the loop goes round his neck now.

6 July 1995

In the end, Major won, but sufficient MPs either voted against him or abstained to leave his leadership in question once again. Gyles Brandreth, in his fascinating diaries, Breaking the Code, describes the scene on the eve of the vote. Major was sitting alone, apparently ruminating. A whip asked Brandreth to go over and cheer him up. He failed; Major seemed to be lost in a morose world of his own. Then an older Tory MP arrived and began to chat about Surrey cricket players of the distant past. Major perked up immediately and spent a happy hour or so talking about something quite different from his own political problems. You may recall that two years later, after he lost the premiership in the Blair landslide, he went straight to the Oval to watch Surrey play cricket.

However, having won re-election he had a cabinet re-shuffle.

'It's over now to Downing Street and our political editor, Lance Boyle. Lance, is the prime minister using this reshuffle to assert his authority?'

'Yes, Barry, he is. It's looking like a very good day for the Nerd wing of the Conservative party, which is, of course, where the prime minister himself stands. He called this election because he was fed up with the endless sniping from the Interesting wing and of course, as we saw, he managed to rout them. So it looks as if we'll be saying goodbye to raffish figures such as Jonathan Aitken and aristocrats like Douglas Hurd; in come prominent Nerds such as the new Welsh secretary, William Hague.'

'Is Mr Hague one of the people the Nerds most hoped to see promoted?'

'Definitely. Remember, Barry, in 1977, at the age of 16, he made a speech to the Tory party conference in which he managed to sound like a 70-year-old – "rolling back frontiers of state", that kind of thing – but he has lost most of his Yorkshire accent and nearly all his hair now he's about to become District Commissioner for the Cambrian tribes.'

'And he's a Meatloaf fan?'

'He certainly is, Barry. Every Saturday morning, Mr Hague puts Bat Out of Hell on the stereo and dances round the room on his own. Seasoned observers are saying this may be the most Nerdish hobby ever admitted by a senior minister.'

'The foreign secretary's job, Lance. Is that a case of Hurd to Nerd?'

'Yes, Barry. Malcolm Rifkind is certainly the most Nerdish foreign secretary since the War, so it's a very big plus for the Nerds to see him offered the Great Anorak of State. He also has the most astonishing vowel sounds: he's known at home in Scotland as Loyd Grossman.'

'This promotion also removes a question mark that's been hanging over Mr Rifkind's head, doesn't it, Lance?'

'Yes, for years Mr Rifkind was famous for having breath which could stop a runaway horse. Clearly he'd done something about that, possibly by invasive surgery, or else there'd have been a problematic situation: that whenever he went into top diplomatic negotiations and said, "I want to make the UK position absolutely clear," other foreign ministers would have run from the room shouting "*Sapristi!*"'

'And the new agriculture minister, Douglas Hogg, is a rare example of an Old Etonian Nerd. When he first came to the Commons, his desk was in a division lobby and other Tory MPs played a game of throwing rolled-up order papers at him. You scored five if you got him on the head. And, of course, he is married to former Major policy chief Sarah Hogg, who's celebrated in her own right as a nerdette.'

'But do the Nerds entirely trust him, Lance?'

'There was some talk that Mr Hogg was so incredibly rude that he was almost interesting. But friends said that he didn't realise he was being rude, so the Nerds decided to accept him. And there was his starring appearance on the controversial shock Channel 4 late show, The Nerd, in which men go trainspotting naked.'

'And the other jobs, Lance – what are your sources saying?'

'Well, there's Michael Heseltine's new title, first secretary of state. As Hezza gets further away from power, Barry, his titles get even grander. He's now said by friends to be holding out for 'the Godfather' next time. Virginia Bottomley has the crucial National Heritage portfolio, so expect to see Stonehenge closed and moved to more modern facilities 100 miles away. And Mr Portillo's a big disappointment here, Barry. Many viewers had hoped he would get the job that has gone to Brian Mawhinney, so they would have had the pleasure of hearing us say, "Mr Portfolio, the Minister Without Portillo". As it is he has been moved sideways to defence. So that must be something of a let-down for him, Lance.'

'Yes, but at least he has 20 new phone lines, for people to call him with messages of condolence.'

3 October 1995

New Labour was full of surprises, as we discovered yet again at the Labour party conference.

'How the Labour party has changed.' The moment I wrote that – the actual moment, and I am not inventing this – a man from the Country Landowners' Association dropped by as part of his lobbying operation here. Who next? The Confederation of Beer-Waterers in Silk Hats?

Gordon Brown left his prepared speech towards its end and said, mistily, 'I want a Britain awash with opportunity, alive with compassion; a Britain in which people can dream dreams that can be fulfilled.' It sounded like the end of a Hollywood movie. Grizzled yet lovable old guy on his deathbed turns to young hero and, as his eyes close murmurs, 'Just one thing, Billy. Don't forget to dream.' Cue violins, tears, stampede for bar. It's not what we usually associate with Gordon Brown, in the way we don't expect tap dancing from Norman Tebbit. But this is New Labour's world, in which dreams come true and the magic never ends.

For example, the Guardian fringe meeting included a lengthy analysis of the pivotal role of the BMW owner in New Labour politics. Judith Church MP had been canvassing recently and had meant to skip a house which boasted huge new Beamer in the front drive. But she was glad she hadn't, because the owner turned out to be an enthusiastic Labour convert. 'Who are these people who haven't voted Labour, who have never voted Labour?' she demanded. 'Tories!' shouted some unreconstructed dinosaur from the back.

Then Ms Church began heavy-duty dreaming on behalf of every BMW owner, a maligned and misunderstood group: 'The BMW owner doesn't think he's rich. He doesn't feel he is going to be able to hold on to his house much longer, or to his job. He has suffered more under the Tories than he has under us.' Just as we expected stewards with collecting tins – 'For the cost of little more than a few artesian wells in Africa, you could provide a BMW owner with leopardskin seat covers' – Roy Hattersley cut in and said that he hoped it would be possible to improve pensions, child benefit and employment without any penalty falling on BMW owners. 'But I have my doubts. If helping the poor means hurting BMW owners, are we prepared to do it?'

'Yes!' shouted the audience – dinosaurs, every one. No wonder Mr Blair despairs of getting his message across.

11 October 1995

Michael Portillo had been made defence secretary. His speech at the Tory conference was thought so demented, so over-the-top, it probably ended any chance he had of becoming Tory leader. He had also

*lost vital loyalty points by installing phone lines in a Westminster
house in case he decided to run against John Major which, in the end,
he didn't. His defeat in 1997 was the last straw; since then he has
re-invented himself as a much-loved, liberally minded TV presenter.*

As Michael Portillo sat down, the audience rose. Then we
heard, somewhat late perhaps, a sound similar to a gang of
football hooligans descending on an Oslo bar. The defence
secretary had won his stamping ovation. Someone made
retching motions, but he was only a hack and doesn't count.
I asked another minister, 'How about belonging to the same
party as Portillo?'

'Ours is a very broad church,' he murmured.

It was an anti-Brussels rant, of course. Miguelito could
turn the welcome speech at a Tupperware party into an anti-
Brussels rant. It was also designed to appeal to the adolescent
Tories who like Portillo so much. Here was the authentic voice
of a schoolboy boasting about his toys: 'Three letters send a
chill down the spine of the enemy – SAS. Those letters spell
out one clear message: don't mess with Britain,' he said, snarl-
ing like a schoolboy bully.

Only three nations including Britain, he gloated, will have
Tomahawk cruise missiles: 'A weapon so accurate that it can
be launched from a submarine a thousand miles away and
guided down a single chimney.' He even declared that Labour
had not really changed its mind on CND: 'Anyone, they say, is
entitled to change his mind. Not about the defence of Britain,
you're not. You either feel it in your heart, in your bones, in
your gut, or you don't.' This diatribe from someone who was
such a pacifist in his youth that he refused to join the school
cadet corps, his biographer claims.

Portillo ended by again quoting the SAS, which appears to have become the military wing of the Conservative party: 'Who dares, wins.' My imagination was seized by a picture of Mr Portillo being launched from a submarine then dropped with astonishing accuracy straight down a chimney, a thousand miles away.

1 November 1995

Victory in his unwonted and unwanted election did not seem to make John Major any more relaxed or affable.

Mr Peevish woke up in a bad temper. Mr Peevish always woke up in a bad temper. Nothing ever pleased Mr Peevish. 'My toast is not inconsiderably cold, Mrs Peevish,' he said to his wife. Later, the prime ministerial car came to pick Mr Peevish up. 'I don't like the ashtray,' he said, 'and the seat cover makes my bottom itch.' The driver mumbled something to himself about knowing another way to make his bottom itch. He was very glad when he'd dropped Mr Peevish off. Next, Mr Peevish answered prime minister's questions. He was very peevish indeed. Mr Winnick asked if Mr Peevish had done a nuclear deal with the French President M. Chagrin. 'You are the person who saluted the courage and determination of the protesters at Greenham Common,' said Mr Peevish.

The Labour MPs loved to tease Mr Peevish. They knew it made him more and more peevish. They laughed and cheered at his peevishness. The leader of the opposition, Mr Blair, asked Mr Peevish a question about railway privatisation. (If I may interrupt the story, it's fascinating that as rail services are run down, the larger stations are being turned into Arab souks. At Water-loo, for example, it is common to see thousands of people milling about, searching vaguely for non-existent trains, surrounded by stalls selling ladies' underwear, tie racks, pick 'n' mix, candies, Indian jewellery, coffee pots and stationery requisites.) Mr Blair said that the government was lurching to the right. That made Mr Peevish really cross: 'The centre-right is our ground, and there is no way a squatter like you will be able to rest on it. You may regard yourself as the Trojan Horse of socialism, but you will find that it's our land you are parking on.'

Labour MPs adored hearing Mr Peevish talk like this. They specially liked his funny metaphors. Did he imagine that someone might put a yellow clamp on the Trojan Horse of socialism with a sticker: 'Warning. Do Not Attempt to Move This Trojan Horse'?

Mrs Winterton asked Mr Peevish about Labour's all-women shortlists: 'Will you promise that we will never impose all-women shortlists by diktat?' Mr Peevish agreed that female shortlists were 'all tat and no dick', or words to that effect. 'We will not follow the policies of the opposition because, daily, they are following our policies,' he said very peevishly.

Mr Ashdown asked if it was true that the allies had abandoned the people of Srebrenica and allowed 8,000 of them to be massacred.

Well! You should have seen Mr Peevish! Do you remember when you trampled mud over your mother's clean carpet? That was what Mr Peevish was like. Furious! 'What you are saying is not correct. You have been wrong throughout the whole of this episode. Time after time after time, you have denigrated what the British government has done and what British armed forces have done.'

Mr Sutcliffe told Mr Peevish that we should have a job skills audit because this country had poor job skills. 'I think you have just demonstrated a skill shortage in answering questions,' he said. The Labour MPs were hooting with fun and merriment. It was Mr Peevish who was supposed to answer questions, not Mr Sutcliffe. Mr Peevish had become so peevish he didn't know what he was saying.

Later the Speaker, Miss Testy, accused Conservatives of leaning to the opposition, which was not their job. She accused them of total abuse of the House. It was lucky Mr Peevish had gone away by then. He might have exploded.

2 November 1995

Mr Michael Fabricant (Mid-Staffs) had tabled a question for answer yesterday afternoon. Looking down on him from the gallery, you could tell how excited he must have been all day. Imagine the moment of waking up, and that spell of a few seconds in which we recall what the coming day is due to bring us. Another ordinary day at work, perhaps, or a party, or even a wedding. Mr Fabricant must have opened his eyes and thought, 'Today I am going to ask a parliamentary question!' The mounting excitement over breakfast. Rehearsing on the bus. Trying to drop it casually into chats with colleagues: 'Yes, as it happens I have tabled a question to the president of the Board of Trade. I'll be putting him on the spot with a no-holds-barred query about his plans to visit the USA for discussions on North American Free Trade. He won't wriggle out of that!' Then lunch... almost impossible to eat. Taking one's seat at 2.30. The agony as question

2 follows number 1, followed in turn by 3 and slowly, inexorably, by question 4.

At this point I took my place in the gallery. Mr Fabricant was fishing nervously in his jacket pockets. He knitted his fingers together, as if making a cat's cradle. Then he leaned back, adjusted his order paper and plonked it down on the bench. Next he brought out a bunch of keys and put it on the other side. Then he put the order paper on top of the keys. And still we had only reached question 10. He made a chin strap out of his hands and inserted his chin. He leaned forward as prelude to leaning back. He stretched his legs out before drawing them back beneath the bench.

He was so excited and nervous that he even laughed at a joke by a Labour member. We had reached question 12 and I could actually feel the tension radiating upwards. He studied the order paper yet again, making sure that question 14 had not vanished in the 20 seconds since he had last looked for it. He tapped the back of the bench in front. Then he started twitching in a slow, almost formal manner, like those in-seat exercises they suggest you take during long flights. He clasped his hands as if congratulating himself.

Question 13 arrived. By this time I was worried. Mr Fabricant's hair, never very securely anchored to his head, began to shake. His whole body was twitching like a steam engine about to explode. He coughed. He shuddered. He clasped his groin like a nervous slip fielder who sees Brian Lara emerge from the pavilion. Then, the moment arrived. 'Mr Michael Fabricant,' said the Speaker. 'Number 14,' said Mr Fabricant. Mr Ian Lang replied that he would be going to the USA before too long. And at this point Fabricant blew it.

He was delighted that Mr Lang was going to America. He was delighted, too, that he would be going to Canada as well. He discussed how the US is our second largest trading partner and the fact that Britain is the largest investor there. It all came burbling out: the pent-up excitement, the planning, the nervous energy. He couldn't stop himself. Our common language with the United States. Our shared culture. The common legal system. He was starting to blather. Labour MPs began jeering. 'Gerronwivvit!' they shouted. None of this would have mattered, except that the Speaker herself then rose: 'I must adjourn the debate on this interesting topic,' she said politely.

Mr Fabricant tried to make light of it. 'I stand chastised,' he muttered, in what he thought was a jovial manner. But, in the gallery, we knew that all had been lost.

16 February 1996

For months the arms-for-Iraq scandal had been rumbling on. Ministers were accused of turning a blind eye to British exports to Iraq of equipment that might be used for military purposes. One minister, the late Alan Clark, admitted in court to being, as he put it, 'economical with the actualité'. *A judicial enquiry led to the Scott report. Though it was highly critical of the government, the Conservatives claimed it as a great victory. But they were up against Robin Cook, the nimblest debater in the Commons.*

At 3.30, Betty Boothroyd suspended the sitting and MPs dashed into the lobby to get hold of their copies. First in line was Edwina Currie, who signed 'Best wishes, Edwina', and handed it back. (Sorry, I made that up.) Then Ian Lang rose to give the government's account, painstakingly prepared over the past eight days. The report did sound a little unexpected: 1,800 pages of praise for ministers' unblemished honesty, integrity and sincerity, interrupted only by the occasional murmur of distress about the way events had actually turned out.

It was one of those rare and almost magical occasions when the House of Commons becomes again the nation's debating forum. Heaven knows, this doesn't happen often but, when it does, the Chamber carries a power and authority no TV studio can ever match. If this is what MPs can do when they haven't read the report, we ought to keep them in ignorance more often.

'He makes no criticism of government policy,' Mr Lang purred. There had been no attempt to gag anyone; no conspiracy to jail innocent men. The central charges were not, in Sir Richard's opinion, well founded.

How, we began to wonder, had any of us come to believe they might be? Of course, it must have been the fault of the opposition: 'For three years, ministers have had to endure abuse and attacks upon their honour and integrity of the most offensive and unpleasant nature; they now stand wholly vindicated.' There was an uneasy stirring on the Labour side. The opposition began to resemble Timon of Athens' guests, invited to a banquet and served bowls of tepid water. Mr Lang admitted that Scott felt a few matters could have been better handled. The government would be tackling these in the future; in the meantime, the important business was to rub Labour's nose in its own moral turpitude. The mood of Labour MPs was deeply gloomy. Could it be that Sir Richard Scott, their white knight on a bike, had allowed the ministers to scuttle off?

Robin Cook's reply was, I would judge, the best parliamentary performance made by anyone since the last election. To his enemies – Tory ministers, Peter Mandelson, various bookmakers, among others – every word must have been galling. 'I have spent the last three hours studying it, and I do not recognise the report read in the statement we have just heard.' He recited one of Scott's charges after another. He talked about the supergun, saying the government had known about it for year before it was seized. The evidence was so strong that for ministers to say that the parts were possibly for civilian use was the equivalent of turning a blind eye. Labour morale, which had been sagging, was climbing through the roof. They began to wave their copies in support – no mean feat, since the full set weighs 17 lb. Mr Cook had done a job of gutting any fisherman would be proud of. As he produced each new choice paragraph, MPs began to cheer and even to whistle. The Tories had fallen silent and sullen.

Mr Cook ploughed briskly on. Scott had said that Mr Waldegrave's claim that releasing the crucial documents would cause damage was risible. 'If the secretary of state does not think that the word "risible" is a criticism, when will he recognise criticism?' Mr Cook's art is thinking on his feet, which makes him like a nimble boxer – hard to hit. Mr Waldegrave had sent dozens of misleading letters to MPs. 'And they tell us that he could remain in office as if nothing had happened. They misjudged Saddam, they misled MPs and they misdirected the prosecution.' Then, as a *coup de grâce*, he pointed out that ministers had blamed civil servants for failing to draft correct replies. Yet the civil servants criticised had been told that any reply they made must not criticise ministers. His voice rising to a squeak of moral outrage, Mr Cook asked: 'How *dare* they criticise civil servants while ordering these civil servants not to criticise ministers?' He sat down, to a storm of cheers from one side and a morose hush from the other.

Mr Lang began by pointing out that Mr Cook had spent 10 minutes talking to the press before he had started to read. Somehow this didn't quite fit the bill. Compared to the events in the report, it seemed – how can one put it? – pusillanimous and silly. It appeared Mr Lang's reply to Mr Cook's reply had also been drafted in advance, possibly before Mr Cook had even read the report. He had, Mr Lang said, twisted and distorted everything. No doubt, but so have both sides. It just happens that Mr Cook did it much better.

Absurdly, Mr Lang said that Mr Cook had now 'blighted his career in this House'. I would say that yesterday Mr Cook emerged as a possible Labour leader. Any doubts about who'd won were dispelled when Tory MPs – admittedly all mavericks – joined in against the government. Richard Shepherd (Aldridge) read out a chunk of one of the more lethal paragraphs (4.42 if you have your copy to hand). 'Does this not go to the very heart of democratic and accountable government in parliament?' he asked drily. Rupert Allason (Torbay) pondered whether the government agreed their use of the PII certificates was 'bizarre and unacceptable'. Nicholas Budgen (Wolverhampton SW) felt that whatever differences there might be about what information was available to a sovereign parliament, 'shouldn't it be up to parliament alone to decide?' Having dropped that poison pellet into the trout pond, Mr Budgen left. Robert McCartney, the independent Unionist on the Labour benches, pointed out, sweetly, that Scott's defence was that ministers were honest but incompetent and negligent. 'If ministers are to be lauded for their honesty and good faith, should they not be punished for their incompetence and negligence?' We shall soon know.

29 February 1996

In 1996 the Guardian faced a spate of libel cases – Jonathan Aitken, Neil Hamilton, Stoke Newington police and a little-known MP called George Howarth, who claimed I had libelled him. We lost that one, though I can say that if our editor had been able to choose three victories and one defeat, this is the defeat he would have picked. All the others ended in triumph for the paper.

Readers will find elsewhere in this paper an account of the settlement we have reached with Mr George Howarth, the Labour MP for Knowsley North. Naturally, I congratulate Mr Howarth on his victory. I would go further. It seems to me that the lesson from the short trial is that we, as journalists, should start behaving responsibly and stop hurting MPs' feelings. Plumbers, accountants and teachers don't expect to find vicious personal attacks on themselves when they open their morning paper. If you're a greengrocer, you don't read sarcastic comments about your personal appearance in the public prints. Why should MPs?

Reproved yet inspired by Mr Howarth's 'Mr Hoggart is more nasty than funny', I have decided it is time to reform. I arrived in the Chamber yesterday, just in time to hear Rachel Squire (Lab, Dunfermline) ask a question about registration and inspection procedures for nursing and residential homes in Scotland. I have rarely heard such a question on that fascinating subject. The same goes for the answer provided by

James Douglas-Hamilton, junior minister at the Scottish Office
– junior now, but not for long, I fancy.

His answer covered many aspects of procedures for nursing and residential homes in Scotland, with a thoroughness
and detail that won gasps of quiet admiration from the whole
House. Those of us who have been all too ready to hold glib
views on this vital topic will have been forced to think again,
and not before time.

Next, we were enthralled by a statement from Virginia
Bottomley, the secretary of state for the National Heritage. As
ever, Ginny won the hearts of members with her description
of the millennium exhibition at Greenwich entitled 'The Circle
of Time', comprising 12 pavilions all on the theme of 'Time'.
As Mrs Bottomley announced that the government's role in
this event would be co-ordinated by Mr Michael Heseltine,
spontaneous cries of applause broke out. Here was yet another
richly deserved title for the well-loved deputy prime minister,
First Time Lord. Mrs Bottomley pointed out, with her unfail-
ing good humour, that the last millennium had been presided
over by Ethelred the Unready. Now, a thousand years later, we
have an improvement: Heseltine the Unbalanced.

Michael Jopling (Westmorland and Lonsdale) pained those
of us committed to the New Courtesy by an unkind reference
to Birmingham, some of whose MPs were upset because the
fabled City on the River Chad has been passed over in favour
of Greenwich.

'Northerners much prefer London to Birmingham, which
they think of as somewhere you go through on the way to
London,' he said. Thank heavens for Mrs Bottomley, who
quickly restored the mood of good fellowship which we shall
soon expect from the Commons. 'Perhaps you are unduly

harsh on the joys of Birmingham,' she said. It certainly is a magnificent city. To me, the saddest moment came when she was making a series of moving remarks about the National Lottery. Eyes raised to her vision of the future, she said, 'The Lottery provides the means by which the dreams and hopes of the people of this country can find their realisation.' As we pondered the profundity of this thought, the harsh voice of George Foulkes (Lab, Carrick) cut through our reverie. 'What a load of garbage!' he shouted. Has he not heard of the new guidelines?

14 May 1996

I quite often speak about politics to audiences around the country, and one of the questions they most often ask is: 'What is Peter Mandelson really like?' It is almost impossible to answer, like inquiring, 'What colour is a chameleon?'

For someone who is supposed to be the smooth, behind-the-scenes Mr Fixit of the Labour party, Peter Mandelson has an extraordinary gift for making enemies. He has been known to boycott people for fixed lengths of time, by way of punishment. We learned this weekend that he has not spoken to Gordon Brown, the shadow chancellor, for 18 months, although both men have important roles to play in the party's election campaign. As for his relations with Mr Prescott, we are told these have 'improved'. Well, they can hardly have got worse. Possibly they began as incandescent hatred on Mr Prescott's part and have since been downgraded to rancorous resentment.

A mutual friend tells me that Mr Mandelson's greatest skill is in nurturing the people he does like: 'If he wants you on his side, he lavishes all his charm, his affection and his hard work on you,' this friend told me. 'He is like a little puppy.'

The Labour team was facing Michael Heseltine, who was curiously downbeat. He perked up only with a question from Jacques Arnold (Con, Gravesham, or the 'Unquiet Gravesham' as we now call it) who had been dug up by the whips yesterday morning to ask about Mr Mandelson's feud with Gordon Brown. 'An interesting thought,' said the Hezza genially. 'I would like to hold a reception so that they can get together in convivial circumstances and iron it all out.' Mr Skinner snarled that the prime minister had talked about having 'three bastards' in his cabinet. Yet the last year implied there were fully 89 bastards. Mr Heseltine beamed at him. 'I will invite you to the reception as well,' he said.

Yesterday's questions ended with my favourite monthly session, as Michael Alison (Con, Selby) answers for the Church Commissioners. The moment came and the sun suddenly poured through the windows, bathing the Chamber in a radiant light.

Tony Banks (Lab, Newham NW) was at least pretending to be outraged by the fact that the Bishop of Chelmsford had said he was dissatisfied with his episcopal palace, although it has six bedrooms and sits in three acres: 'If a manger was good enough for the Prince of Peace, then whingeing from princes of the Church is not good enough for us.' I had always assumed that a manger was where, in his grumpier moods, Mr Mandelson kept his dog. Mr Alison replied, in that slow, fluting voice reminiscent of the more old-fashioned Anglo-Catholic priests, 'The Bishop occupies only a small part of the palace which is impossibly close to the A12, a dual carriageway, so you cannot hear yourself speak or pray.'

Mr Banks snorted with scorn. 'It's only the Lord who needs to hear you pray!' he shouted. Some people just don't know how to behave in church.

7 June 1996

Another somewhat sinister figure is Michael Howard, who was home secretary under John Major and went on to lead the Tory party to its third successive defeat in 2005. His colleague Ann Widdecombe famously said that there was 'something of the night' about him. I always imagined him in the drawing room of a great Gothic pile, offering a decanter of something the same colour as red wine, but strangely different, more viscous...

Home office question time has become like some awful horror movie; not a Hammer film of the 60s – in improbable colours with busty starlets getting bitten in the neck – but one of the sombre, expressionist black and white classics of the past.

Jack Straw is Jonathan Harker, the innocent young man sent with letters of introduction to the Count of Castle Dracula. Dusk is gathering. As he walks upward, clouds swirl down the mountain towards the tiny village, misting his glasses. Cackling squeegee merchants push towards him, waving their greasy dripping sponges in his face. Knots of ragged boys, some as young as 10, cluster at street corners, pointing at the stranger, jeering at his nervous, blinking eyes. He makes a mental note that he will have his friend the Count lock them all up, or possibly eat them. Outside the tavern stands a loutish fellow – David Evans (Con, Welwyn). He is bellowing at the crowd, trying to persuade the peasants to rise against incomers.

'We are sick and tired of immigrants who come 'ere, pay nuffink and take everything. Immigrants should stay 'ere for five years before they can use our 'Elf Service. We know that lo' over there' – he points at Straw – 'would let 'em in and the taxpayer would pie the bill.' Straw shudders and resumes his march up to the castle. But even as he climbs onward, he can hear the voice of the sinister Tim Kirkhope (Con, Leeds NE), a minister who is using the simple bigotry and ignorance of the lower orders to pursue his own dark ends. 'I congratulate my friend on his robust remarks,' he says, silkily. 'If only the honourable gentleman and his colleagues opposite had been more supportive, we might have been able to deal with matters more effectively.'

It is cold now, icy cold, though that is not the only reason why Straw shivers as he continues on his quest. Finally he reaches the castle and hammers on the door. It is opened by a woman as wide as she is tall, capped by mane of jet-black hair, quite unlike any creature he has ever seen. Yet he gives a start of recognition, for she is the Count's most faithful servant, once christened Ann Widdecombe in who can say what century, but known to mortal man by other names: Doris Karloff, Bela Lugosi, Yvonne Chaney Jr, Glad the Impaler.

Glad is obsessed by the distant past. She shrieks at an innocent retainer, Greville Janner (Lab, Leicester): 'He seems to think that we are responsible for overcrowding in prisons! Under the last Labour government there was a 15 per cent increase in prison population but capital funding was cut!' She shuffles down the dank, stone-flagged corridor to the dungeons, muttering as she goes: 'Callous neglect of the opposition… neglect of overcrowding…'

Inside, manacled to the wall, is David Ashby (Con, Leics NW), condemned by a court for unnatural practices, his political life about to be brought to its end. Pathetically he tries to curry favour with Glad in the hopes of a reprieve. 'Does she not agree that this shows that Conservative policies are the correct policies?' he whinges. Glad yells back in rage. 'We inherited this from the last Labour government!' she screeches, before the other prisoners drown her with their moaning and their jeers. For she has spent most of the last few decades living in a coffin and, to her, events of 17 years ago are as fresh in her mind as yesterday.

Dark has now fallen and, moments later, young Straw is face to face with the Count! 'Your schimm is full of difficulties,' he says in his weird sibilant accent. 'The only ciffew the Libber party is likely to impose on is – you!' Terror sweeps through the young traveller…

2 October 1996

One of Tony Blair's most famous speeches came at the Labour conference, the last before he became prime minister. This became known as the Old Testament Prophets speech. It was so mocked by the anti-Blair wing of the party that one of them, Bob Marshall-Andrews, set up a luncheon club of similarly stroppy MPs and called it The Old Testament Prophets. They met in the upstairs room of a pub in Whitehall, ate mediocre food and made jokes at their leader's expense.

It wasn't the fault of the chairwoman, Diana Jeuda, that she introduced the leader as 'Tony Blur' – a natural slip of the tongue. And Blair was neither blurry nor bland. He was evangelical. He invoked the names of the ancient prophets of the Old Testament, who first pleaded the cause of the marginal, the powerless, the disenfranchised. We remembered all those wild-eyed men in animal skins descending from the mountain to declare, 'I am here to empower the disenfranchised! And, incidentally, we in New Labour's Old Testament pledge insulation for every cave, free birch twigs for self-flagellation at the point of use, and a stone jar full of parchment scrolls in every school.' At every point, Mr Blair claimed a link with destiny. After the next election, he said, we would have '1,000 days to prepare for the next 1,000 years'. We knew he wanted two terms, but this was ridiculous.

The speech started hesitantly. The barrage of camera flashes was clearly causing him real distress. But he scored a good ad lib – 'Be careful, they're making my eyes red' – and he had won them over. To be fair, they were so keen to applaud that they'd have cheered if he had read out the Tory manifesto. Some dinosaurs would claim he *had* read out the Tory manifesto. This was one of the few speeches I recall which consisted almost entirely of perorations. Indeed, every Blair speech these days becomes more of a parody of itself. He is Tony Blair imitating Rory Bremner imitating Tony Blair.

For instance, his habit of dropping verbs has now become pathological: I counted 115 verb-free sentences in the speech, some of quite sensational vacuity: 'New challenges, new ideas... the future not the past... New Labour, new members... the age of achievement at home and abroad...' A verb, as our teachers always told us, is a doing word and these verbless phrases convey atmospherics without action, plausibility without promises. Feeling good. Looking forward. Rampant sex with no strings attached. (I invented the last bit to make it more interesting.)

The climax came with his salute to the England football team's performance in Euro '96 – another sign that New Labour has written Scotland off. Labour coming home. Seventeen years of hurt. Never stopped us dreaming. Three Bambis on my shirt. Never stopped us screaming (must stop making this stuff up). I gather that the idea for the football analogy came when Mr Blair and team attended the matches at Wembley and saw that the crowds were not football hooligans but well-to-do folk, i.e. perfect New Labour material. What Mr Blair perhaps forgot was that England lost the semi-final in a penalty shoot-out. If, say, John Prescott does a Gareth Southgate and manages to lose the election in the closing minutes, sympathetic team mates will gather round and kick the daylights out of him.

There was a curious passage where he seemed close to tears remembering the day his father almost died of a stroke. It seemed to have no political purpose, though it was more dramatic than John Major's paean to his father: all he remembered was that he made garden gnomes. All party leaders recall individuals who affected them over the years. In Mr Blair's case these were almost all Tories: businessmen, a JCB plant manager, a man who was washing his car. The message seemed to be: 'We are the party for careful car owners who vote Conservative but can't stand the Tories.'

Out in the hall there were the lines of suits, the smart women's outfits, the prosperous middle class of Britain who are now in the happy position of having both main parties dedicated to their continuing welfare.

21 January 1997

Sometimes little of interest is going on in the Commons, so I pop across to the House of Lords. I am rarely disappointed.

One of the many pleasures of visiting the House of Lords (others include speeches which are generally coherent, well-informed and mercifully short) are the free guidebooks in foreign languages made available to tourists. Somehow, the workaday amendments to the Police Bill seem impossibly exotic when seen through the pages of *La Casa de los Loros*. Apparently the Chamber *tiene 80 pies de largo* – not a description of Nicholas Soames' figure but a statistic: the House is 80 feet wide.

On the *Gobierno* benches sat Baroness (PD) James, looking severe. No doubt she was reflecting that, since many of their lordships appear to be already dead and since the benches are blood red in colour, it would be possible for one of her villains to stab a peer to death and no one could tell. Barbara Castle glowered at Jim Callaghan; if looks could lacerate, her old enemy would already resemble an unlucky porcupine.

The main debate concerned authorising the police to bug people's premises. This was the committee stage of the Police Bill; it will be followed by the *Lectura y la Aprobación,* which conjures up a wonderful image of peers waving their capes, shouting '*¡Bravo! ¡Olé!*' By Lords standards it was an angry, rancorous debate, which means that it was conducted throughout with exquisite politesse.

Lord McIntosh, speaking for the *Oposición*, made a good fist of covering up the fact that Labour has done a flipover and now opposes the *Gobierno* plan to allow chief constables to approve bugging retrospectively. They and the *Liberales* insist there should be judicial authorisation beforehand. Normally, any measure which united former home secretaries with the legal profession would be opposed by all right-thinking people. But almost all of the *Pares Vitalicios* (they sound so much more vigorous than mere 'life peers') were against the bill as it stood. Lord Rogers said, 'Where there is conflict between two concerns, the freedom of the individual must prevail.'

From *los Bancos Transversales* Lord Browne Wilkinson (a law lord, or member of the *Corte de Apelación Suprema del Reino Unido*) warned that bugging had never been lawful and the bill would legalise it.

In the first hour only one peer, Lord Gisborough, supported the *Gobierno*, but he suffered from a speech impediment. So it was a big mistake for him to say 'intrusive surveillance' quite so often. But we enjoyed it.

6 February 1997

Back in 1997, full independence for Scotland was scarcely an issue. It was a vague aspiration for the Scottish National party, but in those days few imagined it would ever seem possible. Yet the signs were there.

I called into Scottish question time. This used to be a Festival of Whingeing. From the purple mountains of Skye to the gentle lowlands of the Borders, from the stews of Glasgow and the grey pilasters of Edinburgh, the nation's finest whingers assembled once a month for the Great Scottish Whinge.

The message always was that the English didn't understand them, didn't like them, and constantly mistreated them. For an hour, the high-pitched skirl of the whingers would echo round the Chamber, as stirring and evocative to an exiled Scot as the sound of a cat being strangled.

But times have changed. The government's line now is that far from being deprived by London, the Scots have been ripping off the English for years. The Scottish secretary, Michael Forsyth, claims that £8 billion more in public money is spent each year in Scotland than the Scots pay in taxes.

This, of course, is number crunching with a commercial-strength Magimix and means very little. On the other hand, the Scottish Nationalists' counter-claim that Scotland is running a surplus is obvious nonsense, too. To back up his allegations, Mr Forsyth is accompanied by a phalanx of Tory MPs who sit for constituencies such as Finchley and Hendon: 'Oh, ye'll tak' the M3 an' I'll tak' the Westway / An' I'll be in Chiswick afore ye…' Their job is to explain at every opportunity how their constituents are delighted to subsidise their Scottish friends but only as long as they can control where the bawbees go – in other words that the English will not accept a Scottish parliament.

So Peter Luff (Con, Worcester) solemnly said that he could justify to the citizens of Worcester 'this very good deal' so long as this parliament maintained control over the way the money was spent. MPs can always persuade themselves that whatever it suits them to believe also reflects the gut instincts of the people they represent, as if the people of Worcester thought about Scotland from one millennium to the next. Mr Forsyth told him that the Scots received an extra £2 billion a year for local government and a bonus £1 billion for health.

Indeed, we had learned earlier that some £15 more per head is spent on each Scot's health than is spent on every poorly English person. The minister said this was because Scots had a higher risk of heart disease and cancer and because there was a greater need for dental care. And who's surprised by that? The extra money may be accounted for entirely by that popular Scottish delicacy, the deep-fried Mars Bar. As Burns almost wrote, 'Fair fa yon sweetmeat, fine an' dandy / Proud bar o' chocolate-battered candy!'

As question time progressed – a steady alternation of Scots complaining about Scotland ('the fobbed-off spiral downwards of public services' said George Galloway) and English voices insisting that Scotland was awash with Sassenach money – we became aware of a noise that was dark and deep and rumbling. It was so deep and rumbling it was at first hard to detect what the voice was saying, or even where it was coming from. We finally tracked it down to Tommy Graham, who sits in the Labour interest for Renfrew West. Mr Graham is an enormous man who consists entirely of rolls of fat. Lovers of Rudyard Kipling's Just So Stories would recognise him from the picture of Small Porgies, the lovable sea monster who rises from the waves and smiles at all the little boats. 'Aye,' he said. 'Noooo.' Then 'because it's all lies!' followed by 'an' that's the truth!' The voice grew louder and more resonant until it filled the Chamber. Mr Graham had clearly had a good lunch, possibly including two pints of heavy and a deep-fried Mars Bar.

11 February 1997

One curious result of the 18 years of Conservative rule was that its achievements, or at least its decisions, had come to resemble those of the old Soviet Union. We were offered fantasies about the new, efficient, low-cost privatised industries, all of which demonstrated the wisdom and far-sightedness of our rulers. I came to think of it as 'Capitalist Realism'.

Thanks to Richard Branson you can now live your entire life through his Virgin companies. You could fly Virgin to New York, meet a beautiful woman, woo her with love songs on a Virgin CD (tucking a few Mates brand condoms into your wallet), marry her with Virgin Bridal services, insure her life for a million quid with Virgin Insurance, then throw her out of a hot-air balloon. This weekend, the papers carried drawings of a shiny, scarlet, high-speed tilting Virgin train. These will be equipped with luxurious club cars, where businessmen can drink vodka and make those annoying calls on their mobiles. Yes, on the train.

No one doubted that the privatised companies would find a way of catering for people who could afford £200-odd for a train journey. But what about the rest of us? Pictures like those are the Tory equivalent of the Socialist Realist school in Russia after the revolution. Vast canvases showed strong, handsome, bright-eyed comrades standing together under the Red Flag, cheerily hewing coal from the mines, the fires in the steel mills reflecting from the honest sweat on their muscles. Meanwhile, in the real world, workers had little to eat or drink and peasants were being shot. Because the reality was so different from the dogma, art was used to fill the gap. There might be nothing but rotting cabbage for dinner, but we can offer you the myth of glorious victorious comradeship instead.

In the same way, Capitalist Realism offers us a gleaming vision of what the ideology claims to provide but doesn't. Among the leading exponents of the Capitalist Realist School are ministers in the Department of Transport. Take John Watts, yesterday answering questions about the privatised railways. 'I would like to congratulate the directors of Chiltern Railways on exceeding their targets; their passengers are now enjoying the fruits of privatisation... The heroic workers of Steel Mill 872 in Kryashkov have exceeded all targets for the third successive year!'

Andrew Robathan (Con, Blaby) recalled the dark, prerevolutionary days of British Rail. Did the minister recall BR sandwiches, the wrong kind of snow and Cossacks cutting down unarmed passengers (I made the last bit up)? Mr Robathan paid tribute to the glorious achievements of the East Midlands Main Line, which was now forcing passengers off the road and on to the trains. I had a vision of the privatised engines being fitted with cow-catchers, veering off the tracks to scoop up bewildered motorway drivers.

'The key to the success of rail freight is privatisation,' said Mr Watts. 'By following the correct teachings of Marxism-Leninism, mineworkers in the Yakutskaya region have increased coal production by over 800 per cent.' Teddy Taylor (Con, Southend) congratulated the LTS railway which transports his constituents. Now the line was so reliable they could take jobs in London. And, added Sir George Young, the minister, there had been a 66 per cent fall in assaults on passengers. In the new era of socialist brotherhood, under the wise leadership of Beloved Comrade Leader Josef Stalin, all workers have jobs. And crime is at an end.

Throughout this Great Leap Forward to a Glorious Future, I noticed my old comrade Michael Fabricant jumping up and down. Sadly, the Speaker didn't call him until Question 15, which concerned traffic in the Pendle area. Surely even the Polymath of the Potteries could not be an expert on that? But he is. To loud Labour barracking he declared that road congestion in Lancashire would not matter since the train service would soon be wonderfully improved, unless Labour got in and ruined it. As the old Communists used to say, under capitalism it's always jams tomorrow.

4 March 1997

Now and again, I devote the column to questions from readers, all of them made up by me, of course. Stephen Dorrell, the health secretary, was often in the news, for reasons largely forgotten.

Once again, today's column is devoted to questions from readers.

Who is Stephen Dorrell when he's at home and why is he on every BBC news bulletin, whether it's about the European currency or Broadmoor?
I can help here. In the late 1970s I was on roller coaster at a fair near Loughborough, where I had gone for some Saturday night fun with Mr Dorrell and several other members of the Tory Reform Group, whose conference I was reporting. During the ride, Mr Dorrell threw up over me and former minister Richard Needham. Mr Needham says it was the other way round, but we were all fairly merry at the time so cannot

be absolutely certain. After this event Mr Dorrell disappeared from the public gaze. However, it seems he has rediscovered the delights of spattering his colleagues from a great height.

Why don't you have a cool strapline on your column, like your so-called rivals on the Daily Mail ('The Pundit the Politicians Dread') and the Mirror ('The Columnist Who Makes the Politicians Tremble')?
Yes, why not? I first suggested 'The Pundit Who Makes the Politicians Throw Up Over Each Other'. When that was rejected, I asked for 'The Columnist Who Covers Politicians With Hot Shame and Obliges Them to Commit Hara-Kiri in Front of Their Supporters According to Ancient Samurai Rituals', but the editor said it was too long.

Was that Cruella de Vil answering National Heritage questions yesterday?
It was Virginia Bottomley, but since she was wearing tight black trousers, a long scarlet jacket and high-heeled black boots I can understand your confusion.

What culinary disaster did Michael Fabricant MP tell his local paper would befall the leafy lanes of Lichfield if cable companies did not take care of the city trees?
He said they would become a concrete dessert.

What was Fabricant on about yesterday? He seemed to talk an awful lot.
He asked a question about the British pop music industry, which was appropriate since older readers in the Brighton area will remember his appearances as Mickey Fabb the mobile DJ

during the early 1970s, especially his Ballroom Blitz (Club Dub) and his magic mushroom loon pants with fluorescent highlights.

'In the 70s, rock and pop stars left this country because of punitive taxation under a Labour government', Mickey protested. 'But under the Conservatives the Spice Girls have stayed in this country. Will my right honourable friend congratulate the Spice Girls on winning the Brit Award last week and was she heartened to learn that Margaret Thatcher was the original Spice Girl?'

By contrast, some of us take the view that the 70s was the Decade of The Damned, but if it had anything to be said in its favour it was that lots of the Worst Pop Singers in the History of the Universe quit these shores. (Apart from the ones who drank eight bottles of vodka and choked on their own vomit first ... which is better than choking on a cabinet minister's vomit.)

If Margaret Thatcher was a Spice Girl, what did she mean by 'I really really really wanna zig-a-zig-ah'?
Dunno. But I expect that Lord McAlpine could tell you.

Is it true that Lord McAlpine erected a life-sized statue of his gardener in the garden which he had restored?
Yes. Isn't it sweet?

How should Mr Major react to Lord McAlpine's barb that he made no contribution to internal Conservative strategy: 'John Major was often at Chequers, pretending to be a pair of curtains'?
He should pull himself together.

2 April 1997

The 1997 election campaign began in early April. Everyone's eyes were on the exciting new party leader who seemed certain to win.

Our day out with Tony Blair began at Labour's news media centre in Millbank, London. As we waited for the leader, we watched a video film of the party's rally in Kent on Monday. What a happy occasion it was, with confident, prosperous people arriving in late-model cars. Past Labour broadcasts used to show derelict factories and crumbling hospitals; now they depict an idealised, sunlit Britain, designed to force home Mr Blair's key campaign message: 'Life's better under the Conservatives. Don't let the Tories ruin it.'

Britain's favourite battling granny, the Founder and President for Life of the World Institute of Thatcherology, was out to help. When the Tories are in trouble they always call on the Baroness. But so does Labour. 'Can you imagine,' Mr Blair asked scornfully, 'Mrs Thatcher saying, "There are candidates I would very much like not to stand, but I'm sorry, there is nothing I can do about it"?' What a shame, then, that the object of his admiration holds him in such apparent contempt. So much of what he says precisely resembles what she used to say.

Yesterday he told us that the way to get a better standard of living for the poor 'is not to stop people being wealthy at the top; it is giving others hope and opportunity'. So very like Lady Thatcher's 'You can't enrich the poor by impoverishing the rich', which she had embroidered on all her flak jackets.

Mr Blair announced that Labour's policies were 'mainstream, costed, sensible', and with that battle cry ringing in our ears we set off for the leader's cavalcade. This consists of three buses, each with a slogan on the side: 'Leading Britain', 'Into the Future,' and 'With Tony Blair'. As we sped north, we sometimes changed order, or a lorry would slide between us so that the convoy would read: 'Eddie Stobart Leading Britain into the Future' or 'Daily Wet Fish Deliveries Throughout the UK With Tony Blair'.

In the bus, Mr Blair was busy lowering expectations. This is his current strategy. 'All the way through I have said that we do not promise a revolution; I don't say I can wave a magic wand and put the world to rights.'

We arrived in Northampton, ready to lower a few more expectations. 'You're going to win!' one woman shouted. 'I hope so,' he said dubiously. He'll probably be saying that it's too early to predict the result if Labour takes Huntingdon.

He plunged into the crowd. 'It's that bloke off the telly, wossname?' a loutish youth yelled, but most people seemed pleased. One woman actually gave him her baby to kiss, something that politicians rarely do, since what voter wants to see her child covered with MP's slobber? A voter from hell arrived with another child in tow. She harangued him. There was no escape. 'I want to see you keep your promises!' she yelled. Clearly her expectations were very low, but he lowered them some more. 'That's why we're only making promises we can keep,' he said.

He kept tight hold of Cherie, encouraging her to wave, as if they had just spotted someone they knew in an upstairs window. This is something else politicians share with children: they too have imaginary friends. Back on the bus a spin doctor climbed on board to spin for us not just what the leader had said, but what the public had said about him. For instance, a Mrs Rowlands had reported that he seemed 'not too bad, really'. Obviously her expectations were none too high, but even so that's not exactly what she had intended to say. 'She *meant*,' said the spin doctor, 'that he was very nice and trustworthy.' In this election nothing, least of all the public, can be left to chance.

24 April 1997

Martin Bell, the celebrated TV reporter in the white suit, ran in Cheshire against Neil Hamilton, the Tory former minister who was accused of taking money in brown envelopes from Mohamed Al Fayed, something he always denied.

'You'll notice,' said Martin Bell, 'that all Neil Hamilton's posters are on trees and hedges, never in people's houses. Unless I'm mistaken, trees and hedges do not have a vote. Nobody wants to admit that they support him.'

If the posters mean anything, Bell will triumph. Last week Hamilton threatened him with several libel writs. 'I didn't know what to do. I don't even have a lawyer. I'm 58, and he's the first enemy I've ever had.'

We went to canvass in Great Budworth, a gorgeous old village, usually solid Tory territory. Apart from one blue placard on a tree, all the posters were for Bell. His reception was astonishing, quite the best I've seen for any candidate in this election apart from Mo Mowlam. A smartly dressed woman in a BMW screeched to a halt. 'We are definitely voting for you!' she said, evidently a founder member of Beamers for Bell.

The campaign has clearly been the most tremendous fun, involving several mini pub crawls between bouts of canvassing. Bell himself, his huge minder, a cameraman called Nigel Bateson, the various 'Bell belles' who include his daughter Melissa, and the substantial press entourage, spend a great deal of time pondering the campaign over refreshments. In one pub, two old geezers looked up from their pints. 'I couldn't vote for a man who drinks,' said one. (Northern humour does tend to verge on the predictable.)

'This is medicinal,' said the other.

'Then you must be very ill,' the candidate snapped, but amiably.

'I expect you'd rather be dodging bullets,' said the first man.

'Oh, I would, I would,' he replied. But it's not true. He's having the time of his life.

29 April 1997

Labour was determined not to take any chances in this election. All candidates, including the party's most senior members, were to be kept on the shortest possible rein. Robin Cook, who went on to be foreign secretary, was among those who pooh-poohed the notion that he might be directed from central control in Millbank, London. I caught up with him in the far north of Scotland.

Many people say that New Labour is a party of control freaks. New Labour resents this. They particularly resent the implication that people who expect to be cabinet ministers next week have less freedom than a crocodile of school children on an outing.

Possibly so. But to put the theory to the test I went out with Robin Cook, who is likely soon to be our foreign secretary. He was in Inverness, drumming up support for the Labour candidate, David Stewart, in Britain's only four-way marginal. Last time, Sir Russell Johnson, a Liberal, got only 26 per cent of the vote and still won the seat.

We drove miles out into the countryside, then turned left across open fields and wound down to the Moray Firth. Here, in the middle of nothing, is Barmac, Europe's largest maker of oil rigs. It is almost as far from Westminster as you can go while remaining on the British mainland.

We were to rise 270 feet in the air, hauled up by a gigantic crane in a 'basket'. This turned out to be a large steel tray, perhaps 5 ft by 12 ft, with fencing round it. Rather low fencing, I thought. We were given steel-capped boots, industrial goggles, protective jackets and hard hats. Then we were strapped into harnesses, which grasped us cosily round the back and the crotch. Finally, they hooked our reins to the rails.

We began to climb, swaying gently. Mr Cook asked, reasonably I thought, if the crane driver was a Labour voter. By this time we were about 150 feet up, suspended from the top of the crane by a single hawser. 'I'd have thought it would be pretty hard to fall out of one of these,' said Mr Cook, hopefully.

'Oh, no, it would be quite easy,' said our guide, a Labour activist who works at the site.

Loch Ness was to the south, Easter Ross in front of us. Seagulls cut the air far below us. Even the workers on the rig looked minute. Mr Cook thought it would be a good idea to get closer to them, no doubt to solicit their votes. Instructions were radioed down. 'It'll be a bit rocky, I'm afraid,' said our guide. The basket began to swing from side to side, as we swerved dizzily between the struts and pipes that make up the rig. We clanged noisily into something. Fifty feet below an arc welder sent up a shower of sparks.

And at that very moment, as we stood suspended in the heavens, swaying at a height that would give a mountain goat vertigo – no, would make a condor queasy – Mr Cook's bleeper started its urgent electronic pinging and flashed this message:

'Call Millbank, as soon as possible.'

Tony Blair I

8 May 1997

Labour duly won its enormous landslide majority.

The Commons was full of bewildered bunches of people, drifting around, uncertain what to do or where to go, desperately seeking their group leader. Normally these are tourists. Yesterday they were new Labour MPs. When they finally reached the Chamber, it was full to bursting as never before. Those lucky enough to find a seat were stuffed buttock to buttock, so tightly that if anyone had wriggled, half a dozen new members would have popped up like bread from a toaster, described an arc, and landed on the Tories. At the Speaker's chair they were jammed like a Cup Final crowd. They filled the jury boxes, usually kept for civil servants, and spilled over from the galleries. They actually looked like a landslide. It all resembled a great Frith canvas, perhaps depicting Derby Day. The 120-odd women stood out in this summer's chic shades of orange, fuchsia and lime green.

Then, on closer inspection, we could see the fascinating detail. Angela and Maria Eagle, identical twins, both in black costumes with white blouses, both capable of creating massive and pleasing confusion. Anne Begg, the first MP in anyone's memory to be a wheelchair user, tucked up by the Bar of the House, tiny and sparkling with happiness. Dennis Skinner, now promoted to the Edward Heath Memorial Sulking Seat.

The Tories looked furious, with the exception of Alan Clark, who was aiming his heat-seeking eye contact at Virginia Bottomley. Surely not? He has reformed. Probably. The new prime minister arrived to cheers and clapping from Labour members, who didn't know that the rules forbid applause. But what do they care? They make up the rules now.

Then it was time for the election of the Speaker. Gwyneth Dunwoody, the first seconder, announced, 'This is a beautiful day. God is in his heaven, and a majority of this House are wearing the right colours.'

Next Tony Benn stood up to make the historic first attack on the new government. It was, he said, the first time he had spoken from the government backbenches since 1 August 1951. 'Then, the British government controlled the lives of millions in Asia and in Africa. Why, we even controlled the Bank of England!'

The Tories were slightly consoled by this and cheered him mightily. (So, inwardly, must a few Labour MPs have felt, on the grounds that they were not swept into office to give more power to bankers.)

Then came the moment when the re-elected Betty Boothroyd had to be dragged ceremonially and as if unwillingly to the chair. No drag queen, she. Never has anyone marched more merrily in that direction. Indeed she almost dragged her seconders along until, on reaching the Despatch Box, they retired, panting and defeated.

10 June 1997

John Major had swiftly resigned and disappeared to the Oval to watch cricket. The Tories held a crowded leadership contest, with each candidate offering a reception with drinks and nibbles for the voters – other Tory MPs – on the same evening.

All five leadership candidates held parties for Tory MPs last night. For an indecisive alcoholic, it must have been four hours of bliss. A lot of effort was being expended in pursuit of a job that will confer on the winner, for five years at least, roughly as much raw power as the Hon. Sec. of a crown green bowling club.

The air crackled with malice. John Redwood started with tea and Pimms in a private room at the Commons. One of his supporters marked our card: 'Michael Howard has been economical with the *actualité*, as usual. He's claiming at least two people who we know are committed to John... Ken Clarke's giving a beer and crisps party. Don't you hate that carapace of affected ordinariness?... Hague? Oh dear, the human embryo...'

The press hung round outside while the members arrived with their wives. People kept reminding us that this was the most sophisticated electorate on the planet. They looked more like Ladies' Night at Hartlepool Freemasons. The wives tend to a fashionable plumpness, like Sophie Dahl only with clothes on. They all had that glossy air of people who know exactly where their next meal is coming from.

Like many other MPs, Peter and Virginia Bottomley went to all five bashes. 'Michael Howard had the best champagne, Peter Lilley had the nicest garden, and John Redwood served some squidgy passion-fruit thing,' observed Mr Bottomley.

Outside the Lilley party three young men, not yet shaving I would guess, appeared with placards marked 'Portillo 4 El Presidente'. They were dressed as Mexican peasants and were swigging from a bottle marked 'tequila' but which looked suspiciously like cold tea. They spoke to the MP for North Essex: 'Meester Jenkin, what about Miguel, 'e is our 'ero. Why you no vote for Miguel? In our country you would be shot.'

They turned out to be Young Conservatives from Streatham, which leaves another mystery: where do you find four Young Conservatives in Streatham?

William Hague arrived at the Carlton Club with his fiancée, Ffion Jenkins. She did not look happy. His expression was relaxed, cool and confident. Her expression seemed to say, 'If you don't leave *now*, I shall call security!'

Ken Clarke had the biggest turnout of former cabinet ministers, including Willie Whitelaw, now very old and frail. There was a surreal moment when we were briefed by Peter Luff on the food: 'There were those little Indian oniony balls, bhajis is it? And some hammy, cheesy things, and those vol-au-vent thingies, and stuffed cherry tomatoes.' This was the real cutting edge of political reporting. Walter Bagehot, thou shouldst be living.

20 June 1997

Ten days later we learned who had won.

The result was announced, and in the committee corridor a woman of a certain age, described as a Tory MP's assistant, let loose a blood-chilling cry. 'Y-e-e-e-s! There is a God looking after the Conservative party!' I was reminded of the famous scene in When Harry Met Sally, except that this time the orgasm was real. 'Urghhh! Ohh!' went the woman. 'I don't want what she's having,' murmured a few listeners.

Moments later the new leader marched past us to speak to MPs and peers. His remaining hair was yellow and glossy, his tie was yellow and glossy, and his pate seemed to have been french polished. Give him glasses and he'd look like the comedian Harry Hill, with the same surreal undertow to much of what he says.

After the speech Jeffrey Archer told us, 'I wish you could have been there. He was marvellous. He grew another foot.'

A third foot, to go with the triple-breasted suit! He spoke to us, and our minds rolled back twenty years to that speech in Blackpool. He sounded only slightly younger now. 'The Conservative party has placed a grave responsibility on me... done me a great honour... road to unity and confidence... collective responsibility...' The phrases poured slowly out, like sludge from a sump. There was a certain frozen look on the faces of his campaign team. Could it be that he is – above all else – terribly, majestically, thunderously boring?

We moved over to Conservative Central Office, where John Major was to make a ceremonial handing over of the leadership. What form would this take? A gavel? A sceptre? A brown envelope full of £50 notes? It turned out to be an exchange of flattering speeches.

'Whichever way we chose today, we could not lose,' Mr Major said.

'Yes, because you weren't standing,' muttered one party disloyalist.

Finally the new leader addressed us. He warned that there would have to be changes. That everyone would need to work hard. That he would sweep away 'a lot of old cobwebs!' (Has anyone ever promised to sweep away new cobwebs?) Then he produced one mighty, resonant line: 'I will tolerate no bellyaching!'

If he's so young, why does he sound like an elderly house master in a minor public school?

11 July 1997

We parliamentary sketchwriters tend to ignore the long-serving left-wing Labour MP Dennis Skinner, one of the old place's great institutions, on the grounds that we do the funnies. But he is quite often good copy.

Dennis Skinner intervened in the British Airways strike yesterday. 'People who work for a living should be treated properly,' he said, 'not by Pontius Pilate!' (Or possibly by Pontius Pilot. 'Good morning, ladies and gentlemen, and welcome aboard. We'll be on our way to Malaga just as soon as I've finished washing my hands…')

Mr Skinner was referring to 'that evil man, Ayling', who had been 'hounding and intimidating the people down at

Heathrow, the stewards and stewardesses who have been on strike, many of whom vote Labour'.

The Tories hooted with glee, not only because Bob Ayling, the BA chief executive, is a Labour supporter, but because of the image conjured up by Mr Skinner's words. To him strikes are not merely a means of bargaining for better pay and conditions, but an affirmation of traditional community solidarity. We could picture the villagers in the old, tight-knit, flight-attending villages of Weybridge, Chertsey and Egham, huddled round braziers, stamping on the snow in their complimentary slipperettes, glugging miniatures of duty-free Baileys to keep out the cold, as their loyal womenfolk hand out plastic trays of lasagne made out of recycled inflight magazines. These people are engaged in a noble, if doomed, attempt to preserve their traditional, fast-vanishing way of life.

Anyhow, his intervention should be enough to get Mr Skinner a complimentary upgrade if he ever decides to go abroad. (He's tried abroad in the past, but didn't care for it.)

'Our in-flight film presentation this morning is Ken Loach's The Price of Coal. Songs of Defiance, with Arthur Scargill, can be found on Channel 7 on your headsets. A protest march against the appalling conditions suffered in economy class will begin from the forward galley shortly after the service of canapés. And can demonstrators please keep the aisles free for the drinks trolley...'

10 September 1997

Margaret Thatcher might be gone, but she was most certainly not forgotten. Less than a fortnight after the death of Princess Diana, she turned up to address the American Association of Travel Agents who for some strange reason had decided to hold their annual conference in Glasgow, and for some stranger reason still had invited her to address them.

Since the dreadful events of 10 days ago, she may well be the world's most famous woman once again. Perhaps that is why her fee is £50,000 per speech, which worked out yesterday at £1,136 a minute. Campaigners for a 'yes' vote in the referendum currently being fought in Scotland were desperately hoping she would speak to the cameras on behalf of the 'noes'. For years now, her mere existence has been seen by many Scots as the conclusive proof that they need independence. Indeed, she did talk about a proud, hard-working people under the jackboot of an arrogant, distant government. But it turned out she meant Hong Kong.

I settled back to enjoy a treat, since most of her lucrative speeches are closed to the press and public, who cannot afford the £7.57 each word costs at normal talking speed.

She began with a tribute to Princess Diana. This lasted 90 seconds, or £1,704. Then she displayed the breathtaking chutzpah familiar to those of us who are not American travel agents. She launched a paean of praise to herself. Politicians, she said, always get things wrong. 'There are, of course, exceptions. Ronald Reagan, for example. And, er, there was a woman who worked along the same lines!'

Then she announced that the Blair government was also working along those lines laid down by her. 'That is why we have the lowest unemployment in Europe and, all things considered, the highest standard of living in Europe!'

What? asked the handful of Brits in the audience. Who was she kidding? But it didn't matter. We had reached £6,618 and the meter was running fast. Leadership, she mused, was difficult – for some. 'I know politicians who lead by following the opinion polls. It's called 'followership'. I prefer to lead myself!' Loud applause; meter reaches £15,904.

She had wanted, she told us, 50 years more on the lease of Hong Kong, 'for which I had the temerity to ask!' Loud and prolonged applause reminiscent of Castro speaking to the party congress in Havana. Meter hits £21,584.

The next 20 grand took us on a *tour d'horizon* including China and the Middle East. The travel agents, having topped up their frequent groveller points, were getting restive and hungry. At £45,440 she quoted Bette Davis: 'I always attempt the impossible; it improves my work!' and they recovered enough to roar with admiring laughter.

Then came the jaw-dropping peroration. We had just reached £48,848, and she got on to the Pilgrim Fathers. 'They didn't go to America for subsidies! There weren't any. Instead, they founded the greatest nation on earth!

'My friends, I salute you!'

Massive, roof-raising applause, cheers, yelling, foot-stamping, with discreet barfing from the Brits. And 50,000 smackeroonies for her!

1 October 1997

In the autumn, Tony Blair spoke to his party conference for the first time as prime minister.

The prime minister walked on to the music of Saint-Saëns, specifically the part used as the theme of Babe. This is the popular film about a shy talking piglet who learns to round up flocks of docile, disciplined sheep. Just a coincidence, of course. We had just seen a video depicting Five Months of Glorious Progress. Election promises honoured! Blair triumphs in Amsterdam! Ragged cheers greeted these declarations, a reminder that Labour has always had trouble distinguishing between a decision and an achievement.

He walked onto the platform and the audience rose to him in a standing ovation which was, perhaps, slightly more enthusiastic than the one at the end. He kept waving them back down. You half expected him to say that the hall was only booked for half an hour, and if they didn't mind he'd crack on.

His whole style is muffled and subdued, even the loud bits. It's not so much a speech as a presentation without slides.

The audience is like the congregation in an evangelical church. They want to be writhing on the floor in ecstasy but find they've got a Church of England vicar who doesn't even have a tambourine. By the end he was talking about the importance of giving.

'Make this the giving age...' He sounded as if he was announcing Harvest Festival next week: 'Not too many vegetable marrows this year, if you don't mind.' Soon the congregation realised that they weren't going to get very much in exchange for their giving. He used the phrase 'hard choices' and even 'harsh choices' 11 times. In the past this has always been Labour-speak for 'No more money'.

And so it is today. But under Mr Blair, harshness is also a virtue in itself. 'Ours must be a compassionate society. But compassion with a hard edge. A strong society cannot be built on soft choices.'

Compassion with a hard edge! The razor blade in the duvet! I wonder what it's like at the Blair breakfast table.

'Which cereal would you like, dear?'

'I want the hard choice, and that means Shreddies. But Shreddies without milk, because otherwise they would become the soft choice, and soft choices are no basis for break-fast for our people.'

As well as being harsh and hard, we must be modern. Being modern is an absolute good in itself, and he used the word 21 times. 'We must modernise – and take the hard choices to do it.' Civil servants are to be replaced by computers. Soon a quarter of all dealings with government will be performed electronically. Members of the public can be asked:

'Do you want your choice to be (*click on one*) (a) hard, (b) harsh, or (c) downright pitiless?'

There were curious Blairish phrases: 'The gates of xeno-phobia, falling down', which was almost Blakean. We had anointed him to lead us into the next millennium. 'That was your challenge to me. Proudly, humbly, I accepted it.'

Vainly, modestly, he set to work. Harshly, compassion-ately, he took the tough choices. Loudly, softly, he spoke to conference and, fascinated, bored, they gave him a standing ovation anyway.

19 November 1997

One of the most controversial measures that Labour had promised to bring in was the abolition of fox-hunting.

Fox-hunting is a gut, emotional matter. You loathe it or you don't. It is not susceptible to rational debate. You cannot discuss the pros and cons as if they were interest rates.

But MPs didn't half have a go. The House was almost packed and simmering with excitement. Cometh the hour, cometh the man. Unfortunately the man was Michael Foster, whose bill they were now debating. Mr Foster is a new boy, so there is one excuse. He is also a former accountancy lecturer, and there's another. Unfortunately you can't address the Commons as if they were a group of promising trainee accountants. And Mr Foster had over-prepared.

Even the apparently spontaneous interventions by his supporters were marked 'Intervention' on his script. Beside him sat a colleague who, every few moments, presented him with a fresh sheet of facts, in case he might run short. He used cliché like an aerosol: 'the hand of fate... we must put over our core message and restate our key pledges.' He plonked down truisms like dominoes: 'As many people have pointed out, dying is a natural activity.' At the end he was loudly cheered by supporters of the bill. I know that cheer; it doesn't reward a speech well made, but covers up for a turkey.

This might have mattered more if Michael Heseltine had not, for once, made a bad speech, and if Ann Widdecombe had not made a brilliant one. Mr Heseltine started, as ever, slowly and solemnly. With his bristling eyebrows and bushy hair he looked a little like a fox, but a very grand one with quite the bushiest tail in the wood.

He attacked the bill for allowing 'flushing out'. 'Why do you flush something out?' he demanded, and foolishly left a pause, no doubt designed to add gravity to the reply he was to give us.

But it was too late. 'Ask Mrs Thatcher!' shouted Denis MacShane, and the place dissolved into laughter, the kind of nerve-shredding, speech-destroying, morale-deflating laughter that takes away all hope. Heseline ploughed on regardless, but people chattered happily among themselves like mice who've seen the cat locked in its basket.

Soon afterwards Ann Widdecombe rose to support the bill.

Magnificent in scarlet and bottle green, she was consumed by a terrifying rage. She didn't just scorn the hunting lobby; she poured whole carboys of nitric acid over them. Their argument about jobs was ludicrous: 'If you abolished crime, you will put all the police out of work. If you abolish ill-health, you'll put the doctors and nurses out of work!' Her whole body rocking, she invited the bill's opponents to go and stand near the lions in Africa, 'and see if they enjoy the hunt! I know I would enjoy watching it.'

She sat down to roars of applause from the Labour abolitionists and – strictly forbidden, this – clapping. I doubt if she changed a single vote, but she didn't half cheer up the abolitionists.

We finished with a Home Office minister weaselling his way out of a promise to make time for the bill. But that doesn't matter just yet. In the meantime it will meet its fate in the Lords, where it will be seized on by savage peers, ripped to pieces, its sub-clauses torn out and eaten.

4 March 1998

One of the new administration's most colourful figures, in every sense, was the lord chancellor, Derry Irvine. He was a complete stranger to what are nowadays known as self-esteem issues. He was asked to give evidence to a select committee, the subject nominally being constitutional affairs; in actuality it was about the immense sums he had arranged to be spent on his private quarters in the House of Lords.

Lord Irvine might have adopted the approach humorous, with a few self-deprecating jokes about his £650,000 redecoration. He could have turned up to the public administration committee in white overalls and paint-spattered shoes, carrying an old radio smeared with putty. They'd have loved him.

Instead he took the approach pompous. He had not merely been right to demand his refurbishments; he was working 'in a noble cause', like extending the franchise, or defeating Hitler. 'Future generations will be grateful,' he intoned. (Of course future generations are grateful when we spend our money on them. Sod 'em, is what I say. Let them buy their own £8,000 beds.)

The lord chancellor does not so much answer a question as unroll a speech, as if it were precious hand-blocked wallpaper. Nothing is ever so humble as to be merely 'true', but instead 'is the case, across the board, as it were, for all manner of reasons'. He never does anything so mundane as to agree with someone. Instead he examines himself and declares, 'I find myself hospitable to the idea.' Unlike us mortals, he cannot just say yes, but instead informs us: 'Right or wrong, that is the view I took. Other views could, however, be expressed.'

He treated the committee as if they were all junior barristers. Or rather, he spoke to them as if he were the grandest of grand QCs, up before a particularly young and callow judge who might be expected to quail before his admonitions.

'That is a speech, not a question!' he snapped at one whipper-snapper, who just happened to be an elected member of parliament. He instructed them to pause for his answers. The more he was attacked, the more blameless he appeared, in his own eyes, at least.

Andrew Tyrie, a Tory MP, asked about the letter the lord chancellor had written to Black Rod, explaining that he and Lady Irvine were connoisseurs and how important it was that great works of art should be shipped to decorate their quarters *instanter*. Had this proved embarrassing?

Embarrassing? What a bizarre concept! A pigeon defecating on his wig, perhaps. That might be embarrassing. But not suggesting the expenditure of huge sums of money upon his official residence. What could be embarrassing about that?

'I was not even setting out an argument. I was setting out the facts, the pros and the cons, as dispassionately as I could...

'Future generations will agree, and will see this as a storm in a teacup,' he vouchsafed (the style is catching). He could well be right. Peter Mandelson may be sitting in a sperm bank now, canvassing the views of future generations.

Mr Tyrie persisted. Was it not an embarrassment to his party?

Heaven forfend. 'I think that people up and down the country believe this has been blown grotesquely out of proportion.'

Mr Tyrie wondered whether his attitude amounted to 'Je ne regrette rien'. Once Lord Irvine had untangled the accent (11th-century Norman French is the only dialect lord chancellors are allowed to understand), he affirmed: 'I do not think that my apologies are due. I read the commentators who say, "Three cheers that this work has been done! And three cheers for the committee that chose to make the decision!"'

Suddenly we had a picture of a nation rejoicing. It was like VE Day. There would be school holidays to celebrate the pasting of the last roll on the wall. Marchers would descend upon London, demanding the right to go fox-hunting and for hand-sewn tapestries to line Lord Irvine's bedroom.

But though the lord chancellor is as pompous as it is possible for a man to be without actually bursting, he may have a point. When Pugin did the interior decoration of the Palace, he insisted on standards that today cost £4 million to maintain. Either you keep it up as it is, or you go for chipboard and Formica. As Lord Irvine said, 'You are not talking about something down at the DIY store,' though to our delight it turned out that he had never even heard of B&Q. I suspect that the lord chancellor has T'ang Dynasty hand-blocked wallpaper in his potting shed.

30 June 1998

The Millennium Dome was not quite the disaster it was sometimes painted; now re-named the O2 Arena, it has become the greatest pop music venue in Europe. The mistake was, perhaps, to give the task of organising the interior to Peter Mandelson, who has always regarded appearance as more important than mere substance.

Yesterday Peter Mandelson was attacked, as usual, over the contents of the Millennium Dome. How, asked Tim Loughton, a Tory from Worthing, could anyone enjoy contemplation in the Spirit Zone, with the roar of the Blackwall Tunnel under-neath, a circus nearby 'and not a crucifix in sight'?

Mr Mandelson said solemnly that there would be, some-where in the Dome, a place for private prayer. (Though if it's like other theme park attractions, the queues will be endless, with signs saying, 'At this point you are 90 minutes away from the Lost Orison Experience.') Mr Mandelson added, 'Churches are setting up many events, centred on Pentecost 2000.'

Pentecost 2000! It's a perfect New Labour name, being pure PR-babble and also quite inaccurate, since Pentecost happened 30 years after the birth of Christ. (Though of course 'Pentecost 1970' wouldn't work, since it would make everyone think of flared trousers and Sweet records, and the time when Michael Fabricant was one of the top disc jockeys in the Brighton and Hove area, appearing as Mickey Fabb.)

You could rename all the events in the Christian calendar. Christmas would become 'Nativity Year Zero'. Good Friday would be the 'Hanging On In There '33 Tour', and cast-ing the money-lenders from the Temple would be entirely re-themed and launched as 'In Partnership with the Business Community'.

Mr Peter Ainsworth is a man of whom I had not heard before. He has a magnificent head of hair, like a female Ameri-can TV newsreader, and surprisingly he appears to be the member of the shadow cabinet concerned with culture, media and sport. He complained about the lack of government support for seaside towns. Indeed such places were suffering from tremendous over-regulation. 'Far from receiving a Kiss-Me-Quick hat, any minister visiting the seaside this summer is likely to be told exactly where he can stick his rock!'

I wondered briefly what Harold Macmillan would have made of Mr Ainsworth. I suspect he would have told his gardener to spray him with something.

30 September 1998

We became used, over the years, to the prime minister's strange, somewhat hypnotic speaking style. This was at the 1998 Labour conference.

The first Labour conference session yesterday was closed to the public, though I turned on the TV feed anyway. You could see the hall, but all you could hear was a bored technician somewhere, repeating over and over again, 'I have been asked to say, "This is the BBC control room, identifying conference sound."' A few minutes later he said it in Robin Day's voice. Then he did the gormless people from Monty Python: 'Diss. Ish. Durr. BBC. Control. Wooomb!' Then he did an excellent John Cole.

An hour later we got a brilliant Tony Blair impression. So it took me a while to realise that this was the real thing. Like many politicians who are insecure in their style, he has begun to copy his imitators. The long legs (he is much taller than you think if you've only seen him on television) march forward to the front of the stage, then back again, like Michael Flatley in slow motion. He is beginning to sound like Margaret Thatcher, though with 1960s diction and a mid-Atlantic vocabulary. He never meets a man, but always a 'guy'. The conversational tone is 'aw shucks' and self-deprecatory. He had, he told us, been made overconfident by the success of his speech at the

French National Assembly. Afterwards, he said, 'Ah got me French muddled up and said, "I desire Lionel Jospin."'

The line 'No backing down. Backbone, not backdown, is what Britain needs' must surely have deliberately echoed 'The lady's not for turning'. He is becoming a cross between smiley, cuddly, toothy Richard Branson and Miss Whiplash.

Most of all, the verbs disappear. The number of verb-free sentences rises every year. Yesterday there were 112 syntactical orphans in the speech. Verbs are cut down like earthworms under a lawn strimmer.

As my old English teacher used to tell us, a verb is a doing word. Leaving verbs in your sentences implies a promise of action or a record of achievement past. But no verbs, so no pledges. Instead, fuzzy, well-meaning word pictures. New investment. Holding firm. Modernisation. Reform. The best in the world.

These sentences tell us nothing. They are the equivalent of the copy in ads for expensive cars: 'Luxury. Prestige. Performance. A promise of the future, with you in control.' There is no commitment, nothing concrete, nothing to attack or to demand. Instead we are offered a vague evocation of a better world, as if the fantasy were the reality – a trip to Utopia without a map.

After the speech, Alastair Campbell, the prime minister's press secretary, stopped by our part of the media room to tell us that it had been a 'self-spinning speech'. What a technological triumph that is, along with the self-cleaning oven and the self-basting turkey! What he meant, I suppose, is that it was written in terms so simple even mere voters would be able to understand it, and did not need to rely on hacks to interpret it as 'Blair's triumph' or 'My pledge to our children – by Tony'.

Afterwards I eavesdropped on the delegates, many of whom seemed genuinely moved. 'Wonderful' and 'truly uplifting' were among the remarks I heard. And indeed it was uplifting, in the same sense as a Wonderbra, creating a marvellous appearance with the minimum of raw material.

8 October 1998

One of the great political hatreds was that between Edward Heath and Margaret Thatcher, made all the more poignant and fascinating because it was essentially one way. He detested her; she simply regarded him as a grumpy nuisance. At one of the dinners he held for political journalists at party conferences, the hacks jokily presented Heath with a chocolate bust of Thatcher they had found in a Brighton sea-front shop. He unwrapped it, grinned, then picked up his table knife and demolished it, in the manner of the shower scene in Psycho.

The prime minister who gave away our national sovereignty to Europe sat on the platform yesterday. Ted Heath was a safe 10 feet behind her. Margaret Thatcher sat serene and poised, receiving plaudits from speaker after speaker, who have each remembered her triumphs and forgotten the disasters. Ted Heath sat at the back, scowling and sinking as deep into those nasty Ikea armchairs as it is possible to go. I was put in mind of one of those beached whales who turn up at seasides now and again. You half expected Greenpeace to send a crane to pick him up, load him onto a boat and offer him a hearty lunch of plankton. Speakers would say the kind of weird, dysfunctional things people say at Tory conferences, and his arms would stay still, draped along the sides of the chair.

'We say no to Labour's nannying attitude to British beef and the meat-eating public!' someone said. The conference whistled and cheered. Ted sat still. Even his eyes were motionless. Like the stranded whale, he is in a wholly alien environment.

The speakers attacked Europe. Some imperceptible muscular movement caused the expression on his face to register faintly more distress and contempt than it had before.

'How ebsolutely splindid it is to si Margaret Thetcher and Tid Heath on the plitform,' said Michael Howard. This compliment to himself was greeted by Sir Edward with what, for him, amounts to wild applause: that is to say, he placed his palms together twice, very slowly indeed.

'We votid overwhilmingly to support William Hague's policy on the single currincy,' said Mr Howard. Lady Thatcher applauded. Mr Hague tried to look stern and resolute. In a frantic burst of activity, Ted turned his head three degrees to the right. For some reason I formed an image of Lady Bracknell taken hostage in Beirut, determined to give no satisfaction to her captors.

'Tin years ago, Margrit Thatcher lifted our eyes…' said Mr Howard. Liddy Thatcher's own eyes, always gleaming madly, seemed lit from within by a phosphorescent glow. Sir Edward's eyes widened sceptically by a millimetre, which, for him, is the equivalent of leading 10,000 people on a protest march to Downing Street. The speech ended and the conference rose for a standing ovation. Faced with the prospect of being the only person seated in the hall, Ted was obliged to stand, which he did with unwilling yet stoical lethargy, in the meantime flapping his hands together like two dying flounders twitching on the dockside.

At that point, Michael Ancram, the new party chairman, started to execute a curious little dance, a sort of stately onstage gavotte, which puzzled me until I worked out that he was trying to steer Lady Thatcher out to the exit while simultaneously blocking Sir Edward's progress, so they wouldn't have to be in proximity to each other for even a few seconds. He did this with such success that I half expected him to sweep off a tricorne hat and bow in triumph.

Soon afterwards John Redwood made his annual rabble-soothing speech. It must be hard to fail at a Tory conference by making an attack on Peter Mandelson, but the shadow trade secretary managed it. The biggest laugh, evoking a sort of ghastly rattle like a rat trapped in a dustbin, came for this line: 'For Peter Mandelson, Dome is where the heart is.' It got the biggest laugh because it was the best joke, and that tells you all you need to know.

15 April 1999

John Prescott's position as deputy prime minister meant that in Tony Blair's absence, he took prime minister's questions. These occasions came to be hugely popular, not least because of Mr Prescott's unusual way with the English language.

The prime minister was in Brussels, working with Kofi Annan on the plight of the Kosovo refugees. Back on the government front bench another humanitarian disaster was unfolding. His deputy, John Prescott, had taken over question time.

It was terrible. It was also ghastly, chaotic, miserable and floor-staringly, mouth-puckeringly, gaze-avertingly awful. In any civilised country a trained SAS squad would have abseiled down the Chamber walls, tossing smoke bombs, grabbing Mr Prescott and hustling him to safety.

As it was, many people felt sorry. He is, after all, someone who has got where he is by dint of hard work, dedication and political flair. Others take a sterner view.

He is, nominally, the second most powerful man in the land, and should at least be able to patch a sentence together. Or be vaguely aware of government policy on the kind of vital, world-changing issues to which the rest of us devote slightly less thought than whether we want salt 'n' vinegar or original salted flavour. Being a soggy, Guardian-writing liberal, I agree with both points of view. Yes, it was hilarious. Yes, but only an arrogant, boorish oaf would not feel a twinge of pity for the man.

He began by flannelling well enough. Labour's David Chaytor asked him about the role of the Russians in the Balkan war. 'I think that on a number of occasions there has been a concern and it has been a subject of discussion in these discussions,' he said, in what was basically pidgin Prescott. He was reading from a script, and though he skipped several words, the average brain, accustomed to the Prescottic dialect, supplies the missing syllables.

At this stage, Labour MPs were calmly discussing whether Peter Lilley (William Hague's deputy and the Niles Crane of the Conservative party) was wearing make-up for the cameras.

Things were calm. They had no idea of what was to follow.

Then nemesis arrived in the unlikely shape of the genteel Alan Beith. The Liberal Democrat deputy asked him to confirm that average class sizes are, in spite of Labour's promises, actually increasing.

'I can confirm that we are on target for reducing class sizes,' Mr Prescott said, to Tory jeers.

'But that is not the same question,' said Mr Beith, who rattled off a series of figures which seemed to make his case.

'You asked if we were on target,' said Mr Prescott, changing the subject again. 'And that is the answer you are going to get!'

The Tories were chortling, even glistening with pleasure.

Then Michael Spicer demanded a guarantee that the withholding tax would never be introduced in this country.

Mr Prescott scrambled desperately through his notes but couldn't find the page. 'Well, as someone who is now the secretary of state for the environment, that disastrous poll tax is one that I am constantly having to deal with. You should bear in mind that what we have now settled with the local authorities is the most generous settlement they have ever received!'

The Tories suddenly realised that he was talking not about withholding tax (which is to prevent people using offshore holdings to dodge tax) but about the council tax. He probably didn't even know what the withholding tax was.

They collapsed in tucks of mirth, some genuine. Ann Widdecombe kept clutching at her own face, as if to hold the hysteria in. 'More, more!' the Tories yelled.

Soon afterwards, Mr Prescott paused for 30 agonising seconds, then answered the wrong question. 'There are different ways of doing this at different times,' he said in reply to a query about a new National Forest.

'It's the way I tell 'em,' he said plaintively. 'I have caused some confusion.' (More confusion was caused by Labour's David Taylor, who asked for 'the government cavalry to ride to the rescue of a scheme which is becoming becalmed in a quagmire'. Oh, those poor horses!)

Mr Prescott stalked angrily from the Chamber to further Tory cries of 'More!' Am I just imagining the quiet glee with which this debacle will have been welcomed by Mr Blair and his staff?

30 September 1999

And it wasn't just in parliament that he could perform with such elan. The annual party conference was always the occasion for one of his blockbuster speeches.

John Prescott was furious. Mr Angry. Kebabbed. Off his trolley. Out of his pram. This is a man who has brought bad temper to a fine art. He should be the author of a self-help book: 'Oo You Lookin' At? – How to Liberate Your Inner Consciousness through Constructive Rage. Think of Victor Meldrew seeing the last bus of the night sail by his stop. Visualise Basil Fawlty when a guest with a nose ring arrives at reception. Nikita Khrushchev at the UN. John McEnroe debating a line call. Truly, seriously cross.

Mr Prescott is often tetchy. He has threatened in the past to kill me, or at least so I am told by kind friends, who look forward to the memorial service, followed by drinks and a wide range of canapés in the church hall afterwards.

But for heaven's sake, what has he got to be angry about? This is a man with two Jaguars, one chauffeur-driven. He went to Oxford. He earns a salary that would make most former members of his profession, barmen on cruise ships, drool with envy, though there are fewer tips. He is even – in name at least – deputy prime minister of the United Kingdom, which is, as

Labour ministers never tire of reminding us, the fourth-largest economy in the world.

As I watched him yesterday, shouting furiously at the conference, bellowing from the podium, I decided that he is angry because angry is what he knows how to do. For years he raged against the iniquities of the Tories. Now, more than two years after coming into government, he has to rage about the successes of New Labour. He has no other style.

Urghhhhh!

Gosh, he was angry. 'Under Labour, our air is getting cleaner. Our rivers and beaches are less polluted!' This is appalling, I thought. Where can we all march to protest in favour of all this?

Gak! 'Five billion pounds of capital receipts to help improve 2 million homes!' No wonder he was beside himself. The better the news, more spittle poured from his mouth. Aaarghhh! He announced the creation of two new national parks the way you might declare the annexation of the Sudetenland.

He told the railway companies, which have been left almost entirely alone during his stewardship of the transport department: 'You! Are! Still! On! Probation!' He really stuck it to hypothermia – 'an obscenity': that was telling them. All those in favour of hypothermia must have been shaking in their shoes. As for asbestos – 'Britain's biggest industrial killer' – if I were a lobbyist trying to persuade schools to offer asbestos spread in children's sandwiches, I'd be really worried now.

Everything made him furious, even the new miracles of public transport. 'The Docklands Light Railway crossing the river to Lewisham!' he barked before scowling at the audience.

Not since Caesar crossed the English Channel have we had such cause for alarm. Rage, rage against the crossing of the Docklands Light Railway!

'We have a name for it! We call it "democratic socialism"!'

And having daringly used the S-word, he sat down. Tony Blair led the applause – so no threat there, then.

21 October 1999

Sometimes in idle moments I would imagine how one of the great fictional detectives would have tackled a parliamentary debate, or in this instance, question time.

The great Norway mystery consumed the Commons yesterday afternoon. Parliament was abuzz with the rival theories. All we could say for sure was that no Tory leader had been so troubled by that sea-girt, pine-clad, troll-infested land since Neville Chamberlain was obliged to resign after the Norway debate of 1940.

It had been a good session for William Hague. But who left it in ruins? I handed the conundrum over to my old friend Nero Wolfe, the gourmet detective who solves most of his cases without even leaving his brownstone mansion in New York. Wolfe's legman has always been the hard-bitten, fast-talking Archie Goodwin.

'"I decline", the great detective said, "to have lunch interrupted by the exigencies of mere business. I shall attend to the client's request after we have eaten."

'When he had added another inch to his waistline so that he looked more like the Goodyear blimp than ever, which is saying plenty, he grunted at me, which I knew meant it was time to talk.

'"Proceed, Archie, and kindly err on the side of brevity."

'"OK, boss, here's the story. Prime minister's questions, almost over, the chief is getting both barrels from Hague, the Tory capo – for now. Usual story. Europe. Big turf row going on there. Hague swears he can renegotiate the deal. Blair says five gets you twenty he's talking through his fedora."

'"Be so good as to spare me some of the more colourful details, Archie," Wolfe said, pulling on his beer and closing his eyes. This is the only guy I know who gets paid more for being asleep than Michael Jordan gets for shooting hoops.

'So Blair goes nuclear. "You can cut a deal with the EU mob, huh? Name one other country in Europe supports you. There isn't one."

'Next thing, it's hell on a skateboard in there. "Norway?" shouts Blair, 'cos he's heard some bird yell it out. "Norway? Norway isn't even a member of the European Union!"

'So the Labour gang collapses in a heap like a girls' school outing who just spotted Brad Pitt through the bus window and Blair gets himself cheered out the room. He looks great, and Hague looks so damn dumb that if you took off his base-ball cap his head would fall off.

'"So who yelled 'Norway'? That's what the client wants to know, and he'll pay 15 big ones to find out."

'"Eyewitness reports, Archie. You know the procedure."

'"You'd get more reliable eyewitness reports if you put LSD in the coffee at St Dunstan's. But here goes.

'"Some say it was Forth, the guy who has his ties run up out of boarding house curtains. A couple reckon it was Bercow, the bird who took a 'copter to his selection meeting to make himself look stacked, though the bag lady on our stoop has more; at least she's got pizza coupons.

'"Some of the reporters figure it was Hague saying 'No way!' He likes American talk; he's going to tell Blair 'Eat my shorts' over tax rises next week."

'"Pfui!" said Wolfe. "Folderol and balderdash. It was none of those things. The mystery is that there is no mystery."

'"OK, even for you, that's crazy. You sat here, you didn't go outside the house, no one came by and you didn't pick up the phone. But you know the answer, right?"

'"The answer", said Wolfe wearily, "is that nobody exclaimed 'Norway!' Blair claimed he heard it in order to use a line he had, no doubt fortuitously, arranged to deploy. It worked satisfactorily; he won a round of applause at the end of a difficult session. He invented it."

'"You certain? The hacks say he doesn't have the smarts to pull a stunt like that."

'"Possibly so," said Wolfe. "But there is one man who is quite cunning enough to construct a foolish heckle in order to facilitate a crushing riposte. He is a tall, sinister individual with a perpetual sneer."

'"You mean…?"

'"Yes, I refer to Alastair Campbell. I think you will find that he was present throughout the exchanges in order to make certain that his 'boss' did exactly as he had been instructed.

'"You may bank the client's cheque tomorrow. Meanwhile, Fritz has prepared beluga caviar blinis with a juniper-scented sour cream mousse, and I suggest we proceed to supper before Inspector Kramer eats them all."'

25 January 2000

People sometimes ask how sketchwriters find something new and fresh to write about every day. But the fact is that even on the dullest day there almost always is something to catch the attention. Often it is when you are closest to despair that one tiny incident occurs, around which you can build an entire sketch.

It was one of those dreams that make ministers wake up at 3.30am, sweating and perhaps even whimpering with fear.

'Darling, what is the matter?' ask anxious wives and mistresses, as their menfolk wipe the clammy moisture from their brows and crawl downstairs for a cup of tea and 20 restoring minutes of Judge Judy on all-night television.

The dream is always the same. There they are in the Commons, confidently beating off Tory attacks, poised, assured, the facts disposed in well-marshalled files, the arguments deployed like a chessmaster's pawns. Their quiet glow of satisfaction sends serotonin, the happy drug secreted by the body, into the correct receptors of the brain.

'The whips are listening,' murmurs the serotonin. 'They'll be telling Number 10 about how brilliantly you laid about the Tories. Who knows what will happen to them in the next reshuffle? Tony's bound to need someone as intellectually nimble as you to promote to the cabinet.'

John Spellar, the defence minister, dreamed on as peacefully as any child. In his nocturnal lucubrations, he was being assailed by Robert Key, a Tory spokesman. Mr Key was complaining about a cut in the amount of money being provided for service hospitals.

'We discover that as long ago as last December Admiral Sir John Brigstock confirmed that there had been £1.5 million cuts. I for one feel misled. Who is right – you or the admiral?'

Mr Spellar grunted gently and rolled over. Outside the first notes of the dawn chorus could be heard, and the soft whine of a milk float wafted from a nearby street. A distant shriek told of urban foxes fighting over scraps of rubbish. In his dreams he formulated the perfect reply.

'We recognised that these cuts in defence medical services had gone too far,' he said – except that horribly, unimaginably, nightmarishly, he had inserted an extraneous letter N into the word 'cuts'.

The mistaken word was clear and crisply spoken. What made it even worse was that the sentence as it came out made just as much sense as what Mr Spellar was trying to say. There was a short but terrible silence. Mr Spellar must have felt like a man who dreams he is falling out of bed, then realises that he is, and that his bed is on a clifftop mountain bivouac.

Then the Tories exploded, laughing riotously, slapping their thighs amid a barrage of stage hilarity. Frontbenchers scanned the gallery to make sure we had caught the words he had used.

At the end you could say that the government had survived a damaging assault on its credibility. Or you could argue that the opposition had mercilessly exposed its shortcomings. Or, as I beg Mr Spellar never to try to say, you could take your pick.

26 September 2000

Spool forward to September 2000, and the Labour conference heard, in short order, from its future and present leaders.

Gordon Brown sat down to a massive ovation after a dazzlingly successful speech. He had tackled the twin problems of the Ecclestone fib and the petrol crisis head-on – by ignoring them.

Was he contrite? No, he was not. His speech was as packed with contrition as a frog is full of toothpaste. But the Labour party has decided it adores him. The stamping and applause and cheering continued for ages, and became even more hysterical when his wife Sarah ran to join him on the platform.

As they descended, a vast, heaving mob of cameramen climbed up on top of each other.

The Browns saw the tottering, lurching phalanx advance towards them. They fled backstage, and finally the cheering stopped.

The reception was as demented as the prime minister can expect, and possibly more so. And it can't be coincidence that he ended with the last words John Smith uttered in public: 'The opportunity to serve: that is all we ask.' (This is politician-speak for 'The chance to grab power: that is all we demand.')

Mr Blair sat on stage clapping and beaming as if his life depended on it, which it possibly does. One imagines him saying sibilantly to Mr Brown afterwards, 'That was jolly, jolly good, Gordon. Now I'm afraid I'm going to have to kill you...'

Earlier we heard from Peter Mandelson, who spoke about Northern Ireland. For most of the delegates this was the equivalent of having a guest speech from Beelzebub on the subject of flower arranging. He did not receive a standing ovation; instead the applause resembled the sound of empty crisp packets blowing across a deserted playground.

By contrast, John Prescott's speech was received with rapture. Under Labour, he said, you'll have noticed – 'no water bans or hosepipe crises'. That's because we've had all that rain, I wanted to shout. It's certainly a first – even this government has never before taken credit for the weather.

'Citizens make cities and cities make citizens,' he raved, adding, 'How true that is!' Yes, how true, we thought. I wonder what it means? In the exciting world of John Prescott nobody ever makes a mere decision: on trains, 'We shall make a decisive decision!' he told us.

27 September 2000

I sat in the front row for Tony Blair's speech. It was like the monsoon in a Somerset Maugham short story. Hot, steaming sweat flew all over the platform. His shirt was so damp you expected him to rip it off in mid-speech and call for horse blankets.

His eyebrows were on fire, blazing with commitment. At times he was excitedly hopping from side to side like a lonely line dancer. The cabinet (remember them? They used to have a minor constitutional role in government) were herded into a set of seats below the leader and to his left, so that they were obliged to gaze adoringly up at him, with the exception of John Prescott, who took time out from beaming at his leader to glower at the sketchwriters.

The prime minister began with a ringing battle cry. 'We're crap!' he told the delegates. 'Yes, we're crap all right, but we're not so crappy as the other lot!' He didn't quite put it like that, of course, but that was what he meant. It was that rarest of moments, an apology from a politician. The Dome, the fuel crisis, pensions, even prime minister's question time. But he was sorry, God he was sorry. He would never, ever do it again.

Would a bunch of flowers help? He was feeling our pain. 'There's the mortgage to pay… inflation may be lower, but the kids' trainers don't get any cheaper.' (How true that is. There's the riding trainer, the personal fitness trainer, the ski instructor – do you know what they charge these days?) He set a new record of 163 verb-free sentences, those phrases which, by omitting any doing words, appear to offer a promise without making a commitment.

Once he'd got the grovelling out of the way he was transformed. He leaped around as the sweat poured off him like a lawn sprinkler. Would he be the first party leader whose own perspiration made him slither off the stage and crash into the photographers?

Suddenly he departed from the text of the speech to put in what was meant to be a deeply felt, personal statement. 'If you ask me to put tax cuts before education spending – I can't do it… If you ask me to give two fingers to Europe, I can't do it' – except that he pronounced 'I' as 'ah', which is meant to indicate sincerity, as in, 'If you want me to reintroduce slavery, ah can't do it. If you want me to take little Leo's pet hamster and hurl him on the barbecue, ah can't do it.' Oddly enough, he didn't go on to say, 'If you want me to link pensions to the rise in incomes rather than inflation, ah can't do that…'

He has always had a love of clunky phrases, verbal Ladas. He banged on about his 'irreducible core' of beliefs. It sounded like something out of The China Syndrome. 'Bweep, bweep! The prime minister's irreducible core has gone critical! Put on this lead anorak!'

Moments later he told us that 'Before us lies a path strewn with the challenges of change.' That's the trouble with Blair speeches; they become pastiches of themselves. 'And it is littered with the beer cans of opportunity, knee-deep in the burger boxes and irreducible apple cores of hope,' you expected him to say.

At the end he told us we were on a journey, a journey worth making. But as well as a journey, it was a fight, 'a fight worth fighting'. So the Labour party were to resemble British football hooligans, who also believe that no journey is complete without a fight. 'We shall hurl the bar stool of opportunity through the plate glass window of privilege,' he didn't say but presumably meant.

It was over. He stayed briefly for his standing ovation, then quickly marched off the platform, no doubt for an urgent swab-down and a bath in a tub full of Lynx.

8 November 2000

Before she became a national treasure, Ann Widdecombe was better known as a committed right-wing Tory minister who had once recommended shackling female prisoners while they were giving birth, to prevent them from escaping. In fact, as we now know, she was much, much more than that.

I went to the Conservative Women's national conference to catch Ann Widdecombe's speech. These gals make no concessions to the feminist *Zeitgeist*. Here were fund-raising books of recipes to tempt your hubby's jaded palate, all the chairwomen were addressed as 'chairman', and the only clothes stall sold cut-price neckties. You couldn't get near it for elderly women stocking up on presents for their menfolk, many of whom probably wear ties in bed.

There was not a dungaree to be seen; instead they were dressed in the kind of sensible clothes advertised near the back of the Daily Mail, the newspaper for old women of both sexes. At the bookstall, where you could still buy jigsaws of John Major, Miss Widdecombe had installed herself in front of a pile of her best-selling novel, The Clematis Tree. It has sold a remarkable 20,000 copies so far. 'Get your copies of The Cannabis Tree!' she shouted wittily. 'Sorry, I mean The Clematis Tree. Roll up, roll up, no sex or violence in The Clematis Tree!'

As a line of women formed, drawn by this unmissable offer, I reflected that, surprising as it might seem, Miss Widdecombe has become the Britney Spears of the Conservative party. Consider: she is not so much an object of desire for the opposite sex as a role model for her own. She has hordes of admirers who would love to dress like her, but don't quite dare. Like the American diva, she makes a great deal of her chastity.

Similarly, she is not blessed with a huge amount of talent, but makes up for it by giving everything she's got on stage.

Indeed, the principal difference between her and Britney is that at the Ann Widdecombe show, it's the performer who does the screaming.

26 November 2000

One of the more depressing aspects of our political life is the way that toadying, greasing, and general obsequiousness, instead of bringing contempt and obloquy, often leads to promotion. Take the case of Caroline Flint, who rose from a position of all-round boot-licker, to a prominent position in government and later to the shadow cabinet.

All through prime minister's questions yesterday, Caroline Flint, the Labour MP for Don Valley, had been bobbing up and down, desperate to catch the Speaker's eye and ask a question.

Even in the new Labour party, Ms Flint is regarded as something of a hardline toady, an aardvark-tongued bootlicker, a member of an active service unit in the greasers' provisional wing. Colleagues mused idly about what form her question might take. 'Is he aware that my constituents are ecstatic about the new spending on health care? And that there have been several examples in the Doncaster area of the dead rising from their graves to praise my right honourable friend?' Or perhaps something about the prime minister walking on the flood-water to bring aid and comfort to the victims? Both would have been choice examples of the Flint oeuvre.

So there was a frisson in the air when the Speaker called her. Like experts in the work of Fabergé, we connoisseurs look to see just how many jewelled words she can cram into a single question, the way in which her craftspersonship lets the phrases sparkle and gleam from every angle, each reflecting back the glory of her leader.

Instead, she astounded us in a totally unexpected way. 'Mr Speaker,' she said, 'my question has already been asked, so I will sit down.'

Sit down? *Sit down?* Without a single congratulation, felicitation or compliment to anyone? Just resume her seat, in silence? I saw members literally slack-jawed, their chins slumped onto their chests. Some raised the energy to flap an astonished arm in Ms Flint's direction. In an old HM Bateman 'The man who...' cartoon, the Tory front bench would have been depicted with great, bulging eyes and scarlet faces. Other MPs just looked very, very bewildered. And no wonder.

Imagine the late Oliver Reed saying, 'No thank you, I've had more than enough,' or Tam Dalyell saying, 'Oh, sod the Belgrano. The Argies had it coming.' The stars seemed to shift in their courses and the solid earth trembled slightly beneath us.

18 May 2001

The 2001 election was upon us, and the big event came when John Prescott physically attacked a voter in Rhyl. Admittedly, the voter whom he hit had attacked first by throwing an egg at him. It's an intriguing 'what-if?' thought – Prescott used to be a useful amateur boxer. If he had hit the Rhyl farmer with his right, he could have severely injured him and sent him to hospital. This would probably have required Prescott's resignation, and the departure of the one man who could sell Tony Blair's policies to the old, traditional Labour party. But he hit out with his left, so we went to war in Iraq anyway.

Covering the Tory leader William Hague, we were able to see the fight literally 37 times on Sky News, showing on the battle bus, as we headed north-east.

The Tory campaign went to East Anglia. It was a big success. Everywhere Hague goes, people are happy and excited, craning to catch a glimpse of that beguiling, infectious smile.

They are less pleased to see her husband. Sometimes they even shout rude things at him. But everyone is thrilled to see Ffion. And she, who I assume is really bored out of her tree, looks overjoyed to see them.

Take the welcoming Tories at a hotel car park in Peterborough. There are some strange-looking people in this town. The local Labour MP is Helen Brinton, whom I like personally but whose wide mouth, always slathered with scarlet lipstick, makes me long to post a letter in it.

But she might be Helen of Troy compared to the people who turned up to greet the Hagues. Old men in battered straw hats. Oddly shaped women with angry faces. Two younger men with earrings, whose clothes could have come from Ronald McDonald's skip. Yet when Ffion stepped off the bus and caught sight of them, instead of shuddering and scampering back on board she smiled as if they were her 20 oldest friends shouting 'Surprise!' at a birthday party.

When he speaks she sits in the audience beaming at him, laughing at his little jokes, applauding at the end as if she can't quite get over what a wonderful speech she has just heard for the hundreth time. She is the Tories' secret weapon. If they lose badly, they should make her promise to be the next leader's wife – if necessary, Ann Widdecombe's.

The Hagues arrived in a fleet of two helicopters. The first, the staff chopper, was marked 'Common Sense'. We wondered what the other would be called. 'Sheer Unbridled Lunacy' perhaps, or 'Political Correctness Gone Mad'. It turned out to be named 'Common Sense' too. The buses are all called 'Common Sense', and the phrase appeared several hundred times behind William Hague's head. As a slogan, 'Common Sense' sounds like simple common sense. But, as someone pointed out yesterday, common sense tells us that the moon is as big as it looks.

The Tory leader had planned a walkabout, but it had been mentioned in the local paper so people might have heard about it. In this election, anything that alerts ordinary people to the presence of a politician is like plain text wrested from an Enigma machine: it's a potentially lethal intelligence failure.

The walkabout was cancelled in favour of a photo shoot. He moved on to St Albans. There was to be a walkabout there instead. But it was raining, and common sense dictated that the walkabout should be held indoors, without any walking about. Common Sense, the bus, debouched the leader at the town hall door. No members of the public could even see him.

In all elections, the nominal contest conceals more complex and interesting battles. Now, in ascending order of bitterness, we have Labour v. Tory, Portillo v. Hague, Blair v. Brown and, what may be the most significant struggle of all, the people v. the politicians. The voters are rancorous, not against Tory or Labour, but against the lot of them.

So it was only a matter of time before the politicians started to retaliate. John Prescott was the first. 'I know where you live,' is particularly threatening from someone who has the electoral roll in his office.

21 May 2001

One of my favourite candidates, and certainly the most aggressive, was Bob Marshall-Andrews, a wealthy lawyer who sat for Medway in Kent. I went to watch him in action. It was a terrifying sight. In spite of the incidents described here, he held the seat quite comfortably.

Britain's most aggressive candidate stalked across the street in search of new voters to offend. According to the Voter ID sheet (the guide to every single elector provided by Millbank, listing name, address, phone number, political preference, star sign and favourite member of Hear'Say – well, most of those), we were visiting someone the computer had described as 'a firm

Tory'. I asked Bob Marshall-Andrews why. 'Because I like to,' he replied grimly.

And he does make a scary sight. With his gimlet eyes, prop forward's build and lawn-strimmer haircut, the Labour candidate for Medway has been compared (by me, admittedly) to a cross between Dennis the Menace and his dog Gnasher.

The voter, a male pensioner, didn't stand a chance. As always, Mr Marshall-Andrews starts gently, to catch them off balance. 'Just came round to say hello,' he began. 'Things going all right here?' With any other politician, this would be small talk. With this one, it sounds like a demand for protection money.

'Not really,' said the man. 'Your lot ent done much for me. For a start they took away my mortgage relief.'

'But your mortgage is much lower now. How much is your mortgage? How much? It's not been lower for 20 years.'

The voter didn't recall. 'But they've done bugger all for me. Nah, leave it out.'

Even though it was now clear that he was like Alf Garnett without the ethereal charm, I wanted to shout out, 'Sir! You are tangling with the wrong man.' But he could not be stopped.

'I am definitely not voting Labour. All these bloody asylum seekers coming in, taking all, taking all – all our bits and bobs.'

'You don't want to send them home to be tortured, do you?' asked Mr Marshall-Andrews, his tone by now rather unpleasant.

The man looked as if he could live equably with that prospect, but forced himself to say 'no', before going on: 'What about the rest of them, then? Coming in by train, under the train, on top of the train.'

'What', demanded the candidate furiously, 'do you expect me to do? Do you want me to lie on the track, wait for the train and, if I see an asylum seeker, pull him off? Do you?'

The man hurriedly changed the subject. 'They took £5 off on housing, on mortgage relief, put it on the poll tax...'

'The poll tax?' roared the candidate, but as he gathered breath for the next onslaught, the man asked, 'Have you had a pension increase?'

'I. Am. Not. A. Pensioner!' Mr Marshall-Andrews said, as if explaining to a congenital idiot that he wasn't Liza Minnelli either.

'Well then,' said the man, with an air of triumph, 'you don't know what you're talking about!'

'I rebelled against my government, so don't you dare start talking to me!' Mr Marshall-Andrews bellowed. At some point the door slammed, and I wouldn't be surprised to learn that it was the candidate who did the slamming.

'Of course,' he said, as he stamped away, smiling the smile of one who has just enjoyed the fight he had picked, 'after Prescott you can't get inside anyone's house. Knock on the door and you hear them shout, "I give in."'

The Labour canvassers spoke with awe of their man's encounter with a send-the-lot-of-them-home voter the previous day. 'The difference between you and me,' said Mr Marshall-Andrews, 'is that you are a racist and I am not.'

'What did they do for us in the war, then?' asked the man, and was told about the Indian and West Indian regiments.

'While we're at it,' Mr Marshall-Andrews continued, 'what did you do?'

'I'm too young.'

'Well, you don't look it. And under no circumstances are you to vote for me. You will not vote for me!'

'I'll vote for who I please,' the man had ended lamely, making him, I suppose, a 'Don't Know' on the magical Millbank chart.

Mr Marshall-Andrews's majority is 5,326. At the present rate of attrition he should have it down to zero by polling day.

26 May 2001

The election had been delayed for one month by the outbreak of foot-and-mouth disease, which caused tremendous loss to farmers and involved the closing down of large parts of our green and rather unpleasant land. The minister in charge was one Nick Brown, a colleague and ally of his namesake Gordon. He did not perform very well.

Mr Flabby, the minister of agriculture, arrived at the centre of the latest and horribly unexpected foot-and-mouth outbreak.

It was a glorious day in the Dales, and if it hadn't been for the soldiers striding around Settle, the army vehicles packing the car park, and the lorries hauling mounds of dead animals away, you would have imagined you were in some Elysium, an English Brigadoon, miraculously preserved from the other horrors of modern life.

We had been told that Nick Brown would do a short walkabout, presumably to glum-hand the voters. He did, if you count 10 yards as a walkabout. He made his way from the ministerial car to the town hall door in around five seconds.

This was just enough time for the locals to tell him how they felt. 'Boo!' they remarked. Mr Brown scowled at them in his flabby fashion, and then flabbed his way up the town hall steps. Here the voters of Settle missed a trick, because right opposite was Sidwell's Bakery. A tempting tray of custard tarts was displayed in the window. Yet not one, not a single one of these, flew in Mr Brown's direction. Rightly are we Yorkshire folk celebrated for our dour forbearance.

Outside there was a gathering of farmers. One was in tears as he talked about having to kill his flock. Others were inchoate, barely capable of putting their feelings into words. With some, the tragedy has, perhaps, removed their powers of reason. Geoff Burrows, a farmer in Malhamdale, has had nearly 4,000 cattle and sheep shot. 'It's just a total excuse,' he said. 'They want to get rid of us. They've let it spread and spread and spread. They've been trying to get rid of us for four years now.'

Did he really think that Tony Blair wants to get rid of all farmers? 'Why else are they doing what they're doing? It's all these animal rights activists behind it…' This isn't so much an argument with holes as a colander, but then people here are desperate, capable of believing anything. One rumour says the disease was started on purpose. A woman was seen waving around a test tube full of the virus. Why? Nobody knows.

They take it very personally. 'On the day the Labour manifesto came out, Tony Blair was on TV, grinning and laughing and smirking and laughing at us, *at us*! He said that was the first day there were no new outbreaks, and 12 farms in our valley were taken out that day. That same day!'

Finally we were ushered into the Flabmeister's presence. He sounds a little more purposeful these days, less anguished, but still fairly flabby. 'We are bearing down on the disease,' he said, about 20 times. We were 'culling out cohorts' (neighbouring animals). Nationally we were 'on the home straight', he claimed a dozen times. Someone asked if he would still be in charge after the election. He replied – was he being wishful or just shell-shocked? – that he had enjoyed every minute of the job. 'It's been full of incident,' he said with flabby understatement.

Mr Brown is a protégé and ally of the more powerful Brown: Gordon. Whether he survives depends on the Great Post-Election Settlement between the prime minister and his chancellor. A culling out of cohorts is possible.

30 May 2001

I was privileged to attend one of Margaret Thatcher's last public appearances. The film Return of the Mummy was showing in cinemas around the country, and she had decided to award the 'Mummy' title to herself.

It was Return of the Mummy II. Margaret Thatcher's Jaguar pulled up in Northampton market place. She was immediately surrounded by Tories, protesters, television crews, reporters, uniformed policemen, special branch officers, a man waving a four-foot cardboard cut-out of her, twin girls performing karaoke versions of Abba hits, a chap with an anti-Kenneth Clarke poster, a Scot with a rasping voice who accused her of hiding bribes from General Pinochet in a secret bank account – in short, a typical cross-section of modern British society.

She clambered out. A woman stepped forward and shyly handed her a banana skin, which she accepted as if it were a bouquet. So when the woman began to harangue her about Tory education policy she swerved smartly away.

'God bless Margaret Thatcher!' Conservatives shouted.

'Boo! Out, out, out!' others yelled.

'But she is out!' one of the Tories raged.

Somehow she made her way to a bald man and stroked his head. (I saw him half an hour later, but he was still bald.) The noise was like Omaha Beach. Mobile phones wheezed classical hits. Booing and jeering was answered by cheers. Photographers shouted: 'Here, Lady Thatcher!' A hundred shutters clacked. The Scotsman screeched: 'In a private account where no one has access!' The karaoke twins, Felicity and Jessica, performed to Money, Money, Money at top volume.

A local TV reporter got close. 'Why are you afraid of the euro, Lady Thatcher?' Foolish fellow.

'Sterling is better!' she barked. 'If you're a broadcaster you should know that. Go on, out you go!' She poked him in the chest, hard, three times. He tried to flee into the crush, but she grabbed his microphone and held it aloft, like the spleen of a vanquished enemy.

'We wish you were still prime minister,' someone managed to yell above the din.

'Did you hear that?' she asked rhetorically. That's the merest common sense in her book. But things were getting dangerous. What Americans call a goat-fuck, an unstable, tottering, towering pile of photographers and TV crews, had appeared. Like a tornado, the GF requires the right extreme conditions, but once it has formed, it swirls across the land, menacing all life in its path. Somehow we pushed along with her into the market. A little girl with panic in her eyes was shoved through to give her carnations. She handed them to someone I can only call a lady-in-waiting. The child fled from the GF.

'You're as good as the Queen!' a man shouted.

We neared the stalls. 'We must get away,' she said, 'we're *affecting their profits*!' This is the greatest offence in the Thatcher criminal code.

Much of the chat is surprisingly banal. 'How nice to see you!'

'Yes, haven't we been lucky with the weather!'

Then it all goes haywire. The face is deathly white these days, and her dark brocade outfit looked as if it had been run up from the curtains in a posh undertaker's. The effect is crepuscular, until the eyes blaze like a panther with a coke habit. A bold young woman asked her about Europe. She snorted, majestically. 'What if there were 15 people who could decide what you did in your own house?' she demanded. The woman came back at her. It was madness. I couldn't hear what she said, but the Thatcher eyes spat fire.

'THAT would never allow any liberty to anyone! What a ROTTEN thing for any British person to say!'

We passed a stand advertising 'Any bag here, £2.99' but who needs any old bag for three quid when we had the greatest old bag in the land for free?

We were swirling now, faster and faster. Stalls were in danger of toppling as the GF heaved from side to side. Someone thrust a copy of her memoirs at her. 'Have you read this? It's a VERY good book,' she said as she signed it. More flowers appeared so that the lady-in-waiting looked like a Garden of Remembrance. Felicity and Jessica had reached Take a Chance on Me. A brave man in a hat and a quite unnecessary green nylon-knit cardigan said we should join the euro. 'Just because

Europe adopts the euro is no reason why we should! We have a *much older history!*'

What on earth did that mean? Who can say? And who cares?

She asks: 'Are we heading in the right direction? I don't know.' This is a remark she probably never made while in Downing Street.

'What would you say to Mr Blair if he came here?' a reporter asked, or rather bellowed across the abyss of noise.

'Not much!' she replied, to gales of laughter from the local sycophantic tendency.

The Scotsman kept shouting about Pinochet. 'And she's not even an MP,' he added.

'She's a baroness,' someone else said.

'No, she's a pain in the butt,' said a stallholder. The twins started, aptly enough, on Mamma Mia 'The NHS is a disgrace,' said an elderly woman. 'They should bring back Matron.'

'Things were run very well when we had Matron,' said the Mummy, before returning to her car. For that, I suppose, was precisely the point the whole visit was intended to make.

Tony Blair II

10 June 2001

Not long after the election, Ann Widdecombe resigned from the Tory front bench, in somewhat spectacular fashion.

Lesser politicians have campaign launches. Only Ann Widdecombe would hold a campaign sinking. She called the media together in, appropriately, a sink estate in East London in order to scupper her political career, to send it to the bottom of the ocean. Last night, a backbencher once again, she slept with the fishes.

In years to come the underwater cameras that found the wreck of the Titanic will discern her superlative staterooms, the mighty engine housing, the allegedly watertight bilges, which failed at the critical moment.

It was magnificent. How we are going to miss that woman! She claims that she will be more effective from the backbenches, but that's meaningless – nobody is more effective speaking at 8.45pm when all their colleagues are having dinner or getting drunk. We have lost her from the high seas; no more will we gaze at her billowing sails, admire the brasswork on the cannons, stir with pride as the ensign flutters proudly from the poop deck!

What made it perfect was that as she went down all the guns were blazing, specifically at Michael Portillo, a pocket battleship that had made the terrible mistake of approaching her broadside.

Crump! 'I don't believe that Michael Portillo is the right person to lead the Conservative party!' Thump! 'This is nothing personal; all I can say is that this is what I sincerely believe.' Nothing personal? She loathes him. 'I don't want today to turn into a personal denigration of Michael Portillo,' she added, to the sound of a 12-inch gun firing shells into foot-thick steel. This means, in translation, 'I want you to take it personally.'

'I don't want to campaign negatively, but I don't have confidence in the way he wants to lead the party.' You could almost hear the screams of the trapped seamen, almost watch the ocean begin to churn as the great vessel shipped water and began its long journey to the sea floor.

Was she not sticking a knife into her colleague? someone asked. Perish the thought. 'If not supporting someone is sticking the knife in, then an awful lot of people will be doing that,' she said. Vendetta! Portillo! Armada! This was turning into a Mediterranean blood feud.

We had come to the Arden Estate in East London because she has been here a few times before and because she wants to make the point that Michael Portillo neither knows nor cares about the desolate lives led here. One woman, Vera Falk, aged 59, described how one local boy's hobby was setting his neighbours' cars on fire.

'Is your life really "a daily hell", like she says?' a reporter asked another elderly woman.

'Yes,' she replied quietly, as if agreeing that it looked like rain.

Ann Widdecombe was back on the attack. 'I have had quite enough of the people who surround him,' she said, meaning of course, Michael Portillo. We left the estate, perhaps imagining a few bubbles breaking the surface of the waves. All it needed was the band playing Nearer My God to Thee, and sparks as the seawater reached the ship's generator. By this time there were only a few survivors bobbing around on the swell, watching the ship's terrible yet eerily peaceful end.

27 June 2001

The traditional Labour landslide was followed by the traditional Tory leadership contest. Among the perennial candidates was Ken Clarke.

Ken Clarke rolled up, literally. Everything about him is round. His face, his body, his belly, his eyes, even the movements described by his torso as he circles a room, are all spherical. If Lucian Freud had been there, he'd have grabbed his brushes, ripped Ken's clothes off and shouted: 'I want a crack at that!'

Mr Clarke was announcing his candidature for the Tory leadership. His platform – I hope readers will not mind if I use complex psephological jargon here – was 'Fuck the lot of you.'

To summarise his philosophy: 'I am the only candidate who can win the next general election, and if you don't agree you are even more stupid than I thought you were.'

It could just work. Tories love to be insulted, at least by the right people. He is the proles' version of the red-faced squire bellowing at the village idiot. Someone asked him, 'Surely you can't lead the party you so regularly insult?' and he replied that, so far as he could see, the Tory party had no idea of how humiliating their defeat had been. In fact, the Tory party had failed to realise anything much at all.

(The American comedian Henny Youngman had a joke: 'I said, "What's the matter with me, doc?" He said, "You're ugly."

'I said I wanted a second opinion. He said, "All right, you're stupid too."'

This is a perfect summary of the Clarke campaign, which is against the party as a whole, not just his rivals for the leadership.)

Boris Johnson, the new MP for Henley and a popular television performer, was at the back of the room. Boris, I hear, had a difficult session last week with Michael Portillo, who told him he had to decide whether he wanted to be a politician or a comedian. This is terribly unfair. Why is Boris the only MP out of 659 who had to make that choice?

Mr Clarke rumbled on. His oratorical style contains several different elements. Sometimes he chooses random words and barks them out in mid-sentence as if suffering from Tourette's syndrome. 'Can a pro-European like. MYSELF! Successfully lead the Conservative. PARTY?' This is based on Michael Foot's old style. It's as if the speech had fallen into a deep slumber in a comfy armchair, then suddenly woken up with a great harrumph.

Then there's the Winnie-the-Pooh, in which the words are dragged backwards down a staircase. 'AAAAS far as I can see

the issue-of-the-sing' currency...' Bump, bump, bump goes
the speech until it winds up in a heap on the landing.

He really doesn't mind whom he insults. Adam Boulton
from Sky News pointed out that there was not much false
modesty in his speech. 'Putting yourself forward for a job is
not an occasion for false modesty,' mused Mr Clarke, 'unless
perhaps on Sky television.' I'm sure Mr Boulton did not mind
this jibe, but it takes a very confident politician to make it.

10 July 2001

*Gerald Kaufman, who would have been foreign secretary if Neil
Kinnock had won the 1992 election, had a rare gift for keeping himself
in the public prints. Gerald is, among his many other accomplish-
ments, such as writing for the old TV satire show That Was The
Week That Was, a great and skilled hater. I once asked him if he had
watched a TV speech by Tony Benn, whom he loathes. 'I feel like a
constituent who once wrote to me saying that whenever he sees my
face on television, he leaps across the room and turns off the set within
three seconds. I feel the same way about Benn. But I have a remote.'*

The House of Commons was rocked yesterday by one of those
events that shock and thrill at the time, then echo resonantly in
the mind for years to come. One thinks of the Norway debate,
or Margaret Thatcher's farewell speech. Yesterday Gerald
Kaufman walked in wearing a suit. Virtually all the other men
in the Chamber were in suits, but none was clad in a garment
remotely like this. No matador in his costume of lights ever
possessed such a suit. Max Miller's wardrobe could have been
owned by a down-at-heel accountant compared to this.

It was only one colour, but what a colour! Afterwards those of us who had seen the vision gathered together, like disciples who had seen the risen Christ, anxious to record each detail so that we could hold it in our memories and pass the knowledge down to generations yet unborn.

The hue was astounding. At first I thought I had never seen it in nature, then I recalled the weird, deep, luminescent pools of water that bubbled to the surface after Mount St Helens erupted, stained with livid chemicals from the earth's very core.

Terracotta would not do the colour justice, being too dull; ochre would be too yellow. Cinnamon came to mind, although the spice is too dark and woody. Someone compared it to murram, the orangey, clay-like surface of many African roads. All we could agree was that Mr Kaufman must be the only dandy who arrives at his tailor's with a Dulux chart.

And it wasn't just the colour. The suit was striped in broad, neat stripes, like a well-mown cricket pitch, one stripe glossy and the next matt, so that as light played upon the suit and Mr Kaufman moved, it shimmered sinuously.

The effect was completed by Mr Kaufman's nut-brown shoes and his nut-brown head, a tribute to the wonderful recent weather in Manchester Gorton. He looked, in short, as if Hannibal Lecter had taken up a job as a TV talent show host. It was a magnificent sight, eliciting gasps of mingled delight and horror from other MPs and from those of us in the gallery fortunate enough to see it.

25 October 2001

The winner of the leadership contest was Iain Duncan Smith. I suspect the Tories recognised fairly quickly that they had made a mistake. The line about the ballpoint pen I stole from the late Bernard Levin who, as 'Taper' in the Spectator, was probably the greatest sketchwriter of the 20th century.

The received wisdom about William Hague was that he was brilliant at prime minister's question time, but hopeless in front of the public. In that case his successor must dazzle the electorate, because at PMQs so far he is a wash-out. He is a bore, a terrible, thumping, ground-shuddering T. Rex of a bore.

Things may change. He is on what the Americans call a steep learning curve. But at present, if there were giant tree sloths in the Chamber they would greet his arrival by dropping from their branches and dashing away. Doctors would use his interventions as a breakthrough for research into insomnia, except that they would need to work in teams, since few could stay awake for more than a minute at a time, like those scientists who collect the poisonous fumes that belch from the mouths of active volcanoes, and yet manage to stay alive by always getting out in time.

I myself propped my chin up on a ballpoint pen and just managed to stay awake, though I kept drifting off close to unconsciousness and had to rely in the end on a tape recording.

It is hard to convey on the page the sheer numbing quality of his boringness. How can you express it in mere words? In Howards End, EM Forster brilliantly described the sensation of listening to a Beethoven concert. Some wine writers risk making themselves look idiotic by using words to describe taste. (As with the Riesling that I once saw described as having 'topnotes of cinnamon and vanilla, with a hint of Nivea cream'.) I must follow their brave example. But first, allow me to quote an IDS question in its entirety:

'The, er, what I say to the prime minister, it isn't going from one extreme to the other, because he has taken, he has given a valuable lead, which I applauded him for, in building this coalition, for example, with the Arab states, so, will perhaps he be aware of this condition, that as I am, their dismay as they look at convicted terrorists using our legal system to avoid their natural judicial process. And when we were asking, this is the point, when we're really asking our allies to make huge efforts in part of their war against terrorism, isn't it time to ensure here that we can make, make sure that they cannot shelter behind our laws? And I so say in that same spirit to the prime minister, we stand absolutely ready to work with him to tackle the problems that there are now being caused by the Convention on Human Rights. Surely, this is the point, when the law is wrong, the law must be changed!'

At the end, his voice rose to an angry shout, but of course this is the bore's fall-back; if you can't rouse emotion in other people, you pretend to create it in yourself.

What makes an IDS speech so very narcoleptic is, I suspect, the way that the voice rises and falls very slowly. This movement is, however, never synchronised with what he is saying. Like the tide on the rocks, it is both rhythmical and arbitrary at the same time. When we listen to someone in a conversation, we expect the tone of their voice to tell us the important part – saying, 'Surely this is the point,' doesn't have that effect.

He is also harmed by small but deadly verbal infelicities. 'So, will perhaps he be aware of this condition, that as I am,

140

their dismay…' is the kind of convoluted phrase we might all use now and again. In a public speaker it is lethal. The listeners' brains, unable to cope easily, switch off and resemble a frozen computer screen, apparently ready for action, but in fact dead to all input from any source.

23 January 2002

The House of Lords rarely lets us down.

They say that the quickest remedy for feeling affectionate about the House of Lords is to go there and hear a debate. But I always enjoy my visits. And their lordships still have a lot of influence. Everything that matters has to go through the Upper House: terrorism, justice, education, health. Its continuing role is vital and its membership is of the first importance. So it was vital to hear what they had to say about the glue on Christmas card envelopes.

As I arrived, Lord Tordoff was on his feet. A Lib Dem, Geoff Tordoff is chairman of the greeting card standards committee, or some such. He was replying to Lord St John of Fawsley, a majestic figure from our imperial past, who should himself appear on a greetings card in scarlet robes with a robin on his mitre.

Norman St John Stevas, for it was he, wanted to know about last year's arrangements for the Lords' Christmas card. Lord Tordoff said that they had been just fine and dandy.

Wrong answer. Norm rose in his full pomp. Did the noble lord realise that he was, like Bognor, his last resort? He had been quite unable to obtain satisfaction from anyone about what seems to have been the Christmas card from hell. The card had followed the 'barbarous' custom of standing on its side (I would point out that, if it were not for the House of Lords, few of us would realise just how barbarous side-standing cards are). And this card wasn't even barbarous in the correct fashion. 'It fell down, and having fallen down, it refused to get up!'

(People as superb as our Norman expect to be obeyed. Only a modern, yobbish, doesn't-know-it's-born type of Christmas card would refuse to rise at his command.)

It got worse. 'The envelopes were too small. When I put the card in them, they burst. And the glue had long ago lost any adhesive quality. I had to send out my secretary' – a word that he carefully pronounced 'se-CRETE-ary' – 'to buy a glue stick, at her own expense!' Peers shuddered at this revelation, not least that Norman's poor se-CRETE-aries have to buy their own office supplies. But they had not yet drained the cup of horrors.

'While the exterior had a beautiful picture of Westminster Abbey, the interior said that it was Westminster Cathedral, which must be the greatest anachronism of the millennium!'

Many of us had thought that this epithet applied to Lord St John himself. Astonishingly, Lord Tordoff seemed less than appalled at all these monstrosities. He referred to George V's views on the last resort ('bugger Bognor') – perhaps a mistake, given their lordships' close interest in buggery. He said that he himself had had no problem licking the envelopes. 'My spit must be more adhesive than the noble lord's,' he mused.

That, we reflected, must be why Norman pronounced the name of his assistant in such a curious way. She was not a shorthand typist at all, but a supplier of secretions, since his own are not up to the job.

Lady Hilton, who is in charge of the arts committee, apologised for the labelling mistake. Peers rallied round her. Lord Tordoff spoke of her 'infinite trouble'; Lady Trumpington paid tribute to her 'extremely hard work and leadership'. You'd think she was Shackleton, leading her men to safety across the frozen wastes, not someone who'd chosen a Christmas card.

Lady Walmsley wanted a card devoted to the Parliamentary Choir. Surprisingly loud cries of 'No! No!' greeted this idea. Lord Tordoff looked pained. He had seen all those calendars 'produced by Women's Institutes, and so on'. He clearly wanted the Parliamentary Choir on a card, but only if its members were naked.

Next to speak was Lady Gardner of Parkes, who as Trixie Gardner the dentist came over from Australia to earn money from the NHS, or 'bash the Nash' as they say, and stayed here to play a crucial role in legislating for modern greetings card technology.

I can't remember what she said, as I was too busy pondering how she might look in a nude calendar, and what a terrible effect this might have on Lord St John's production of saliva. But at least she could advise him to rinse and spit.

And they want to reform the House of Lords. Why?

18 April 2002

Gordon Brown might have been the 'prudent' chancellor, but it didn't stop everything going wrong when he reached the premiership. His technique was to massage the statistics so much that it seemed – even to quite sophisticated listeners – that the economy was in perfect working order. This was a typical budget speech in 2002.

To sum up its contents: this was a budget for a typical bingo-playing small businessman with several children, who has just inherited £249,999 and decides to celebrate by going out in his low-emission van for a few pints at a pub where they brew their own ale. On the way back, pissed, he drives into a tree and is whisked to hospital where, after a 10-minute wait, his hip is replaced. There's no pressure on beds, so he stays as long as he needs, but it doesn't matter, because the chancellor has made VAT optional, or at least told businessmen to think of a number and pay that.

So his night out will have cost him nothing. Or a lot less than before. For the rest of us, with 1p in effect going on income tax, it will be rather a crock, not least because Mr Brown invariably leaves the bad news out of his budget speeches. As Iain Duncan Smith said, 'He has turned small print into fine art.'

All Brown budgets are much the same. There is the tight, taut, anal-retentive language of the boy who probably had his piggy bank bolted to the floor of his bedroom. He used 'stable' or 'stability' 13 times, and we had a welcome return of 'Prudence', who was dropped after he got engaged, but who came back yesterday with five heart-tugging mentions.

In between these there were many uses of 'sustained', 'steady', 'strong', 'cautious' and 'disciplined'. Indeed, he used 'disciplined' so much that the speech began to sound as if it ought to have been blu-tacked up in a West End phone booth.

Take this: 'In the interests of fiscal discipline, I will maintain our cautious rules and lock in the tight fiscal stance... hotel visits arranged discreetly.'

I made up the last four words, but you get it. Moments later he was again promising 'a small tightening of the fiscal stance'.

'I don't know, Doris, I have this one client, Scottish gentleman he is, wants me to get into me Madame Bondage kit and tighten his fiscal stance, and all the time I'm thinking, "Blimey, I could murder a cup of tea."'

The important part of the speech is the bit rarely mentioned in the papers next day: the opening 20 minutes or so in which the chancellor describes the miracles he has wrought for our economy.

This is a tour round what I think of as Gordonland, a happy, smiling, prosperous country in which unemployment is disappearing, debt is dwindling, growth continues at a frantic rate, and all is sunshine compared to the grovelling misery of those condemned to live in the rest of Europe, the USA, and worst of all Japan, where, cast far from Gordonland, impoverished workers have to eat the Toshiba boxes they are too poor to live in.

This is all meant to contrast, I assume, with Blairland, the poor, grimy, crime-ridden country in which we are actually obliged to live.

Gordonland by contrast is isolated and oblivious to all this. It resembles that ship made up of apartments, which cruises the world with its cargo of rich people, now and again reaching port, occasionally glimpsing real life through binoculars from the bridge, seeing but never dwelling among the wretched folk who cannot afford to live aboard.

One day, he is saying, your nightmare will be over, I will be prime minister, and we will all live cocooned from any financial problems, in the great floating Elysium that is Gordonland.

25 September 2002

The war in Iraq loomed. Tony Blair took precious time from his other pressing concerns to address our elected representatives.

You don't realise at first that he is doing his Winston Churchill because the voice is light and skittery; sometimes he throws whole lines away, and says dorky things like, 'That'd be really, really serious,' which you can't imagine Churchill ever getting his throat round. But for the most part the language is straight out of the Bumper Boy's Book of Wartime Speeches. All he needs is a cigar, a watch chain and a homburg. Try reading this, not in Tony Blair's normal voice, but in a low, aggressive growl: 'If people say, why should Britain care? I answer: because there is no way that this man, in this region above all regions, could begin a conflict using such weapons, and that conflict not engulf the whole world!'

Or this: 'At any time he could have invited the inspectors in, and put the world to proof.' Put the world to proof! What on earth does that mean? It doesn't matter. When you are Winston Churchill you can make up the language as you go along.

If we didn't like his famous dossier, that didn't matter either. Our intelligence people might not have got it right, but – who do you believe? Them or the Iraqis? This missed the point – the fact that we don't trust Saddam doesn't mean that the dossier was right, but it skates neatly round the point. He was skating masterfully now: double axels and dazzling twirls.

Then he shivered our goose pimples and made our teeth chatter: 'The biological agents we believe Iraq can produce include anthrax, botulinum, toxin, aflatoxin and ricin. All eventually result in an excruciatingly painful death,' he said with something approaching relish. By that time we realised that the excruciatingly painful political death he might have faced has, for the moment at least, been postponed.

He ended: 'This House, as it has in our history so many times before, will not shrink from doing what is necessary or right,' and you could almost hear the squeaks, the popping, the grunts of the old man in his heyday, or at least how he might have put it if those great wartime broadcasts had been in Blairspeak: 'Hey, you know, never before in the field of human conflict have we owed you guys such a lot, and, well, we're really, really, grateful, you know. Right?'

2 October 2002

Weirdly, the Labour leader's speech always comes on the Tuesday afternoon, making the rest of the conference something of a let-down. This dates back a century, to the days when the speech was entitled The Parliamentary Report, and MPs were only a very minor part of the movement. Much as they are today. It is one of Labour's few time-encrusted traditions that Tony Blair never sought to change, possibly because it enabled him to do what he pleased for the rest of the week.

As ever, Tony Blair appeared as several people. For a large part of his speech he was a mystic, squatting in only a loincloth, a bowl of rice in his hands, the Bentley hidden in a garage round the back. 'Caution is retreat, and retreat is dangerous,' he informed us in that light, high-pitched voice, faintly reminiscent of the Maharishi. 'Influence is power is prosperity,' he said, and we all wished we'd thought of that.

At times he seemed to be in a colloquy with inaudible disciples. His replies, however, were in the speech. 'What is the antidote to unilateralism, oh master?' they must have asked, and he replied, 'Partnership is the answer to unilateralism.'

'Is that all there is to partnership?' they presumably enquired. Apparently not. 'Partnership is statesmanship for the 21st century,' he replied. The disciples must privately wonder what on earth he is on about, though they also know that the path to wisdom is a steep and rocky one.

'Teach us, oh master, what comes from hope!'

'From hope comes change, my children!' (I regret to say that I made the last two words up.)

'Enlighten us, oh caretaker in the mansion of truth, with what must we not drench progress?'

'We must not drench progress with cynicism!' he replies.

'Oh guru, to whom all is known, what is happening?'

'From progress here to life and death, change abroad, it is happening.'

The followers have a spot of bother with that one, but they plough ahead. 'Tell us, what is the time?'

'About 3.25. Sorry, scrub that, NOW is the time. So if you'd like to leave your contributions to promote the spread of wisdom to all peoples of the world in the bucket provided, I'll get on. I've got a boy band wants to know the meaning of life at half-past.'

Then, suddenly the loincloth disappears and is replaced by a tweed jacket. He has become the retired major in the lounge bar. He complained about police officers being hamstrung by civil liberties legislation. 'It's not civil liberties, it's lunacy!'

'You know the problem isn't just crime. Yes, another gin and tonic if you would be so kind, no I'll tell you what the problem is – it's disrespect!'

At this point – the only bit I made up was about the g&t – the audience cheered wildly. Then, just as suddenly, the yogi was back with us. He talked about how Christopher Reeve, the actor, might be able to walk again because of British scientific research, helped by £2 billion of funding. 'I made that choice for Britain,' he said. Tony Blair – not only walking on water, but making Superman fly again.

Next we were whisked off to Mozambique where, he said, a doctor in an Aids hospital had told him, 'Thanks to you, the docks in Maputo are being rebuilt!' So, when they are out canvassing, and grow tired of knocking on doors, they should remember that doctor and feel proud of what they did.

Labour's next battle-cry: 'Rebuild Maputo docks!' We could picture the scene. 'Excuse me, I'm canvassing on behalf of the Labour party. Can we count on your support?'

'Your lot have done nowt for me, nowt!'

'Yes, but sir, the docks at Maputo are undergoing a rolling programme of containerisation. Think on't!'

The end approached, and the guru was back with us.

'When are we at our best, oh swami who is all-wise?'

'At our best when we are boldest!' he concluded.

23 October 2002

In the autumn of 2002, firefighters threatened a national strike. John Prescott was the minister in charge of the negotiations.

Heaven knows what will happen if the people who staff Hansard, the official parliamentary report, ever go on strike. Day after day, with no thought for themselves, these brave men and women go into action, grabbing the words of politicians, cutting them out of the wreckage, rescuing whole speeches in danger of collapse.

Yesterday they were faced by a four-alarm statement by John Prescott about the firefighters' strike. We can imagine the scene in the Hansard office. 'This is it, lads, the big one,' says the station commander (or 'editor' as she is known in their professional slang). Card games are abruptly halted, phone calls ended, cups of tea pushed aside. They scramble for pens, notebooks and stenography machines. MPs, ministers, civil servants and clerks squeeze themselves to the walls as the crack team hurtles down to the gallery, ready to do their duty unquestioningly, without any thought of their own safety.

As they arrive, the situation is becoming desperate. The Prescott has caught hold. It is already smouldering, the temperature is rising, and very soon structural damage will threaten the perilous stability of the whole speech.

'Can I say to him that his last statement about the circumstances of events is totally untrue and he wasn't even in the country at the time, so let me deal with that point to begin with, as to the statement of the wage, most public authority negotiations have all been at least twice the level of inflation, that's the gain they had under this government, and not under the previous administration, so it would be most unusual for me to be opposing it with regard to the Fire Brigade Union, if I was actively involved in it...'

It was already too late to have the Chamber evacuated. MPs were going to have to find breathing apparatus, or run from the Chamber with wet handkerchiefs over their mouths.

'It is true that we have been asked for, but the circumstances are such that we put it back to the employers that it's your judgment to make about the age negotiations that were going on at the same time and were in a different situation.'

Sinister cracking noises could be heard. A fountain of sparks erupted from the roof as one of the speech's central beams crashed to the ground. Now and again there was a roar as air rushed in to fuel the conflagration. The Fire Brigades' Union became the FBU, then the FBO, and on one memorable occasion the FBI. Their general secretary, Mr Andy Gilchrist, alarmingly turned into 'Andy Christ'.

'I made it very clear to him, to be fair to him, he accepted that I hadn't interfered with those negotiations, and has gone on record since to make that precise point, and now he makes a different point at this present in time!'

At this present in time! The Hansard team exchange grim glances. They know what needs to be done. It has to be put into English, and only they can do it. But there is worse to come. As smoke billows from the statement, they hear the sounds that tell a trained ear that the blaze is out of control. 'We believe an independent body should make consideration of that,' he says. 'Let me say quite clear', 'the safety of the citizens are served' and 'denied them in the name that it wasn't a fire service'.

The government has pledged that if the Hansard writers ever do go on strike, they will be replaced by soldiers equipped with crayons, many of them up to 50 years old.

6 November 2002

Poor Iain Duncan Smith was nominally leader of the Conservative party but appeared to be totally out of his depth. The people who should have worked as lifesavers were the ones pushing his head under water. In November several Tory MPs simply defied a three-line whip, always a terrible blow for a leader. He made a rather tragic public plea for loyalty.

'D'you think we've peaked too soon?' asked a Tory peer I bumped into just after Iain Duncan Smith's plaintive announcement. Graveyard humour is the only kind they have left. You can't underestimate the terrible Heart of Darkness horror that has gripped the Conservative party. 'Who persuaded IDS to make that crass, that catastrophic statement?' asked one front-bencher. 'He holds a press conference to say, "I lead a party that is out of control, and there is nothing I can do."' Many Tories recalled with something less than fondness the 46 times IDS voted against the John Major government, or was it 47?

Nobody seems sure. The red mist has come down, and they stagger about the place blinded by fury and despair.

'He was a fifth columnist, a saboteur,' said a backbencher.

'Now he asks for loyalty. Him! Loyalty!' Others were less elliptical. 'That bastard was the most disloyal bastard of all the disloyal bastards John Major had to cope with. And do you know why? Because he's a bastard!'

I had a cup of tea with a Labour MP. 'Whatever IDS thinks, it's not a cabal gathered against him. It's just a lot of individuals who think he's no good. And it's going to get worse. After the battle of Austerlitz Napoleon turned his cannon on the river ice: thousands of Russian and Austrian soldiers drowned while they fled. That's what Labour are going to do to them. There'll be plenty of screaming, but no mercy.'

The statement was indeed a curious and painful affair. IDS was flanked by loyalists who are, for the moment, still loyal, though Oliver Letwin gazed up at him with what was meant to be earnest interest, but actually seemed to be saying, 'I know I've seen this bloke somewhere. Was it on TV? Or at that awful dinner party?' The statement – it lasted all of 2 minutes and 47 seconds – was meant to sound tough and resolute. Instead it was plucking and pleading.

His words were abrasive and authoritative, but his body language was soft, shrinking and defensive. He begged for our good opinion. He had never underestimated the task ahead. He had never flinched. He had sought to do everything 'with courtesy, decency and honesty'. This was getting embarrassing. Napoleon was wheeling his cannon towards the ice, and the Russians' commanding officer was asking us to praise his good manners and tact.

He concluded: 'My message is simple and stark: unite or die!' And with those three words, he became the first leader of the Conservative party to turn himself into a suicide bomber.

27 November 2002

The deputy prime minister again reported to the House on the firefighters' strike.

'Let me be clear!' Mr Prescott said to the House. Tories set up a barrage of mock cheering. But the DPM did put the government's case in some detail, so I thought it would be helpful if we had him reply to your questions about the fire dispute. All answers are verbatim from John Prescott's remarks in yesterday's debate:

Should statutory law be invoked, to end the strike on grounds of public safety?

'The agreement is taking place. I tell him properly that if his judgment to make a judgment on the public interest and the safety of the community. That is not my judgment, it is the judgment given to the Attorney General.'

Should the TUC deploy their own agreement, by which unions do nothing that might jeopardise public safety?

'As for the question about whether the TUC have agreement if the members of the 1978 agreement, that is a matter for the TUC and their agreement, but it is a matter for me to an agreement, as I informed the House, I did seek to find an agreement which I failed on the first occasion, dealing with this really exceptional in conflict.'

What should be done about pay differences between full- and part-time firefighters?

'When I asked for – can't we have the figures? That seems simple to calculate what the money is but then you have to renegotiate the whole allowances that you then find out, that's not easy to do it immediately – I put forward perhaps one understanding.'

Will the government use the law to stop London Tube drivers from taking secondary action?

'I've already mentioned quite frankly there may be a 100, previously, then it was down to one yesterday, now it's no. Not. And I think we should welcome that as a fact.'

Why won't the government get all sides into one room and feed them beer and sandwiches until they agree?
'I think it's more wine and canapés at the moment.'

How can MPs complain about the firefighters asking for 40 per cent when they recently voted themselves a 40 per cent rise?
'The 40 per cent increase was given to the prime minister and only the prime minister. It was done by independent inquiry and not by this House.'

Why can't ministers make sure the army can use the 400 fire engines that are available but standing idle?
'There are 400 engines, some without an engine, some without wheels, I mean, I don't know what you mean by that.'

Might the firefighters be more willing to adopt new working procedures?
'I personally have always had that to my mind, and in particular for the consequences of fire service. I visited my fire stations. They posed the question of what is the work of the firefighter, and that precisely what we have to dress ourselves to this. This should be in front of every one of us. It's certainly to the front in my intentions, and I intend to see we can achieve it.'

16 January 2003

War in Iraq grew ever closer. Tony Blair needed all of his rhetorical skills (and a little sleight of truth) to drag the Commons into line.

Tony Blair is a lucky man – lucky in his opposition, lucky in his friends, lucky in the news of the day. Yesterday he was supposed to face the harshest parliamentary test of his premier-ship. Labour MPs are increasingly angry that he seems to be toadying to a right-wing American president who looks like a chimpanzee that hasn't quite got the hang of bubblegum. But yesterday he walked away with the cheers of his party echoing round the Chamber. It must be an extraordinary sensation – to arrive facing 30 minutes of complaint and to leave hearing huzzas, bellows of applause and the demented waving of order papers. It was a little like one of those documentaries about the last war, in which Winston Churchill thrills the House with his defiant oratory.

The actor with his cheeks stuffed with cotton wool says something like, 'I shay to zish House that I shall never – nevair! – shell the birthright of the Brish people for this mesh of pottage!' The bravos and the hip, hip hoorays are a little too loud, over-enthusiastic, too actory.

My own surmise is that Alastair Campbell has had a silicone chip installed in Mr Blair's Y-fronts. In his Downing Street office, Mr Campbell has one of those revolving switches, like in the cab of old railway trains. Usually he leaves it in the 'moderate' position. Every now and again, however, he likes to swivel it round to 'full speed', if only to see what happens.

It was the Plaid Cymru leader, Elfyn Llwyd, who inspired Mr Blair's triumph. Mr Llwyd is a charming and a witty man, but his mien, lugubrious and slow, reminds one of a morose sheep on a damp Welsh hillside. How, he asked, could Mr Blair justify war in Iraq if it were backed neither by international law nor by British public opinion?

That is the moment that Alastair Campbell hit the switch. The current coursed through the prime minister's private parts. His body tensed. His face went red. He began to thump the Despatch Box. As it happened, he didn't say anything he hadn't said a few days ago, but this time he sounded as if he meant it. If we didn't act now, terrorists would have access to weapons of mass destruction. If, in August 2001, he had warned of the menace of al-Qaida and called for an invasion of Afghanistan, nobody would have believed him.

'Sometimes the job of prime minister is to say the things that people don't want them to say... the threat is real, and if we don't deal with it, our weakness will haunt future generations!'

Passion, commitment, real belief! The PM's pants were on fire. The House erupted, Mr Campbell moved the switch back to 'idling' and for the first time Mr Blair had spoken about Iraq as if he meant what he said, rather than regarding it as just another tedious problem cluttering up his in-tray.

19 March 2003

Then in March came the crucial vote.

At 10.11 the chief whip, Hilary Armstrong, reached across the front bench and gave Tony Blair a note. He leaned back, folded his arms in relief and could be seen to mouth, 'So that's all right, then.' John Reid and Jack Straw, the cabinet ministers nearby, smiled like cats let loose in a dairy. John Prescott scowled, but then he usually does. He probably managed a scowl for his wedding day photos. It was not a great result, but from their point of view it was a perfectly adequate one.

At times in the debate that preceded it, the House resembled a bus which has just plunged off a cliff. Some passengers were insisting that we were headed in the right direction, some that there was still time to turn back, while the rest were shrieking in terror. The prime minister could take much of the credit – or blame – for the result. He seemed to have summoned up unknown reserves of energy. Recently he has looked tired, drawn and drained. His face is still grey, and his hair seems to be shrinking back into his scalp, but yesterday he was alive, roaring, quivering with tension, like a young lieutenant about to lead a platoon into battle. He blazed with conviction and the certainty of his own rightness.

His opponents may be just as sincere, but yesterday their attacks pinged off him like air gun pellets off a suit of armour. By the end he heard a noise which has become unfamiliar of late – the sound of Labour MPs cheering him. At one point he said that Saddam's claim that he had destroyed his weapons was 'patently absurd'. At this point he heard loud Tory applause, but this time even louder Labour silence. Then there was his attack on France, for we always find it easier to forgive our enemies than excuse our friends.

Again, the Churchillian phrases were wheeled out, for every British prime minister has a template for the oratory of war. 'For 12 years, we have been a victim of our own desire to placate the implacable.' At the end he kicked into full Henry V at Harfleur mode: were we to 'tell our allies that at the very moment they needed our determination, that Britain faltered?' Finally the vote: the Labour party more split than ever, but the Commons almost 2–1 in favour of a war.

22 May 2003

I once wrote that Peter Mandelson was the only man I knew who could skulk in broad daylight. At least I must have done; I have no memory of coining the phrase, yet it appeared in a book of political quotations. Then in another, then another and another, since all of them simply copied from the rest.

For years Mr Mandelson has been described as the dark genius behind New Labour, a man whose dazzling knowledge of the arcane political arts and flair for mist-shrouded secrecy have made him irreplaceable to Tony Blair. MPs may beg the prime minister to take one decision or another. Cabinet ministers can, rather pathetically, try to promote their own views. World leaders might plead. But all this is naught compared to a single bleeper message from Mandelson. He is Thomas Cromwell, Cardinal Richelieu and Svengali, all rolled into one, but more powerful than any of them.

And yet his record has been of endless, sometimes hilarious, disaster. Yes, he was involved with two election victories. But these were interspersed with events which would be ludicrous if they weren't so catastrophic. The Sheffield rally, which helped destroy Neil Kinnock in 1992. The Saddleworth by-election, at which an unpleasant negative campaign handed the Liberal Democrats a seat Labour should never have lost. And of course the Dome, which some of us might have forgiven if he hadn't made such ludicrous claims for it. ('Surfball – the game for a new generation!' Surfball never existed, except in Peter Mandelson's head.)

And on top of all that, not one but two resignations from the cabinet, a whiff of corruption clinging to him like stale smoke on a cigar lover's jacket. Evil genius? He is to politics what Mr Bean is to art restoration, or Laurel and Hardy to piano moving.

Two days ago he surpassed even himself, shoving himself into the agonisingly constructed peace accord over our entry into the euro, accusing Blair of being manipulated by Brown, and generally acting, in the words of Raymond Chandler, 'like a tarantula on a slice of angel food cake'.

And afterwards, having unburdened himself in front of 18 political journalists, he complained about his privacy being breached! There are recluses in the deserts of Namibia, anchorites in the caves of Kashmir, who have a better working knowledge of the world than him.

Yesterday Iain Duncan Smith, still miraculously leader of the opposition, took advantage. 'The words of your close personal friend show how vicious and personal this feud has become,' said IDS, offering Mr Blair the chance to spring to Mandelson's support, an opportunity he conspicuously failed to seize. Poor Mandy. He seems to be without any admirers on either side of the Commons. Still, he always has himself.

25 June 2003

In June 2003, a prankster, dressed as an Arab, infiltrated a party being given at Windsor Castle for Prince William. The home secretary was called to the Commons to account for this. Father Brown tackled the case.

Few among the MPs gathered to hear his sombre words knew that the minister, Sir David Blunkett, had sought assistance from my old friend, Father Brown, whose many baffling cases have been chronicled by Mr GK Chesterton.

None noticed in the Strangers' Gallery the figure of a short, plump Roman Catholic priest, dressed in black, a shovel hat on his head, his nondescript appearance emphasised by the tall figure seated next to him, an imposing Frenchman and former jewel thief named Flambeau, whom Father Brown had once rescued from a life of depravity – saving with it his immortal soul.

Flambeau seemed to be in a state of some agitation, since it seemed to him that MPs were not taking the matter as seriously as he did himself. The home secretary was describing the events of that terrible night. 'As Aaron Barschak advanced along the terrace, he was challenged by a contractor. By this time he had changed into fancy dress…'

'It must have been the lord chancellor!' exclaimed one from the Conservative ranks.

'I am not aware that he was wearing a wig at the time,' replied the blind statesman.

'He was! He was, and ladies' tights too!'

'*Sacré bleu, mon ami!*' exclaimed Flambeau. 'They make a *blague* of this outrage!'

'And he kissed him!' shouted another Conservative lout.

Flambeau, goaded beyond endurance, tried to clamber over the rail into the Chamber, being restrained only by his friend's insistent arm.

The minister continued with his grim tale. 'Mr Barschak's actions have exposed an appalling failure in security at Windsor Castle which should simply not have happened.'

'It is a mystery, a confounded mystery,' said Flambeau. A liveried attendant signalled them to remain silent.

'The mystery,' said Father Brown in a low voice, 'is that there is no mystery.'

'I do not know what you mean, my friend! In the name of all that is holy, let us get out of this infernal place!'

Moments later the two men emerged, the priest blinking owlishly in the summer sunlight, his friend striding out towards St James's Park, where his upraised stick sent a flock of ducks into the air.

'At least,' said Flambeau, 'the wretched constable who caught the blackguard then sent him on into the party will be dismissed, and I hope sentenced to a generous term in prison!'

'On the contrary,' replied his friend. 'I hope that he will be spared, for he is the only man in this sad sequence of events to emerge with any credit.'

'What the devil can you mean by that?' demanded Flambeau.

'How would an Arab terrorist arrive at a fancy dress party?' asked Father Brown. Would he come as an Arab terrorist? Of course not. He would be dressed as a comical lion, or as David Beckham. Or even as the Queen herself.

'What he would not do would be to come in a beard and a keffiyeh. The constable who saw him realised this – realised that the only man who would not conceivably harm the Prince was a man dressed as someone who might wish to harm the Prince.

'And he was right. I hope he is promoted in short order.'

16 July 2003

One of the greatest scandals of the Blair years involved the death of Dr David Kelly. Andrew Gilligan, reporting for the BBC, had said that experts in the field believed that some of the intelligence contained in the notorious 'dodgy dossier' had been exaggerated, or 'sexed up'. This infuriated the government who went to some trouble to find Mr Gilligan's source. His name, David Kelly, soon became public knowledge, and he was asked to appear at the Commons foreign affairs committee. Throughout his session, Dr Kelly spoke at barely above a whisper, and as the air conditioning roared, it was hard to make out what he said.

In view of his later suicide I felt sorry that I had been rude about his appearance before the committee. But I have included this sketch because it does reflect the event.

Dr Kelly spread confusion and despair among the committee. Was he one of theirs, or one of ours? Was it a single bluff, a double bluff, or a Möbius strip-style interconnected, self-referential triple bluff? It was lucky that Dr Kelly was not Deep Throat in the Watergate scandal, or else the parking garage would have resounded to Bob Woodward's cries of 'How's that? Come again?' Time and again, the chairman asked him to raise his voice. Though it was a hot and muggy day, they had to switch off the air-conditioning.

Dr Kelly admitted having met Andrew Gilligan in May, in a London hotel. When he read and heard his reports, at least some of the material seemed familiar. That is why he had contacted his bosses, admitting that he might have been one source. But he had not been the main source. That must have been someone else.

One MP asked him about Gilligan's interviewing style. Had he used the C-word? Dr Kelly looked like someone who did not know what the C-word might possibly be, in any context. It turned out to mean 'Campbell', as in Alastair. Yes, the name had cropped up. But, he said, he had not breathed the word in a significant way, as Gilligan had reported his source as doing.

Dr Kelly was asked if he had met any other journalists and spoken in the same way to them. He was evasive. Labour's Andrew Mackinlay was infuriated. 'This is the high court of parliament and you are under an obligation to reply!' The recipient of this magnificent, hand-stitched threat raised his voice to a whisper and gave a couple of names.

Mr Mackinlay returned to the attack. It was clear to him that Dr Kelly was 'chaff' put up by the government to fool the committee's radar. 'You're the fall guy!' he said, loudly. 'You've been set up!'

Dr Kelly looked mildly pained at this, but only very mildly.

My guess is that it was all a mistake. Clearly Gilligan couldn't hear Dr Kelly's hushed voice above all the noise in the Charing Cross hotel.

'We should have a drink. I'll get the barmaid to set 'em up.'

'Aha, sexed up, was it? I guessed as much.'

'We could have some wine. The house white is a bit of a gamble.'

'Campbell, eh! I thought we'd be hearing that name!'

'I've just had a word with the maitre d'. Apparently we can have lunch in four to five minutes.'

'Launched in 45 minutes! Thank you, David, I think that's all I need!'

16 September 2003

Tony Blair, deeply shocked by Dr Kelly's subsequent suicide, set up an inquiry. It was headed by Lord Hutton. Those who suggested he would be a most compliant judge were mocked. In the light of his report, months later, it seems that from the government's point of view he was precisely the right choice.

There were innumerable witnesses, some of them a little surprising.

In an unprecedented move, the chief of MI6 appeared in public before the Hutton Inquiry yesterday. In fact, 'C', as he is known to his friends, did nothing so compromising of his personal security as to actually appear. Instead he manifested himself through his voice. Even the link to the computer screens in the court seemed to have been covered by sacking just in case they inadvertently gave a clue to what he might look like.

We weren't told where he was, though a technician said he was not in the MI6 building, but 'somewhere north of the river', which may be intelligence slang of some kind. My private fantasy was that a cupboard door in the corner of the court would fall open and a very embarrassed spymaster would drop out.

Wherever he was, it was rather noisy. At one point we seemed to hear a toilet flush. Then there were other mysterious clangings and bangings, as if 'C' were using a traction engine rally as a cover for his briefing. At one point, he even had to be asked to speak closer to the microphone. Perhaps he was at home and didn't want his wife to learn what his job is.

The world depicted by 'C' – or 'Sir Richard Billing Dearlove', which is his code name – seems a long way from the glamorous life of James Bond. There was no mention of Aston Martins fitted with rocket launchers, or pistols disguised as pens. Nor did we glimpse the more workaday world of George Smiley, gazing at the Berlin Wall.

'I hear Rczski has gone north of the river.'

'Yes, that was a regrettable lapse in security.'

Instead, the day-to-day life of the average spook seems to consist, as it does for most civil servants, of meetings and paperwork. We learned that intelligence reports are known as 'CX' in the business, and that he had been 'shocked' to discover Dr Kelly had been discussing a CX report with the press. 'It was a serious breach of discipline,' he said, in the same appalled voice as the chief of police who discovers there is gambling at Rick's Bar in Casablanca – that is, not shocked at all.

We also learned that the people who get to read these CX reports are known as 'customers', as in: 'The reference to 45 minutes did not evoke any comment from customers at all.'

This may be another clue. After all, customers sometimes make demands, as in: 'Haven't you got anything stronger?'

'All right, hang on, I'll have a look in the back. Can do you 35 minutes, if that's any use…?'

We had a long discussion about what constitutes a reliable report, and it turns out that a single source can be quite enough. 'Much high-quality intelligence comes from single sources.' This is, of course, the point that Andrew Gilligan and the BBC have been trying to make, without much success. Apparently it's OK when the single source is talking to secret men with no faces; an outrage if it's talking to a reporter.

At the end, the inquiry's counsel, James Dingemans, asks, as he always does, if there is any other light the witness can throw on the death of Dr Kelly. They always say no.

I yearn for someone to shout, 'Yes, it was me! Me, I tell you! But you'll never catch me alive.' (Plunges out of window, last seen heading for north of the river.)

But 'C' simply said there was nothing he could add, and doubtless went for a much-needed cup of tea with two sugars, stirred not shaken.

23 September 2003

Later Alastair Campbell, Tony Blair's chief media adviser and long-time factotum, gave evidence. We had learned that ministers agreed that – having worked out that Kelly was the source – they would not actually name him. But if reporters asked about him specifically, they would confirm the identification. Since only a handful of people were working in the field, it didn't take the reporters long to discern Andrew Gilligan's source.

The Campbell diaries exploded on top of the Hutton Inquiry like a shellburst over the chateau where the officers are billeted. They were sensational! Right in the very first paragraph he wrote 'G[eoff] H[oon] and I agreed that it would fuck Gilligan if that was his source.'

We gasped. We reeled. The thought that a senior official in the British government would use the word only once in the pages of his diaries was unimaginable! This is a man who probably reads his children stories like Now We Are Fucking Six and The Wind in the Fucking Willows. Were the diaries a forgery? It seemed a real possibility. None of us wanted to be caught out and made to look foolish, like Hugh Trevor-Roper with the Hitler diaries.

But if they were, why was he there to launch them? For a launch was what it was. There was everything except the warm white wine and cheesy nibbles. The inquiry clerk began by describing them. 'They were written not for publication, or indeed for anyone except Mr Campbell to see,' he claimed, to cynical laughter. Where do they find these legal types who believe that kind of stuff? In caves? Anyhow, they could use that quote on the jacket.

Authors these days present publishers with a 'proposal', which is a summary of the book plus a few teasing extracts, designed to whet the appetite. But few writers get to offer their proposal to umpteen barristers and the world's press. I suspect that in the space of one short hour he may have doubled his advance. Ka-ching!

Clearly some work will have to be done at the editing stage. For example, Mr Campbell tried hard to persuade the inquiry that he hadn't wanted Dr Kelly's name to be published. But according to the diaries, he wanted to get it out through the newspapers. What could that mean?

'This is diary writing – it doesn't actually express what is going on,' he said. Rather a good example of the Blair spin machine, expressing nothing of what is actually going on.

Mr Campbell persisted. He hadn't wanted 'it' to happen. Lord Hutton asked in a baffled sort of way what 'it' was. 'It is me, at the end of the day, scribbling whatever comes into my head,' Mr Campbell replied. So that's how the dodgy dossier was compiled. I think we'd already guessed.

Earlier, Geoff Hoon, the defence secretary, another lawyer, produced some fine obfuscation. Asked if he thought the government had done anything wrong, he eschewed both 'yes' and 'no'. Instead he replied, 'Having followed your cross-examination carefully, I can see that there may be judgments about the precise timing of particular decisions, the precise point at which those decisions had an effect which are

within what I would describe as the reasonable range of judgment people can make when confronted with this situation.'
So that's all right, then!

He even insisted that his ministry had not released Dr
Kelly's name, which took some tortuous reasoning. In short,
he was both ingenious and ingenuous. For Dr Kelly's outing
was not, as one QC claimed, like 20 Questions. It was more
like Give Us a Clue, in which each player is desperate for the
others to get it right. 'Fingers in his ears? Is it "quiet"? No,
he's tapping his chest, it's a stethoscope. He's a doctor! Now
he's cupping his ear, means "sounds like". He's rubbing his
stomach. Is it "Dr Tummy"? No, I know, it's a belly! Gilligan's
source was George Melly!'

22 October 2003

The House of Lords began its long assault on the hunting bill. Or
rather it began its long assault on the pitiful remainder of the old
hunting bill which had arrived in shreds from the Commons. The
government had wanted a complicated compromise that would have
allowed hunting to continue, but under licence. MPs threw that out
in favour of a total ban.

The peers were trying to put Humpty Dumpty back together
again, or possibly to reassemble someone who had just been
disassembled by Arnold Schwarzenegger. The first part of the
debate was an interminable discussion of what was meant by
the word 'intentionally'. They were worried that some people
might be prosecuted for hunting by accident. As always, they
were at their best describing their own strange lives.

For example, Earl Peel asked what would have happened if his grandmother were still alive, which of course she was not, and she had been walking through the woods with her two chihuahuas. What if the toy dogs had decided to chase a hare?

Well, I thought, it's most unlikely that they would dig the old lady up just to prosecute her. But you never know these days. The police are always on the lookout for easy targets to improve their arrest figures.

Viscount Astor wanted to know what would happen if someone tried to follow a hunt on a motorbike. Not a common occurrence, I'd have thought – you don't see a lot of people in hunting pink riding with motorcycle gangs. And how would they get over those hedges?

Lord Eden described, possibly at greater length than was strictly necessary, a walk by the riverbank with his dog. They had seen many rabbits suffering from myxomatosis. Many of these were blind. 'They were caught and were dealt with appropriately,' he said, which sounded rather sinister, unless he meant that they were taken to Rolf's Animal Hospital.

'Aw, look at these li'l fellas, 378 blind bunny rabbits. Hey, kids, I'll just finish painting Picasso's Guernica over here and then we'll drown the lot.'

Round about this point, Lord Hattersley came in and sat on the steps to the throne, where, I must say, he looked very much at home. Clearly the debate was of some importance to him, since his much-loved dog Buster would chase a rhino if he saw one. Roy could be in jail for years, so putting a dent in his promising writing career.

They got quite technical. Viscount Ullswater pointed out that 'The intention of the dog may be quite different to the intention of the owner, and should not be confused' – as a past lord chief justice had said, when ruling in the case of Rex v. Rex.

31 October 2003

The Tories finally got rid of Iain Duncan Smith, and chose Michael Howard without opposition. The new leader-elect began with a press conference on Halloween.

There he was, along with Norman Lamont, a reminder of why people voted against them in 1997 and why they will take the earliest possible chance to vote against them again. They held the press conference overlooking the Thames in the Saatchi Gallery, home of the wildest off-the-wall art to be found on anybody's wall. It was chaotic. It was, aptly enough, the night before Halloween. We arrived early and apparatchiks told us to get out of the room. Liam Fox, a top Howard booster, told us to get in. Young men in shiny suits, jobsworths without jobs, told us to get out again.

After such a build-up, surely the candidate would not merely appear on stage. He would have to be lying down in his underpants, on Tracey Emin's famous unmade bed, surrounded by empty vodka bottles and used contraceptives. (Sorry, that's just a quiet night in for the more louche Tory MPs. Not Mr Howard, of course.) We were just a few feet away from Damien Hirst's pickled shark. Oh, and a display by the artists Jake and Dinos Chapman. This includes a lesbian couple making love, except that the women share the same buttocks. How inclusive can you get?

I delved into the catalogue. The Chapmans also display Fuck Face, a model of a two-year-old boy with a penis for a nose and a vagina for a mouth. It was back to basics again.

The room was packed and heaving. Michael Fabricant was tugging at his hair, to prove it was 'real'. And there were Julian Brazier, James Gray and other MPs who look as if they should only be allowed out on tonight of all nights of the year.

Fights broke out between some of the cameramen. As the masses heaved from one side of the room to the other, Mr Howard appeared. 'He's coming behind you!' the MC declared. 'Oh no, he isn't!' we were tempted to reply, since we have been to pantos which were more closely in touch with reality.

In the old days, we had press conferences and rallies. They were separate occasions. Now politicians bring their claque to the press conference. Do they imagine it works? Does anyone say, 'I had my doubts about that chap, but seeing all those strange people with bulging eyes laughing at his jokes, I've changed my mind'?

A man from the television asked an aggressive question, which can be summed up as, 'Are you still as odious as you used to be?'

'That's a very generous question,' he replied, and the claque fell about in a hysterical trance of delight, as if La Rochefoucauld himself had delivered one of his most finely chased epigrams. I suspect that the Tories are now so desperate to be united that they would unite behind John Prescott if he was all that was on offer.

And I shan't mention the sculpture, exhibited a few feet away, called Two-Faced Cunt. Except to wonder how any politician in the world, however desperate for a space to announce his candidacy, might want to claim the leadership of Middle Britain within 10 miles of a work of art bearing that title.

11 December 2003

Mr Howard managed to work himself up into something of a frenzy at question time, rather like a lawyer defending a client who is clearly guilty. Rage is the only way the jury might be persuaded to change their minds.

Michael Howard was in a terrific bate. The new Tory leader was furious because the government has started to run ads on commercial radio about the top-up fees. He is certainly on to something, because you aren't allowed to spend public money advertising a policy which hasn't even gone through the Commons. But why should that stop this government? They do what they damn well please.

Even more appalling was the language that the ad uses. It's meant to be a jokey version of teenage slang. 'Ya cough up zip till ya blinging,' quoted Mr Howard, with the air of one removing the droppings of a diarrhoeic sheep from his shoe. In the transcript provided for us, the ad actually says, 'Ya cough up zip till ya minted,' 'minted' meaning 'comfortably off', whereas 'blinging' refers to jewellery. The ad goes on to explain: 'The mega news is that the darty government will help you through uni by shelling out the clam.'

Listeners are exhorted thus: 'So, peg it man, don't veg it.'

Only a civil servant could come up with such a weird mixture of outdated, inapt and entirely non-existent slang. Can you imagine anyone, including a young person, having a clue what was meant?

Mr Blair failed to answer questions about the ad 10 times, so we moved on to Gordon Brown. To paraphrase his report, the clam situation was well wicked. His darty politics had left the whole nation minted. He was blinging home the economic bacon. He produced a flurry of statistics, burying the House in a mass of numbers. They flew past our ears. 'In France 3.9, in Japan 6.9, in Britain only 2.4!' he exclaimed.

His self-satisfaction knew no bounds. The mega news was that the economy had been growing continuously for the longest period since our toothless ancestors lived in wattle and daub houses, eating woad for supper.

The bad news – that he has had to borrow £37 billion, far more than he predicted and rather more clam than seems prudent – was gabbled through in the middle of another passage about the benighted state of all foreign economies.

But none of this mattered. The nation was minted, unemployment was close to zip, and Mr Brown's Treasury was darty as darty could be. As the government's own radio ad puts it, 'Don't sack it, braw!'

29 January 2004

The Hutton report was published at the end of January. To the surprise – no, the astonishment – of those among us who had sat through most of the evidence, it largely exonerated the government and its ministers.

Tony Blair almost never does gloating. He can announce the successful conclusion of a war in the same tone that a vicar might use to say that the church fete has been postponed.

But yesterday he was gloating all right. How he gloated! He didn't just declare that he had been cleared, acquitted, vindicated, washed clean, shriven like the lamb, proved to be utterly moist, fragrant and smelling of roses, but he took the chance to prance and tap dance on the graves of his enemies.

A blizzard was promised outside. Mr Blair was the new Captain Gloats: 'I am staying here. I may be some time.' He was triumphant: Caesar returning from Gaul, Jonny Wilkinson from Australia, the gingerbread man whom no one could catch. As Labour MPs cheered and yelled and almost screamed their support he described in detail his exoneration. And rightly so. The gist of the Hutton report seems to be 'Blair without flaw – official!'

It is no reflection on Lord Hutton's personal integrity that, if the prime minister had been invited to write the report himself, it would have read in much the same way. He declared that the findings were 'extraordinarily thorough, detailed and clear'. It left no room for doubt. 'We accept it in full,' he said. You bet he did. Given that his old pal Charlie Falconer had personally selected Lord Hutton for the job, this was a little like a newly canonised saint praising the Pope's clarity of judgement.

His flail thrashed everyone who had ever attacked him. He had been accused of lying and misleading parliament, but the truth was now out. Anyone who repeated the lies about him should withdraw them, fully, openly and cleanly. They should also cut off their right arms and throw them onto the pyre. (I made up the last bit, but it does convey the flavour of what he said.)

Then we heard one of those marvellous circumlocutions favoured by British judges as a way of not saying 'lie' or 'invention'. Mr Blair quoted Lord Hutton as saying that Number 10's need for a powerful dossier might have 'subconsciously influenced... members of the Joint Intelligence Committee to make the wording of the dossier somewhat stronger'.

Quelle délicatesse! 'Darling, while I might have been in a hotel room with my secretary, subconsciously I thought I was working late at the office.' Or, to give a political example, President Nixon could have said, 'Of course it is possible that I subconsciously authorised the break-in at the Democratic national headquarters at the Watergate building.'

As for the dodgy dossier, if he had lied, which he hadn't, it wouldn't matter because no one had paid any attention. 'Only in retrospect was it elevated to the single thing that conclusively persuaded a reluctant nation to war.' Those who had made false accusations against him should now withdraw them. He was looking straight at Michael Howard.

The Tory leader found himself in the position of a barrister whose client had been caught near the body with a bloody knife, having promised publicly to kill the victim. You can only do your best.

He was met by a sound new to me in the Commons: hissing. This is the equivalent of throwing sharpened pennies onto the pitch. He ploughed onward. He said that the prime minister had misled the House anyway, over the naming of Mr Kelly. This was greeted by such a barrage of loud opprobrium that the Speaker had to beg for quiet.

Mr Blair replied. He snapped into non-gloating but still vindictive mode. 'Nastiness is not the same as being effective, and opportunism is not the same as leadership.'

As they say in the Foster's ad, 'Whoa, that'll hurt in the morning!'

Out on College Green, I did a TV turn with a furious Boris Johnson MP. 'This is a snow job of Himalayan proportions!' he shouted as the first flakes of the storm began to fall.

20 May 2004

In what seem very distant days, members of the public were allowed to watch their legislators at work without being sealed off from them, as if they were attending a football match in southern Italy. A screen had already been built, but the front two rows of the gallery were in front of it. Seats there were reserved for people who could be trusted not to cause trouble, such as peers and the personal guests of MPs. The system proved faulty.

Yes, I was there when the cloud of death swirled around the prime minister. Heavens, we were scared. Some of us actually left the Chamber, humming to ourselves to show that we weren't frightened. If the cloud had actually been anthrax, ricin or sarin, or even blackcurrant flavour sherbet dabs, it could have been a disaster for hundreds. But having walked out, I thought 'This is silly' and walked back in again. I was proud of my colleagues. The attendants were shouting at us all to get out, but everyone stood milling around trying to see what was happening. They were risking their lives to bring their readers the latest tragic events, or at least a jokey paragraph. They should mint a medal: a purple heart for the purple cloud.

Prime minister's questions had been frisky. Mr Howard had said that Brown and Prescott had 'stitched the prime minister up like a kipper!'

At this point there was a commotion in the lower right-hand corner of the public gallery. I looked up and saw two men standing in front of the new £600,000 glass screen that is supposed to protect MPs. Which it does, but only from the people sitting behind it. Suddenly two objects flew through the air and a cloud of purple dust was swirling round the Chamber.

If you look at the tape, you can see that Blair hears the noise, looks over his shoulder, then decides to carry on replying to the 'kipper' jibe – no doubt with another exhaustive description of the economic paradise we live in.

At this point, the first condom filled with flour – for that is what it turned out to be – biffs him in the back, skids off and goes on to spray all over Gordon Brown. What an amazing shot by the protester, throwing from hundreds of feet along a downward trajectory! And how marvellously apt! It had been aimed at Blair but it had exploded all over Brown. The protesters had thrown Britain's finest political metaphor.

The tape continues and the prime minister hardly seems to notice. Then the Speaker, purple smoke billowing in front of his face, announces that the session is suspended, presumably the pre-ordained drill for any form of attack.

John Reid leapt up to spread paper over the – what? Lethal biological poisons? Self-raising flour? But his colleagues said it was John Prescott who was the hero, gathering up and laying down more paper to stop the dust from spreading. There was something very British, very make-do-and-mend about all this. There is probably a yellowing advice leaflet in the cellar of a ministry: 'In the event of terrorist attack, lay down lots of paper.'

The perpetrators were later revealed to be Fathers4Justice campaigners.

6 July 2004

Channel 5 signed up Alastair Campbell, no longer Tony Blair's director of communications, to conduct a series of interviews. One of his subjects was his old colleague and rival, Peter Mandelson.

What a feast of misinformation, exaggeration, mendacity, half-truths, hyperbole, evasion and whingeing self-justification we were promised! And of course we got all that. But what was most striking was the way the pair circled round each other, waiting to strike.

They can't help it. It's in their natures. They were like two cobras rising from the same basket, twisting sinuously to the music. They knew they were of the same species, on the same side as it were, but could not resist the temptation to lunge at each other.

For example: Campbell said that Mandelson had acquired a 'huge' loan to buy a 'nice, swanky house in Notting Hill'. Mandelson: 'It was nice, but it wasn't swanky. It was about half the size of your house in Hampstead.' You could almost see the fang marks on Campbell's neck. Later, Mandelson mused about the manifold failings of the press. 'If you don't talk to them, if you don't return their calls, they think you're…'

'An arrogant, aloof git?' offered Campbell, in a spirit of helpfulness.

Mandelson's first words on air were 'I don't think I'm a particularly loathsome individual' – so clearly he wasn't afraid to plunge into controversy.

Campbell had preceded the question with an avowal that Mandelson was – and is – one of his closest friends and 'a very capable minister'.

'So why', he went on, 'does the Labour party loathe you?'

That was a facer. Mandelson thought that it was probably because he was 'a bit of a loner, a bit remote'. He didn't need to hang around the bars and tea rooms, because he had the leader's ear.

'I didn't need anyone else. I was not a retail politician,' he added. Of course not. No one had suggested that he could be bought!

The fact is that both Campbell and Mandelson have always been courtiers, first of Neil Kinnock, then of Tony Blair. The monarch always thinks the courtiers are terrific, helpful guys. Those outside the circle detest them for their influence; they themselves are deadly rivals for the affection and admiration of the king.

'If I am being honest, which I will be,' he went on, 'I don't think I've anything to lose by being honest at this stage in my political career…'

It was a fascinating insight. He made it sound as if honesty was something you might take up at a certain age, like angling, or DIY. Alarmingly he kept talking about himself in the third person. 'There has always been a fight within myself, and sometimes with others, about whether Peter is going to remain Peter the Process Man, or whether Peter is going to be allowed to become Peter Mandelson, the politician and minister.'

Gosh, I wouldn't mind a ringside seat at that fight – it would be as exciting and unpredictable as Mike Tyson v. Kylie Minogue!

As a boy, I once had an instructional toy called the Visible Man. He had a Perspex body so that you could see the organs inside. Mandy has the Visible Brain; you can see the synapses working together. The synapses have worked out that the future of the Labour party is Gordon Brown. The chancellor, who felt spurned and betrayed by Mandelson at the time of the 1994 leadership campaign, may soon be in power.

'Get in with Gordon!' the synapses were screaming.

'He has the qualities and skills needed to be leader... Gordon is a big person, he is a big politician,' Mandy told us with every appearance of something close to sincerity. In fact Gordon could do no wrong. The news about his house loan ('It wasn't secret, it was unpublicised,' he said to snorts of laughter at the screening yesterday) had been leaked by Gordon's associates. 'That's not the same as Gordon,' he said, and at this point Campbell burst out incredulously, 'You really believe that?'

Yes, he did believe it. Why, he had spoken to Gordon himself on the very day, and had received some good advice. ('Don't resign.') But the real, deep well of bitterness began to gush over his second resignation, after the expose of the Hinduja passport affair. He blamed Campbell for briefing the media against him. He accused him of 'a rush to judgment', adding, 'I think, as my friend of 25 years' standing, you might have given me the benefit of the doubt, and you chose not to.' He had created 'a sort of elephant trap, into which I fell'.

Later Campbell told us in person that he thought Mandelson had not been bitter. If that was him being cuddly and forgiving, I'd hate to see him when he really is bitter. In fact, for either to claim that there was no ill-feeling between them was just a load of old cobras.

14 September 2004

Pretty well every other year Tony Blair would speak to the TUC annual conference. This would always be billed in advance by the press as a great emotional showdown. But it wasn't; it was something quite different.

Tony Blair walked out onto the podium and was greeted by a complete silence. Roger Lyons, who was chairing the conference, said, 'Tony, we are all delighted to welcome you here today!' This was something of an overstatement, and it too was greeted with silence.

It wasn't an aggressive silence, a collective dumb insolence. Neither was it a hostile silence. It was just a total absence of noise. It was the same silence you might expect when one signer for the deaf replaces another at the side of the stage. Nobody objects, but equally nobody sees any reason to cheer. Or even notice.

The speech began, 'As ever, before a speech to the TUC, I am not short of advice!' This line was, presumably, supposed to be met by a warm, affectionate chuckle. Instead it was greeted by more silence. It was slightly eerie; if you ever put on the kind of ear defenders used by aircraft dispatchers, you realise that complete silence can be as loud as noise.

Most speakers put in lines meant to win applause, or 'clap traps' – which is the origin of the term. Tony Blair had 'shush lines', which might have been designed to make the audience, already as quiet as a mausoleum at midnight, even more somnolent than before, sucking any remaining enthusiasm out of the air, like a top of the range Dyson with fitted silencer.

He mentioned the Warwick policy, which the government and unions agreed earlier this year. It was meant to favour 'social partnership', he said. 'So I come to praise Warwick, not to bury it!' he said. This jokette ('Alas, poor Warwick' might have been more apt) was met by another silence, except for one faint, almost imperceptible sound, a minuscule murmur, like a hamster having a bad dream. I reflected that if a 14th-century court jester had written that gag for the king, his head would have been in danger. In these more enlightened times, the author may get a substantial consultancy fee.

He decided to quote himself from 1990, and all the promises he had made then as shadow employment minister – the minimum wage, social chapter, maternity leave, etc. 'We have done every one of those things, as a Labour government!' he said.

At this point, a small claque, fewer than one in 10 of his listeners, some no doubt employed in Downing Street, decided it was time to wake up. A faint rustling noise floated up from the hall, as if a few dozen people had simultaneously decided to open their crisps.

Lines designed to bring wild applause – praise for miners, more apprenticeships, cash for the NHS, help for working families – were received with the same dark sticky silence, like Wellington boots lodged in the mud.

Then it was over. A single man rose in a crazed, doomed attempt to start a standing ovation. And there was a solitary boo. I thought how astonishing it was that a Labour prime minister, speaking at a conference of the TUC, the very begetter of his party, could be received with less excitement than a vicar reading out the parish notices.

16 September 2004

The bill to stop fox hunting was still making slow progress through the House. A group of protesters made use of the fact that nearly all refurbishment is carried out at Westminster during the recess. This had been shortened by the addition of two sitting weeks in early September, so there were still lots of workmen about the building.

When the first protesters ran into the Chamber it was like one of those occasions when a gang of drunken yobs arrive in a railway carriage. No one knows quite how to react, except you can see everyone thinking, 'Pray somebody do something, but let it not be me.'

Four of the young men had run in from the back, apparently from the No lobby at the end of the Chamber by the Speaker's chair. Another, the first to be grabbed, dashed in from the members' lobby at the other end, straight past the deputy serjeant at arms, who, with his sword, is the only armed man in the Chamber. He took an executive decision not to use it. At first, stupidly, I thought they were workmen, arriving to carry out some small repairs, perhaps involving a dangerously rucked carpet. Clearly nobody had told them to wait, not just to storm in the moment they had finished that job in Cricklewood.

Then seconds later, when my brain clicked into gear and I realised what was going on, it seemed quite astounding, since they had emerged from places where even most of us who work at the Commons are not allowed to go. If a platoon of North Korean soldiers had arrived in lock step, it would scarcely have been more surprising.

It took the young men a few moments to work out their bearings – which was the government bench, which the opposition – but having figured it out they stood in front of Alun Michael and Elliot Morley, the relevant ministers. They were bending, twisted with hatred for these enemies. But in spite of having crafted brilliantly successful plans to get past the security system, they hadn't quite worked out what to say.

They had the world to address – the television pictures would be shown everywhere – but they had nothing historic or memorable to hand. It's as if Gavrilo Princip, having reached the running board of Franz Ferdinand's car, had brought only a tomato to throw. One of them shouted feebly, 'It's totally unjust!' like a child told he can't have an ice cream.

Another – or perhaps it was the same young man; it was hard to tell in the mêlée – yelled, 'This government! You've mucked up pensions! You've mucked up everything!' True to a degree, but hardly as resonant as the words of the most famous parliamentary interloper, Oliver Cromwell ('Let us have done with you! In the name of God, go!') Even their T-shirts, the same as those worn by scores of the protesters outside in Parliament Square, were subtly naff, as if composed by someone for whom English was not a first language. Or even a second. The fronts showed Tony Blair with red horns, and the slogan adapted from the French Connection ads: 'FCUK your ban. I'll keep hunting.' On the back, weirdly, was Cherie Blair tricked out as the Queen, wearing a tiara, the words 'I signed the declaration' above her and 'God Save the Hunting' beneath.

But most MPs didn't have time to contemplate the nuances. This sort of thing doesn't happen much in parliament. In fact it doesn't happen at all. By this time, and I mean a few seconds after the incident began, MPs had snapped into action. They gave the young men some very cross looks.

Only Sir Patrick Cormack decided to become a have-a-go hero and grabbed one youth in an armlock. Heavens, we thought, if they had been terrorists armed with machine guns, many of the nation's finest legislators would be dead already.

Sir Patrick addressed one of the youths. 'Get out!' he yelled. 'I am furious! This is disgraceful!' At least he was doing something.

But it didn't matter. By this time a crack team of men in tailcoats and tights had arrived on the scene. They were the badge messengers, and what a proud sight they were, flying into the Chamber, fleet of foot, arms flailing! These men might be middle-aged, retired warrant officers for the most part, but they were tough.

One demonstrator was snatched by the ankle and forced to hop backwards to the door. Another was seized by the throat. A third managed to lie down at the end of the Labour benches, making it almost impossible for him to be budged. And then they were gone.

I suppose I should report that MPs were angry, seething, alarmed. No doubt many reflected that it might have been al-Qaida. But in the end many were laughing. They found it surreal rather than sinister. Whatever you thought of their cause you had to admire the cunning and resource they used to get into the place. And now it might encourage the authorities to take steps against real terrorists.

21 September 2004

The Liberal Democrat conference that year was tinged with more acrimony than usual. And in their ceaseless quest for new hopeless causes to fight, the party had decided to take a stand against 'secondary drinking', which you might assume meant slipping in a pool of vomit in a bus station on Christmas Eve.

It was the day of the *Guardian* lunchtime fringe meeting, chaired by a junior member of the paper's staff, i.e. me. I noticed that there were several members of the House of Lords present, having got there under the popular 'attend 12 Lib Dem conferences and win a peerage' programme.

Many of them had copies of the Orange Book, a work of radical Lib Dem re-thinking that is so controversial that its launch here was cancelled. People hissed when it was mentioned. I expect that some readers had hidden their copies inside a copy of Richard Desmond's Hot Asian Babes.

Sarah Teather MP, who has clearly learned a lot about her party in a short time, said that if God had been a Lib Dem, the 10 Commandments would have been the 10 Suggestions.

Ming Campbell added that if the Greater London Young Liberals had been at Mount Sinai they would have moved the reference back. The discussion turned to secondary drinking. Could it do as much harm as secondary smoking?

Sir Ming said that as a young barrister he had once, along with the late Sir Nicholas Fairbairn, a celebrated toper, defended a man who had fired two shotgun cartridges into a crowded pub. The two lawyers had had a few drinks, then a good lunch, and had gone on to Barlinnie prison to meet their client.

After outlining the defence, they asked if he had any questions. 'Aye,' he replied, 'Sir Nicholas, would ye mind breathing on me again?'

12 April 2005

In 2005, Tony Blair announced another election. Both main parties launched their manifestos, in rather differing styles.

The Tories launched their manifesto yesterday. All their pledges are on the cover, and rather badly hand-written, to make them seem more sincere. Voters are supposed to think, 'I think Tony Blair has done a pretty good job, all in all. But his pledges are neatly printed, and you can't trust that.'

Michael Howard turned up at the launch, all gleaming and polished and shiny, so it looked as if there was something of the bright about him. Members of the shadow cabinet were brought in to support him. They were plonked down, like computer equipment being delivered on little trolleys. 'Where d'you want this Ancram, guv? I've got a Letwin 'ere as well. Print and sign please.' They sat in a mute row and gazed up at their leader. He is a shade frightening.

But this has nothing to do with his being a vampire; more with him being a lawyer, which is much scarier. He uses lawyers' words: 'It does not befit Mr Blair'; immigrants might be coming here 'for nefarious purposes'. These are not words normal people often use ('That next door's lad, he's a nefarious one and no mistake'). He speaks English as if it were a second language, taught by patient specialists so that even lawyers can understand.

Suddenly he remembered all those Teach Yourself English the English People Speak CDs, the ones that instruct you in the demotic, which, as far as politicians are concerned, means football. 'It's like producing Lee Bowyer to talk about proper behaviour on the football pitch!' he said.

('Hmmm,' you can imagine the voters saying, 'I have been tempted by the Lib Dems, but not only are the Tory pledges scrawled on the page, but they can remember things that happen in football matches. They've got my vote!')

He said that he proposed to address 'the simple longings of the British people. They don't ask for much.' This made us sound like hamsters. A few seeds, water, a little wheel to play on. It's not a lot.

'On May the 5th you can let the sunshine of hope break through the clouds of disappointment,' he declared. This line, from the later Wordsworth, or perhaps a Hallmark card ('With deepest sympathy on your coming election defeat. May the sunshine of hope break through the clouds of disappointment'), was too much for the hacks, many of whom began laughing in an unseemly and vulgar fashion. 'Imagine, five more years of it!' Mr Howard added. 'Five more years of smirking!'

He seems obsessed by the prime minister's smirk, and though it may seem a rather self-satisfied grin, it is not technically a smirk, which I think involves a certain relish for other people's misfortunes. A smirk implies *Schadenfreude*: Hubert Lane laughing at William Brown sitting in a puddle.

But we are more conscious of smirking these days. You can see a little group of smirkers outside every office building, huddled together in the warmth, hoping for the sunshine of hope to break through the clouds of disappointment.

14 April 2005

Labour launched its own manifesto yesterday. Or rather, it opened a coal hole and poured several tons of nutty slack down on the voters. Earlier this week the Tories offered pledges that amounted to just 11 words. Yesterday Labour produced a document listing a total of 279 different promises. Yes, 279! Try fitting that onto your wallet-sized pledge card. Imagine what the Durham miners would have had to stitch onto their banners: 'High street chiropody check-ups!'; 'Protect biomass!'; 'Action on dormant bank accounts!' Or this: 'Car pool lanes for cars' (as opposed to what – orangutans?).

I can see, through misty eyes, the men marching down from Jarrow, shouting, 'What do we want? New partnerships to fund workplace training! When do we want it? When time and conditions allow!' As they sailed for Botany Bay, the Tolpuddle Martyrs would have dreamed of a better world, with 'more flexibility in the structure of governing bodies' and 'every pupil offered enterprise education!'

Actually most of these pledges looked a trifle vague, being more in the nature of aspirations than promises. Labour proffers a lot of 'long-term aims', 'promotion', 'bearing down', 'fighting', 'enriching', 'leading reform' and 'tackling'.

Lines such as 'opportunities for pupils in their strongest areas' is not what one's old English teacher called 'a verb clause'. It is a hope, not a commitment, rather like 'more sunny weather for all!'

Tony Blair started with a long meandering speech, which, without warning, would be suddenly interrupted by his colleagues. It sounded as if they were performing the recitative in some terrible socialist realist opera performed in Moscow in the mid-1930s. They all kept banging on about 'decent, hard-working families'. But what about lazy families? Don't they get a look-in too?

4 May 2005

I popped down to the West Country to take a look at a young politician for whom everyone in his party predicted a great future.

'David Cameron is coming here today, to push my campaign – over the edge!' said Stanley Johnson. 'Sorry, over the finishing line!' Stanley, the father of Boris, was in the Devon village of Chudleigh Knighton. He was refreshing himself with his campaign workers in a pub. 'We have campaigned in every village,' he said proudly; 'at least in every village that has a pub.'

David Cameron is the Tories' shadow cabinet member in charge of policy co-ordination, whatever that might be. He is tipped as a future leader. If they lose the election and decide to skip a generation, he could be there this year. He descended on Teignbridge like one of those American tornados that wreck trailer parks. He had been all over South Wales that morning, flown to Plymouth and been driven to the pub for lunch. Inside it was chaotic. Some 19 people were clustered around him and Stanley – aides, agents, canvassers, hacks, photographers, drivers and hangers-on. Mad conversations began.

'And I spent an hour on the local radio station, talking entirely about nappies.'

'Who was the Stilton ploughman's, then?'

'I said I was all in favour of saving the planet, but had they ever tried washing a dirty nappy by hand?'

'Two ham ploughman's and one ham sandwich. Or is it the other way round?'

'So you see, reducing council tax is a massive issue here. That and slaughtering infected badgers.'

'Chicken salad? Somebody must be the chicken salad!'

'I did rather well in the pancake race, and one lady asked me, "Are you a practised tosser?"'

Cameron looks and behaves like a junior minister, and already talks the talk. 'I found that Cardiff was blue, and that Barry was blueing up... the momentum is in our direction. We're talking about what we're going to do in government, while the other two parties are talking tactics. "Don't let the Tories in by the back door," they say. After eight years, that's pathetic!'

We raced on, leaving behind enough food to feed a dozen hungry plough persons. Next we descended on the market town of Bovey Tracey, where Cameron sprinted up the high street introducing voters to the candidate, who didn't like to say that he had worked the shops some days before and yes, most of them had met him.

We passed a pub with a sign outside saying 'Eat the Rich'. Not natural Tory territory, perhaps, though it turned out to be the name of a rock group. A canvasser leapt out.

'We've got a swayer here!' he shouted. Old Terry was precisely that, literally and figuratively. 'Dunno how I'll vote,' he said unsteadily from the stool on which he was more or less seated. 'You could buy me a pint.'

'No, he can't, it's illegal,' said Cameron firmly. 'Old Terry, always pissed as a handcart,' the agent confided.

'Margaret in the fruit shop is *hovering*!' we learned, and faster than a speeding bullet Cameron was among the apples and cabbages to tether that vote. Once outside, he charged back down the street. An ex-policewoman came up. 'I would rather cut my arm off than vote for those lying scumbags who are in power now,' she said.

So not Labour, then, and indeed the party was a poor third last time. Stanley Johnson is just 3,000 votes – 5 per cent – behind the sitting Lib Dem MP, Richard Younger-Ross.

'We've got to go, David,' said his driver. We ran past a stylist's salon. 'I fight shy of hairdryers,' Cameron said. 'Hairdryers and banks. You should never disturb people when they are with their hair or their money.'

Finally the driver dragged him away. He grabbed the candidate's arm. 'Stanley, that was *huge!*' he said, a term which slightly perplexed Mr Johnson. He watched the next leader (or leader but one) with gratitude, but also some relief. 'We can slow down now. I don't know, people from London ...' His voice tailed off as we went into a pub for an urgently needed restorative drink.

Mr Johnson failed to win the seat, though he went on to a successful career as a freelance journalist and environmental campaigner.

A few days later Labour won the third election by a smaller but still substantial majority. Michael Howard immediately announced that he would be retiring, making four Tory leaders whom Mr Blair had seen off.

Tony Blair III

28 September 2005

Summer passed, as it will, and we regrouped by the seaside for the party conferences. Labour was in Brighton.

Tony Blair praised the people of London yesterday for 'locking horns with modernity'. You could see the Labour conference uttering a single collective 'What?' It was a curious phrase. Does he see the people of London as stags, challenging modernity to become the dominant male in the herd? Or was it all a mishearing? Had he asked his speechwriters to come up with gardening advice, suggesting that we dock thorns with impunity, or tips for chiropodists – lop corns with dignity? Or had it been originally about Zen seafood cookery – we should chop prawns with serenity? Maybe he wanted to crack down on the sex trade, both obscenity and swearing – to mock porn and profanity.

I mention this at length because these peculiar constructions he comes up with stop you responding properly to the rest of the speech. It's like being in the middle of a bracing walk and getting your trousers snagged on the barbed wire. Your companion may be marching blithely ahead, but you are still trying to untangle yourself.

Take this. The successful Olympic bid showed that we were a nation 'not just with memories, but dreams'. All right so far – I suppose what he meant was: we don't have to live in a glorious past; we have a future too.

Then he went on: 'Such nations aren't built by dreamers.' So what are we supposed to do? Dream, or not dream? Clearly we must do both, dreaming, but not becoming dreamers. We are to snooze but remain wide awake. We must be alert, yet asleep, on the ball while flat on our backs. Fortitude and 40 winks!

The theme of the speech was his great favourite, change. As a nation we must accept the need for change. We should 'turn a friendly face to the future', asking the future if it needed any help getting that buggy onto the bus, or if it wanted fries with that. Labour as a party had to change too. Indeed we must all face the challenge of change. That way, our country would 'rise with the patient courage of the change-makers'.

(An American colleague tells me that 'change-makers' are those machines that give you coins for coffee, or a subway fare. Our nation should be covered with them, all of them patient and courageous, even when they go wrong and people kick them.)

The only thing that is not going to change is the leadership of the Labour party. There will be no change there. Why? Because of something he learned from Neil Kinnock, which is now 'so ingrained it is like a strip of granite running through my soul'. We did not learn what the granite symbolised (unless, of course, it is real, implanted by doctors to stiffen up his irreducible core). He did however give us a glimpse. 'It's about leadership. Not mine alone. Ours together.'

Once again, the mind found itself stuck on a fence. If a leader has to lead, how can he have co-leadership with the people he is supposed to be leading?

There was a weird and slightly embarrassing moment when he referred to Hugh Grant, who plays a Blairish sort of prime minister in the film Love Actually, and takes the opportunity of a joint press conference to give the US president a piece of his mind. This scene was, I gather, sometimes greeted with standing ovations in the cinemas.

The real Blair said that a lot of people would like him to do the same. But then, he said, he would have 'the next day, the next year, the next lifetime to regret the ruinous consequences of easy applause'.

The *next lifetime*? What on earth was he on about? Is he saying that if he had not joined the invasion of Iraq, then he would have spent eternity regretting it? We know he believes God will judge him. If that would have been such an appalling misjudgment, would he have risked the eternal flames?

But the speech had moved on before we could ponder this. The audience seemed to like it in spite of everything, and even stayed awake. They had no need to block yawns with difficulty.

29 September 2005

The party conferences become more stage-managed every year. The main difference these days is the louder objections from party

officials when the television companies broadcast less and less from
the stage-managed conferences.

The Labour conference was to hold its big debate on Iraq. Did
they discuss it? Of course not. Instead a furious woman from
Unison stormed the platform. 'I want to know why I have
been stopped from bringing a bag of sweeties into the conference! It is bureaucracy gone mad!' she said.

The chairwoman said that the matter would be referred to
the Conference Arrangements Committee, where it will no
doubt disappear like a dead rat in a Bastille dungeon. They
will spend hours debating the issue, then will come up with
a confectionery composite, which will be voted on by, say, 1.7
million block votes to 638,000. We looked rather puzzled at the
whole situation, until a steward standing near my seat said, 'I'll
tell you why they're banned, they could be used as missiles.'

Missiles! What has Labour come to? The party of Hardie,
Attlee and Bevan is afraid that its speakers might be cut down
under a fusillade of Fox's Glacier Mints and Fishermen's
Friends? As Hugh Gaitskell might have said, 'I shall fight,
fight and fight again, no matter how many liquorice allsorts
you hurl at me!' Later I learned that an old woman, a notorious leftie, had had a bag of Mint Imperials confiscated, for
fear that she might create mayhem by rolling them along the
floor. (However, I managed to smuggle in three of those little
Toblerone things, which being triangular and sharp-edged
could be lethal, like a chocolate ninja blade.) The issue may
seem tiny, but it is a reflection of the state of the Labour party,
combining bombast, vainglory and total paranoia.

We finally got on to Iraq. Dennis Skinner made a speech in
which he harked back to the good old days, when he had gone

on endless marches and the miners were perpetually on strike. Glorious days, days of struggle, chaos and power cuts. 'I was very happy, and still am, to participate in the class war. I say this, to every young person in Britain: fight the class war, not the holy war!'

He got a standing ovation. All over the land young men and women will be seizing their Werther's Originals and marching to the barricades. What the class war needs is tactics – and TicTacs!

We heard from Jack Straw, the foreign secretary. Most of what he said was received with the merest polite applause, like drizzle falling on a tin roof. 'We are there for one reason only – to help the elected Iraqi government build a secure, democratic and stable nation!' At this point an elderly man in the gallery shouted, 'That's a lie!'

Dissent? At a Labour party conference? That was definitely right out of order. Building democracy in Iraq is one thing; having it at home and appearing on television is quite another. Two burly stewards grabbed this frail old gentleman. And rightly so – he might have had a deadly belt around his waist containing a dozen sticks of Blackpool rock.

The frail old gentleman turned out to be Walter Wolfgang from West London, a Labour supporter for decades. Incredibly, he was held by the police under the Prevention of Terrorism Act, which ministers had promised would only ever be used against terrorists, and certainly not mere dissidents. Anyhow, Mr Wolfgang received many apologies, and was even elected to Labour's National Executive – which may be a worse punishment than going to prison.

5 October 2005

The 2005 Tory conference was dominated by the leadership contest.
The two favourites were the largely unknown David Cameron and
the largely known David Davis. Not only did Mr Davis make a
markedly lacklustre speech, but he offended many of the delegates by
employing several young women with large busts to walk among the
delegates wearing T-shirts declaring, somewhat unnecessarily, 'I'm
for DD!'

We heard from David Cameron. Most of the delegates had
never heard of him, or rather never quite clocked him,
and they seemed to like what they heard, especially as he
wandered round the stage, speaking apparently without
notes, as if the words were being wrung from every passion-
sodden fibre of his being. He has learned Ronald Reagan's
trick of being dementedly optimistic: 'We love this country
as it is, and our best days lie ahead!' It's morning again in
Blackpool! They even loved him when he started raving, like
a malaria victim who is at the point where he may live or die.
'Let us dream a new generation of Conservative dreams!' he
said, which may be the most meaningless statement uttered
at this conference so far.

'Changing our party to change our country! It will be an
incredible journey, with no turning back and no false stops and
starts! I want you to come with me!' (Though of course if it's
like a Virgin train service south, it will involve an engine failure near Wigan and delays due to planned engineering work.)

6 October 2005

David Davis remains the favourite, but yesterday we could watch his support begin to gurgle away, like oil from a leaky sump. It's not that he was awful; he was thunderously not bad, majestically all right, triumphantly OK, I suppose.

But he wasn't great. They expected more and they wished for more. They wanted to love him, not just to like him. They wished for him to point the way to a glorious future, and what they got was 'Mind if I come along for the ride?'

He is not a natural speaker. You can't throw away your best lines as if you were warning a child not to forget their bus pass. You could almost see them thinking, 'If we choose this guy we will have to listen to this stuff every year for years.' He was clearly nervous, and arrived on stage with a tight little smile. His habit of swallowing words, and letting whole sentences drop alarmingly, like a fat man sitting on a three-legged stool, caused him to talk about 'Margaret Sasher'; bombings became 'bongz'. When he finally finished, the conference wasn't quite sure it was over, so they dragged themselves to their feet one by one. Some didn't even bother to get up. He stood on the stage, hoping to milk the applause, but that cow was already dry.

14 October 2005

Often politicians coin phrases that mean a great deal to them, but can be quite baffling to the rest of us. One that pleased Gordon Brown was 'modern apprenticeships'. Usually the politician doesn't trouble to explain what the term means, and we are free to decide for ourselves.

Gordon Brown said proudly that there had been no apprenticeships when he had come to power; now there were 300,000 young persons in 'modern apprenticeships'. My mind, as so often, began to wander. What would a modern apprenticeship be like?

'I was in my 15th summer when I left the city academy and was 'prenticed by my father to Jeb Haythornthwaite at the old call centre that had stood in our village for nigh on three years.

'"Tek this, lad," said Jeb affectionately, as he handed me a headset, lovingly fashioned in fine grey plastic. He fitted it over my head.

'"Look at them foam ear-pieces," he said. "You don't see craftsmanship like that any more. That thar thang has been in the Haythornthwaite family since the dawn of this millennium. 'Appen it will see us through to 2006. It might even see me out, lessen they close this place and I move to the Tesco Express check-out in Little Burdale!"

'"Mr Haythornthwaite," I asked nervously, "what should I do if ever I call someone up to tell them that our double-glazing representatives will shortly be in their area, and they be eating their tea?"

'His old eyes twinkled with pleasure. "Bless you, child, they will probably fill your tender ears with language that would stop a charging bull! But it bain't half be fun. I once called an old biddy who told me that not one hour ago her husband had dropped dead of the staggers. Didn't stop me telling her about our new range of fitted kitchens, though!"'

26 October 2005

*Politicians also feel an overwhelming need to appeal to young people,
as they are the voters of tomorrow – even if they are not the voters of
today. The fact that none of the people David Davis encountered in
south London had a vote in the leadership election was irrelevant; he
had to be seen to be at home with yoof. It didn't entirely work.*

David Davis arrived at a 'drop-in centre' in Tooting, South
London, the neighbourhood in which he was raised. 'I want
to see the children who go to my old school given the same
opportunities I had,' he said. Exactly the same applies to
David Cameron. In these anti-elitist days many old Etonians
are reduced to managing rock groups or selling dodgy real
estate in Chelsea instead of running the country, their traditional role.

The drop-in centre, which provides advice to young persons,
was festooned with colourful, jolly leaflets about sexual health.
'Don't let an infection ruin your erection!' one of them coun-
selled. Mr Davis took a tour of the computer terminals. 'And
these chairs are just for chilling, I assume?' he enquired. In the
old days Tory leaders probably thought that a chilling chair
was a traditional remedy for piles. I was reminded of the time,
42 years ago, when Harold Macmillan fixed the party leadership for another Old Etonian, Lord Home. 'Alec, I want you to
go down to Tooting and chill with the homies. And bring back
one of those leaflets about how you can get gonorrhoea from
a blow-job.'

Mr Davis met the youths who had dropped into the drop-
in centre. 'So you want to be a social worker?' he asked. 'And
you? Oh, you're just chilling.'

A young woman told him she hoped he would win. He said he wanted the Tories to get back into the inner cities. What could he do for people like her? 'There should be more bus shelters for when it's raining,' she said. He said he couldn't promise that. It's useful for politicians to learn what the public really cares about, and it isn't always crime, health and tax.

He moved past a poster offering to 'pimp your car'. 'It's terrifically embarrassing,' he said. 'I used to scoot down to the pub next door when I was still at school.' Innocent days. A magazine had on its cover: 'He wet the bed – and other drinking disasters!'

Then he gave a short press conference, devoted to barely disguised attacks on David Cameron. 'I do not believe in being an heir to Blair,' he said, adding, 'I have the experience and the principle to win back these areas for the Conservative party,' which means, 'I didn't go to Eton.'

8 December 2005

Having won the election quite easily, David Cameron faced his first prime minister's question time.

The new Tory leader had told us that he wanted the Commons to stop sounding like Punch and Judy. Instead what he offered us was Richard and Judy – cosy and warm, just right for settling down with a cup of tea and a biscuit. Though perhaps the questions were a shade more challenging, and certainly a lot shorter.

Mr Cameron wanted to demonstrate that he was beyond old-fashioned name calling. Instead he wanted to co-operate with the government when co-operation was deserved. He wished to help Mr Blair on education. He yearned to be at his side on climate change. He needed to be in the prime ministerial embrace.

Mr Blair was less enthusiastic. He was like one of those handsome young men on the Dick Emery show, pursued by the star in drag. 'Ooh, you are awful! But I like you,' his female character would purr, as she twined her arms around him. A look of panic would cross the young man's face as he tried to flee.

Samantha Cameron was up in the gallery. She is to give birth in two months' time. They say that babies in the womb respond to their mother's anxieties. This one will be born as if he or she had just drunk eight cups of strong black coffee.

Prime minister's questions is a horrible experience for anyone who might be described as a human being. Mr Cameron had one big advantage: most of his own side were actually on his side. For Tory leaders that is an unexpected help.

He was called by the Speaker. 'The first issue the prime minister and I are going to have to work on together is getting the good bits of your education reforms through the Commons and into law.' Hilary Armstrong, the Labour chief whip, started shouting, as she often does. She is the Commons bag lady, railing against anyone who won't give her a coin. 'That's the problem with these exchanges,' Mr Cameron said. 'The chief whip on the Labour side is shouting like a child. Now, has she finished?' he yelled at her. 'Have you finished? Right!'

It was a terrific coup de théâtre. He was ostensibly offering to help Labour, while actually pointing out how divided Labour was on the issue he had raised. But he had to please his own side too. So he picked on the weakest member of the government, who is in deep trouble for incompetent whipping.

He had spotted the wounded wildebeest and was giving it a good gumming.

For Mr Blair it was a serious problem. If he accepted Mr Cameron's hand of friendship, it would be pushed behind his back to make the half-nelson of revenge. No Labour leader would want to do that. It would be like Liverpool and Everton getting together on match day and deciding that to agree a draw beforehand would save an awful lot of running around in the mud.

Mr Blair flannelled around. He couldn't agree with schools having the right to decide their own admissions. And what about investment? He was desperate to find anything to put clear water between him and this new, Blairite party leader.

Then David Cameron produced a line which was no less effective for having clearly been worked on a long time into the night. 'I want to talk about the future,' he said. 'You used to be the future once!'

This rattled the prime minister enough to cause him to jab a finger at the new challenger on the block. 'Sorry, I'm pointing my finger, breaking up the new consensus,' he said apologetically.

But there is no new consensus. It's just that Edward Scissorhands has taken to wearing mittens.

16 February 2006

William Hague returned to the front bench for prime minister's questions yesterday, for the first time since he resigned as Tory leader in 2001. He was replacing David Cameron, who was on paternity leave.

Paternity leave? The leader of the Conservative and Union-ist party on paternity leave? Can you imagine what Lords Salisbury or Liverpool would have made of that?

'May I inform your lordship that there is no requirement for your lordship to attend the sitting of the House today?'

'Why the devil not, Pettigrew?'

'Because her ladyship has been delivered of a child, your lordship.'

'Good God, Pettigrew, and why was I not told? And what in heaven's name has that got to do with m'duties in the House?'

'Your lordship was shooting with the Prince of Wales, and it was thought inadvisable to interrupt the sport. Shall I bring the nappies to your lordship to change now, or shall I have a footman deliver them to your club?'

In the past Tory leaders probably had only the vaguest notion of how many children they had, if any. But Mr Cameron, being a new breed of Tory, was at home breastfeeding or whatever it is that new men do on paternity leave.

26 September 2006

This was Gordon Brown's last conference speech before he became prime minister. And it seemed to be going so well…

Not since the Potemkin villages were demolished after Cath-erine the Great had gone, not since the old Crossroads motel, has a facade come down so fast. It was a magnificent moment for us connoisseurs of political disaster. Gordon Brown was midway through a paean of praise for his old rival.

'I've worked with Tony Blair for almost 10 years!' he said, waving one of his much-chewed fingers towards the prime minister, as if we might have forgotten who he was.

The words must have been wrung from him like entrails on a torturer's wheel. Then he said, 'It has been a privilege to work with him...' He was not to know that at this very moment, Cherie Blair was walking through the exhibition stands just outside the main conference hall. The chancellor's voice boomed out from innumerable speakers.

It was Mrs Blair's terrible luck that at the moment she muttered to herself, 'That's a lie!' she should be close to a reporter working for Bloomberg, the financial news agency.

Number 10 quickly denied she had said anything of the sort. It claims that she actually said, 'I need to get by.' More cynical observers than me point out that nothing can be thought to be true until it has been denied by the Downing Street press office, but that may be unfair. Possibly she said, 'My mouth is so dry,' or 'Will someone swat that fly?' On the other hand, it is scarcely likely that the press office would agree: 'Yes, the prime minister's wife thinks that the chancellor is a fibber who makes Pinocchio look like George Washington.' On the other hand, Mrs Blair's distaste for Mr Brown is well known – if she could have planted leylandii between Number 10 and Number 11, she might well have done so. And the Bloomberg people have no reason to make it up. What she thinks is unlikely to affect the Dow Jones average, or the value of the Thai baht.

Mr Brown, unknowing, raved on. 'The most successful ever Labour leader and Labour prime minister! Always in tune with the aspirations of the British people!' They had, admittedly, had their differences, and those differences had distracted from what mattered. 'I regret that, as I know Tony does too.' This translates as 'I have been an asshole, but then so has he.'

Mrs Blair scurried off to a fringe meeting, happily unaware of the chaos she had created by saying she could murder a pie.

28 September 2006

For the second time, the former US president Bill Clinton addressed the Labour conference. We were overwhelmed, sort of.

Bill Clinton reached out to the Labour party, reached out and fondled it, told it how much he loved it. 'I have never seen a man flirt with 3,000 people simultaneously,' said one minister on her way out.

It felt like being drowned in a gigantic sundae, with slathers of ice cream, hot chocolate sauce and plenty of fudge. He told them they were fabulous, wonderful, adorable, and of course he would phone in the morning.

'Ah'm glad to be back here, ah lahk this Labour party conference,' he began. Clinton can get away with saying 'ah' for 'I', unlike Blair, who sounds posey. 'The victory you won last year was good for the UK but also for the world as a whole,' he told them. Mmm, raspberry sauce!

'Your prime minister, your government, your party, have all been stunning successes,' he went on. I first saw Clinton speak at the Democratic convention in 1988 and he was terrible. Now he is brilliant. His arms reach out as if he would like to stroke everyone in the hall, tenderly and repeatedly. You might be sitting 50 feet back but he still seems to be making eye contact with you, personally. He uses long pauses, as if searching for precisely the right compliment for the gorgeous, quivering party in front of him. 'I say to all of you. Well done. You should be happy. And you should be proud.' Yum, toasted almonds on top!

The conference, so to speak, crossed and re-crossed its legs. He warned them of the terrible danger that would occur if they ever lost power. 'If you vote another crowd in, surely to goodness, they would keep everything you did right.' Longer pause, for the irony to sink in. 'Yeah,' he said, sorrowfully, and as one they felt his pain. He felt their pain. He wanted to kiss them all better.

He thanked everyone. He thanked Tony Blair, he thanked Cherie and the children. He thanked Gordon Brown for his 'brilliant economic leadership'. He thanked the party for giving all of them the chance to serve.

The gist was that their genius had changed the world, and it was all thanks to the Labour party conference – yes, this very conference! 'You are the change agents in this great nation! You have been, and you will be.' Slurp, slurp, delicious sprinkles and bits of banana! They applauded wildly his applause for them.

Tony Blair was, he told us, 'proud but humble'. Yes, we might have added, and brilliant but useless, truthful but mendacious, level-headed yet crazed. He had been greeted with 'gratitude, devotion and love'. I tried to breathe but had the feeling I was gagging on whipped cream.

Then we heard about Aids, and global warming, and the good work his dearest friend would be doing to tackle both. 'Be of good cheer! Take a deep breath! Be proud of what you have done, and keep in the future business!'

He finished with an African word he had learned. It was *ubuntu*. He didn't immediately tell us what it was. It sounded like one of those huge amalgamated unions you find in the modern TUC: the United Beaders, Upholsterers, Needleworkers, etc. Or possibly it was a reference to the joke about the new district commissioner in Africa who is greeted everywhere he goes with cries of, say, 'Ubuntu!' This enthusiasm pleases him greatly, until he reaches a cattle compound where his guide warns: 'Be careful not to step in that ubuntu.'

It turns out to mean: 'I am, because you are.' No, I haven't a clue either.

24 January 2007

Sometimes question time sessions are so dull that we have to make our own fun.

Older members may remember Frank Muir and Denis Norden's show on Radio 4. They always ended with appalling long-winded puns, which the listeners adored. Probably the most famous was the one about the Eskimo who tried to keep warm on fishing trips with a paraffin stove. Once it fell over, and burned a hole in the canoe, and he drowned. The punchline was: 'It goes to show that you can't have your kayak and heat it.'

I mused about question number 19, which had been tabled by Robert Flello (Lab, Stoke South). How would Muir and Norden have made use of his name?

Mr Flello has a healthy complexion and thick black hair, like someone whose forebears might have hailed from the sub-continent. I thought that he could have gone to visit, say,

Mumbai, where his striking good looks would have caught the attention of local film-makers.

However, he lives in Stoke-on-Trent, and after standing around in 40-degree heat for several hours, he might well have fainted. A doctor would have been quickly summoned.

'Put him in a meat fridge, quick as you can!' he would have said.

'But why?' the director would ask.

'Because you know what they tell you in medical school: "Freeze a Bollywood Flello!"'

Awful, I agree, but a lot more entertaining than local government questions.

24 April 2007

The threat of terrorism was forever held up before us. Conspiracy theorists thought it was a plot to keep the population subdued. Cynics like myself assumed that politicians were covering their backs so that if an incident did take place, they could not be blamed.

The home secretary, responsible for these matters, was John Reid, a man who had survived the Scottish Labour party – a body in its way quite as ruthless as al-Qaida.

I don't know what is scariest about John Reid's disquisitions on terrorism – the 'generation-long' war we are supposed to be fighting against these people, or the preparations he has made to cope. Certainly, as always with New Labour, a massive task force of jargon has been assembled to meet the ongoing, pitiless menace.

Mr Reid spoke to the home affairs committee yesterday. He pointed out that the National Security Board meets weekly, the Committee on Security and Terrorism had met yesterday, and the government is now recruiting someone who will doubtless be known as the Terror Tsar, or Director-General of the Office of Security and Counter-Terrorism to his friends.

It is no wonder that we need so many magnificos with fine titles, since according to the home secretary, 'the level of threat we are facing, and its exponential rate of growth, requires that we re-focus all our efforts'.

And what should these re-focused efforts involve? 'Better oversight, longer strategic planning and thinking, better integrated responses, and central regeneration and capacity to deal with the battle for values and ideas.'

Who should deal with these matters? Why, 'a laterally integrated cross-government centre,' of course. So that's simple enough. But Mr Reid was also in philosophical mood. 'If we had to look at all the changes in the world, and find one defining characteristic, it would be the fact that we are moving from static communities and a static world to a highly mobile world. As the world changes, so we must change our response to the world.'

Here's another one, missus. 'Problems used to come to us. Now we have to go to the problems.' Home secretaries used to bang on about hanging, flogging and prison. Mr Reid sounds more like a hermit on a mountaintop cave, dispensing wisdom to the backpackers and rock stars who have made the stony 8,000-foot climb to consult him.

The threat, the guru said, was so extensive that it could not be handled by only one department. They would all have to have 'a common and overlapping cause: the values that are enshrined in our lifestyle and our liberties, which are common to all of us'.

David Winnick inquired whether we were winning this battle. Any normal, boring, unenlightened politician might have replied, 'yes', 'no', or 'search me'. Not the Swami of Shotts. 'If you will permit me to use one of my favourite quotes to answer your question, I think that the Owl of Minerva will spread its wings only with the coming of dusk.'

I have checked the original quotation from Hegel, and unlike Minerva, am no wiser. But it didn't half impress the committee. They look forward to the terrorists uttering owls of rage.

9 May 2007

One of my favourite characters is Oliver Letwin, an old Etonian of undisputed intellectual skill, but somewhat scatterbrained. He admitted two burglars into his home (they had asked to use the toilet – at 5am) and later was photographed tossing important documents into waste bins in St James' Park. Likewise his speeches sometimes appear somewhat detached from life as it is lived by the rest of us.

The philosophy of the new Conservative party was the theme for the day, and who better to introduce it than the Tories' policy supremo, Oliver Letwin, a man so brilliant that he makes a Cray supercomputer look like an old Amstrad. As with all great intellects, you cannot hear his brain whirring.

We were gathered at a meeting of the Policy Exchange, the right-wing thinktank. There were a lot of young men in suits, many wearing shiny neckties, though no hoodies that I could see. Mr Letwin began by saying that the Conservatives had always been a pragmatic rather than a dogmatic party. A political position, he said, might not be theory-driven, but 'may nevertheless disclose deep theoretical dispositions – patterns of thought which, through their internal coherence, lend strength to pragmatic responses'.

Heady stuff, you will agree, and the audience was rapt. Even their neckties seemed to be paying attention. But Mr Letwin had barely started. We had to move, he said, 'from an econo-centric paradigm to a socio-centric paradigm'. We also had to shift from 'a provision-based paradigm to a framework-based paradigm'. There should be no paradigm lost. Then the best bit: the Tories had to 'internalise externalities'.

I wondered how this would go down in the average Conservative club, possibly planning their annual fete using Mr Letwin's precepts – or 'meta-thoughts' as he called them, as in the phrase, 'a penny for your meta-thoughts'.

'Now, Mrs Trubshott, I confess I am somewhat at a loss to know what Mr Letwin meant to tell us with his "framework-based paradigm".'

'Oh, Major, you are such a silly at times! I am sure it is a misprint for "parasol" and of course it must be mounted on a trellis to stop it from falling over. I'm afraid that several of the ladies felt quite faint from the heat last year!'

'Then what on earth d'ye think he means by a "second-order observation"?'

'Well, the entrance ticket includes only one glass of wine or fruit cup. If someone asks for a second one, they will have to pay for it.'

'Splendid! That seems quite clear. But Mr Letwin says we must also "internalise externalities". What does that mean when it's at home?'

'I am sure it's a frightfully clever way of saying that in the event of inclement weather, the event will be held in the village hall.'

The young persons listened respectfully to all this, paying close attention, and continued doing so until Mr Letwin told us it had all been a joke! Yes, he had been demonstrating that you didn't need 'ridiculous, high falutin' language' to express important concepts, unlike Gordon Brown with his 'neo-classical endogenous growth theory'. The audience laughed at this revelation, as politely as they had listened to all that nonsense in the first place.

But in politics, no good idea goes unpunished. As I type these words, I can hear on the Commons TV feed Chris Huhne of the Liberal Democrats reading out Mr Letwin's words in a mocking tone of voice. And we accuse the Americans of not understanding irony!

11 May 2007

Tony Blair finally left. He made his farewell speech in his constituency.

Trimdon, a neat, spruce community in County Durham, had become a media village. Ten satellite trucks were parked on the well-mown green. Hundreds of journalists and party faithful were amassed inside the Labour Club, where in 1983 an agent called John Burton spotted the potential in the young lawyer and employed sleight of rulebook to give him the last Labour seat going in the imminent election. It has been the chosen setting for all the great events of his political life.

And the audience proved much of what he said. I've been going to Trimdon on and off for 10 years and the people have become noticeably more prosperous – better dressed, better fed, the skin glossier. It's only the old men, the former miners, who look pinched and stooped, their faces lined as if they had never quite been able to scrub the last of the coal dust away.

We waited. Vaguely inspirational pop music boomed out. Search for the Hero Inside Yourself, Higher and Higher.

People appeared with placards, many in suspiciously similar styles: '10 Years, 3 Elections, 1 Great Britain'; 'Britain Says Thanks'; 'Tony Rocks'. Without evident irony they played Things Can Only Get Better at top volume. A woman tried clapping and dancing to this tune – which might be better re-titled Still Some Room for Improvement. Some people joined in, but most didn't, so it looked as if a happy-clappy congregation had been infiltrated by Anglicans.

Then he arrived. He began in folksy style, thanking Maureen, and, er, Maureen's friends. 'She said to me "four more years", and I said, "Maureen, that's not on message for today."' He thanked John Burton. He thanked Cherie and the children, 'who never let me forget my failings'. Surely, there are other people around to do that, millions of them?

Then he was up and away. Most prime ministers are actors, and this was a performance worthy of a Wolfit or a Sinden.

He was revealing about why he had clung on for so long.

'Sometimes the only way you can conquer the pull of power is to set it down.' He made it sound like levering yourself out of bed on a cold morning.

We rushed through the politics of the past few years, and soon realised that this was not merely a description of Blairism – it was a description of Blair. No cabinet colleague – indeed nobody else – was mentioned. Even the word 'government' appeared to have been banned. It was him, him, him! He listed his achievements, all of which we have heard many times. We now lived in a country that was 'confident in the 21st century, comfortable in its own skin', which made us sound like a particularly lazy sausage.

Some thought he had been Messianic. Not so. He had suffered doubts, hesitation, reflection and reconsideration.

Changes had been 'hellish hard to do'. Suddenly and briefly we were on to Iraq, and 'the blowback from global terrorism'.

Had he been wrong on that one? No. 'It is a test of will and belief, and we can't fail it.' So no apology there. But he did say that in 1997 expectations had been 'perhaps too high... apologies to you for the times I have fallen short'.

But apologies for what? He has always been willing to admit being wrong, but will never tell us exactly what he was wrong about. But, 'good luck,' he said to us all, and was away, flanked by a guard of honour mounted by Trimdon's Labour supporters, to cries of 'Thank you!' from them, and 'Move out the fucking way!' from the photographers. And I did see one woman dabbing her eyes.

12 May 2007

Gordon Brown was the only candidate for the Labour leadership. Nevertheless he felt the need to run as if there were dozens of rivals.

Gordon Brown began his campaign in London yesterday. It will be a lonely business travelling round the country asking people not to vote for anyone else, since there is no one else.

But he is a truculent chap, and can easily pick a fight with himself. The launch was at a trendy design centre, all white-painted brickwork and open steel stairways, as if Richard Rogers had created a Victorian prison.

A claque of young persons had been gathered. They were the kind of young people politicians love to have around, but who make other young people look at them strangely, as if they were train spotters, or evangelicals. News came through that Tony Blair had endorsed him on television. The words were warm enough, but the body language was awful. The outgoing prime minister umm'ed and ah'ed. His eyes flickered wildly.

'I am absolutely delighted, um, to give my full support to Gordon. As. The next leader of the Labour party. And – er – prime minister.' It got worse. The teeth were so gritted you could have sprinkled them on a snow-covered motorway. The words sounded as if they had been dragged from the bowels of his being, like a potholer with a broken leg being pulled, inch by inch, to safety.

Finally Mr Brown arrived. The claque clapped him for far too long. It was like a mass Moonie wedding. He looked happier than I've seen him for a long time. He had a new haircut. He worked the crowd, chatting and smiling. He resembled a second husband trying to be chums with his new wife's children. He is the Stepfather of the Nation. ('Awright, I'll have the iPad 2, but I'm not going to call you "Dad".')

His speech was, of course, an attack on Tony Blair. Why break the habit of a lifetime? You had to read between the lines. Like the way he kept talking about 'a new government' with 'new ideas' and 'new leadership for this new time'.

Get the drift? We needed to change. We must embrace change. Communities must embrace change, and 'as the world changes, our priorities must change'.

'We must restore power to parliament,' he said. I wondered who had taken it away in the first place. 'We must uphold civil liberties' – against the tyrant who has been stripping them away, as he meant, but didn't quite say.

But then it was clear that, alarmingly, he was morphing into Blair. He talked about his 'core beliefs' – remember Blair's 'irreducible core'? He spoke with misty eyes, and no evident sense of irony, about 'security with good pensions'. The claque, which had been applauding every line with bright-eyed zealotry, failed to express astonishment at that, coming from the biggest pension-purloiner since Robert Maxwell.

Like Blair, he began to speak in verb-free sentences. 'Faith in people and in their potential! A belief that Britain can lead the world!' He spoke about his parents. Like the parents of every politician who ever lived, they taught him integrity and decency, and provided him with his moral compass. Why does no one ever say, 'They taught me to grab what I can, and look after Number One...'? And the last jab at Blair: 'I have never believed that presentation is a substitute for policy.'

Mind you, if anyone in his team had cared about presentation yesterday he would not have been speaking from behind an autocue that managed to mask half his face. On television it looked weird. But then being there is never any substitute for watching an event on TV.

15 June 2007

We soon got a flavour of the Brown premiership to come. He has never been afraid of demonstrating his command of specialised vocabulary, or jargon as we call it. I wondered how a question session would go if he were invited onto Radio 2. All quotes are verbatim from his appearance at a select committee.

Jeremy Vine: Mrs Figgis of Daventry, it's your call to the prime minister.

Mrs Figgis: I don't know, Mr Brown, everything is so expensive these days. I bought these school shoes for my daughter, and they were £37, and that was in the sale!

Gordon Brown: Well, Mrs Figgis, our long-term policy objectives include the symmetrical inflation target. Inflation expectations have remained firmly anchored to the government's target, and that has enabled us to maintain international best practice.

JV: Does that answer your question, Mrs Figgis?

Mrs Figgis: Yes, it does, it's all perfectly clear to me now.

JV: Jim Bedstead of Surrey, you're talking to the prime minister.

Mr Bedstead: Our local market, it's been there all my life. But the health and safety, they're threatening to close it down, because they say rotten fruit falling off the stalls might make people slip. It's political correctness gone mad.

GB: I have to tell you, we are doing the right thing for the British economy, in a market-sensitive environment.

JV: Now, let's hear from a pensioner. Mr Pettifer of Truro, what's your question for Gordon Brown?

Mr Pettifer: I had a pension scheme, and it's worth nothing now, absolutely nothing. After 43 years in the same job!

To live, I have to eat dog food, and old copies of the *Sun*, mashed up in warm water.

JV: Sounds dreadful. What's your reply, prime minister?

GB: Well, Mr Pettifer, you should know that we have conducted an examination of monetary aggregates in an open economy, which is far more global in its capital markets. The notion that you had a fixed relation between the money supply and inflation was found to be unreliable... and you are ignoring the second-round effect of oil prices on utility prices.

Mr Pettifer: Can't argue with any of that.

JV: Now let's hear from Kerry Skillet, she's a student in East Anglia.

Kerry Skillet: I just wanted to ask...

GB: If I may just say, when we moved from an RPI to a CPI we moved from an RPI of 2 per cent to a CPI of 2.2 per cent.

Kerry Skillet: That is exactly what I was going to ask about. Thank you.

No wonder the Tories are rubbing their hands in glee.

Gordon Brown

28 *June* 2007

After what felt like the longest farewell since Frank Sinatra, Tony Blair finally left.

'We won't miss you at all!' cried Cherie Blair, graceful as ever, as she waved goodbye to the press gathered outside Number 10. They were leaving the place for the last time. As so often, she shouted aloud what her husband thought it more prudent merely to think. Tony Blair played the media with brilliance, so it was a bit like Alfred Brendel's wife complaining about piano tuners.

He arrived at prime minister's questions and began, as ever, with a tribute to fallen soldiers. His voice was on the edge of cracking as he said that there were those who thought that they faced the dangers in vain. 'I do not, and I never will.' Was he hovering on the edge of bad taste, using the dead to back his case for war? He raced on through his list of appointments, adding: 'I will have no further meetings today. Or any other day.' The House, quivering with sentimental anticipation, chortled merrily.

The next 27 minutes were a bizarre mixture of the traditional and the frenetic. We had all the usual lists of higher spending, of shorter NHS waiting lists, of once-failing schools whose alumni could walk into Harvard if they chose.

David Cameron produced an encomium. 'No one can doubt the huge efforts he has made in the public service... considerable achievements that will endure.'

The Tory leader is trying to establish a myth of the golden Blair years, a sort of Camelot, which he can contrast with the dark, dour, dire Age of Brown that we are entering. But this did seem genuine.

Blair thanked him for his courtesy. Clearly 'courtesy' was the word of the moment. Ming Campbell praised his courtesy. Blair in turn thanked him, for his courtesy. And he thanked Ian Paisley. The entire House was leaving some for Mr Manners.

Richard Younger-Ross, a Lib Dem bag person, brain as haywire as his hair, attempted a complicated question about disestablishment. The prime minister emeritus – almost – wearily threw away: 'I am not really bothered about that one.' You can get away with that when you're leaving.

Then it was time to go. He admitted he had never been a great House of Commons man – yup – but he did pay the tribute of 'fearing' it. 'The tingling apprehension I had at three minutes to 12 today I felt as much as 10 years ago.'

'I don't like you, you're scary' seems a curious farewell, especially as they almost never laid a glove on him. MPs have, with a few rare exceptions, been the poodle's poodles.

Then some of his trademark clunky phrases: politics had included 'harsh contentions' but it was a profession where 'people stand tall'. And if there was 'low skulduggery' it was more often a place for 'the pursuit of noble causes'. Again, his voice was on the brink of breaking up.

As he left, by prior arrangement, all Labour MPs stood up to applaud him. Against the rules, or at least against custom and practice, but who was going to stop them? Cameron waved the Tories to their feet, and though only a few clapped, all of them stood. As he left Gordon Brown slapped him on the back, and then again, as if to say, 'There's the exit, that way.'

Over in Downing Street we learned that Mr Brown cannot wave. He raised a hand to hip height, as if patting a passing dog. 'Wave!' shouted the snappers. He tried again, but failed.

Finally he managed to raise an unwilling arm, and disappeared inside – to start, he said, 'the work of change'. By which he presumably meant, 'undoing all the harm done by the last occupant'.

10 July 2007

Jacqui Smith became the first female home secretary. Questions often took an unexpected turn.

The main talking point came from Mr Henry Bellingham, the Tory MP for NW Norfolk, who wanted to know when Ms Smith would meet the local police to discuss illegal raves in East Anglia.

The minister, Vernon Coaker, replied that the police were busy gathering intelligence and car registration numbers. (Haven't they got more urgent work these days?) Then Mr

Bellingham inquired, 'Are you aware that there was a time when raves were generally low-key, good-humoured events?'

At this the entire place collapsed in laughter. What was he talking about? Was there a golden age of raves, perhaps between the wars? Young men in boaters would arrive, carrying jugs of lemonade and a wind-up gramophone with a wooden horn. They would have some records by 'Hutch' which they would play while 'flappers' danced to music so loud that it could sometimes be heard in the next field.

These events were so low-key and good-humoured that the local clergy were often invited, hence the phrase: 'More "E", vicar?'

18 July 2007

It's extraordinary how ministers cling to jargon, almost as a defence against verbal attacks. You can hardly assault something you don't understand.

You can get some idea of how a new administration works by looking at the language it uses. The most important word these days is 'issues'. This appears to mean no more than 'problems', though it sounds more impressive. So Ed Miliband, the new cabinet office minister and brother of David Miliband, the foreign secretary, and presumably of Gummo Miliband too, banged on about 'social inclusion issues' and 'special needs issues'.

Ruth Kelly, the transport secretary, told us that there were 'passenger issues at Birmingham New Street'. Did she mean that passengers were facing difficulties, or that the very existence of passengers was interfering with the smooth running of the station?

Either way, the word is out of control. Suppose you published a magazine like Parents, devoted to the care and upbringing of one's offspring, and your edition about children's problems ran into snags, would you then face issue issues issue issues?

A feast of jargon followed. Mr Miliband announced 'a national programme for third sector commissioning', whatever that might be. Even the Tories joined in. 'Have you consulted the new Volunteering Tsar, Baroness Neuberger?' asked Greg Clark. Only under Gordon Brown could we have such a personage, though of course it should be the Volunteering Tsarina, or possibly a Volunteering Rasputin.

Then John Healey made a statement about giving more power to local councils. The centrepiece was the abolition of John Prescott's regional assemblies, which are, so far as I can see, to be replaced by other equally unelected, unknown and inefficient bodies. Or, as Mr Healey put it, 'We will combine new regional economic strategy into a single integrated strategy.'

So impenetrable was this oratory that another Tory, Tony Baldry, was driven beyond endurance. He quoted the minister's words back to him. 'What does the phrase, "develop proposals for multi-area agreements encouraging local authorities to agree collective targets for economic development priorities and work with interested city and sub-regions on the scope for statutory and sub-regional arrangements which could allow greater devolution of national and economic functions" mean in plain English?' he inquired.

Astonishingly, Mr Healey was able to translate into the demotic. So why use such gibberish in the first place?

19 July 2007

It soon became clear that Gordon Brown was incapable of making a fast decision. Or, sometimes, a slow one.

Time and again Gordon Brown ponders things, promises to give them a bit of thought, to chew them over. Yesterday he was asked if he thought that cannabis should be legalised for medical purposes. 'There will be a consultation document to review our strategy.'

What about serious criminals who are being released from prison early? 'The new justice secretary will investigate.' Will these early releases become a permanent fixture in the justice system? 'We will continue to review it.' Darfur: what is the aid minister, Douglas Alexander, doing there? Like Fagin, 'he is reviewing the situation'.

What about the very large number of missing children in this country? He looked forward to meeting children's charities 'to talk about this very grave problem'.

The death of four cyclists from Rhyl cropped up. 'I will look into this with ministerial colleagues.' Had the Royal Navy got enough ships? 'We look forward to making an announcement.'

But he's had 10 years to sort this stuff out. What on earth was he doing all the time, except sticking pins into a wax model of Tony Blair?

24 July 2007

Brown gave his first press conference at Downing Street. It followed disastrous floods.

He batted aside criticisms of failures by the emergency services by saying, 'In each of these instances where people have raised questions, the answers have been given.' This was the Ted Heath school of debate: 'There are those who disagree with me. They are wrong.'

There would be a review. In Gordon Brown's Britain there is always a review. If he had been stopped by Dick Turpin demanding 'Your money or your life,' he would have announced a review to consider the options. Passing a child drowning in a duck pond, he would leap into action and set up a committee to look at the matter of aquatic safety for the under-fives.

What had been the biggest surprise of his new job, he was asked. 'I think, er, er, it's a new challenge every day, and you're not able to watch sporting events such as Wimbledon and the Tour de France...'

What on earth did he expect? Did he imagine that civil servants would murmur in his ear, 'Pretty quiet day today, prime minister. You just sit down with a nice cup of tea and watch a bunch of drug-soaked junkies pedal up and down a mountain!'

1 October 2007

Boris Johnson was well on his way to becoming the most popular Conservative in the land. Later one could argue that he was the only popular Conservative in the land.

There was a fine symbolic moment at the Tory conference yesterday – the handover of the great blond Mop of State. First we had Michael Heseltine, once the man who could drive the conference into a frenzy of mingled rage and pleasure. Julian Critchley famously remarked that Heseltine always knew where to find the clitoris of the Conservative party.

But he is older, and would need bifocals now. Oh, there were distant echoes of the glorious days past. The hair is as thick, strong and perfectly sculpted as it ever was, propped up like a Suffolk cliff that would otherwise plunge into the sea.

The voice would occasionally peak with anger. But the very thought of socialism, which 20 years ago would have driven him into a spittle-flecked spume of fury, now evokes regret rather than rage. He even stuck to the topic in hand, something he never did before.

At the end he lingered, perhaps waiting for the standing ovation that would once have been his due. A handful did rise, but no one followed them. Perhaps they recalled his part in the fall of Margaret Thatcher. Perhaps some younger delegates weren't even sure who he was. He walked off slowly with – was it my fantasy? – his head slightly bowed.

Half an hour later we heard from another blond. By contrast, Boris Johnson got a standing ovation simply for walking on stage. They cheered and they whooped and they yelled. They love him. The Great White Corona, with its power over men's minds, is now his! What we actually got was his stump speech for Mayor of London – no more high-rise buildings, no more 'jack-knifing, self-combusting, cyclist-crushing bendy buses'.

And we returned to his great obsession – the theft of his own bicycles. Seven since Ken Livingstone had come to power! Had 'the great newt-fancier' been personally stealing Boris's bikes?

We were not told. 'Once they stole my saddle, to whatever voodoo end!'

As slogans go, 'Vote Conservative and stop my bicycle saddle from being nicked' lacks both pith and resonance. But it didn't matter. The conference rose as one, as if bidden by the Mighty Mop. Even David Cameron appeared on the stage, as if to annexe some of that love, fervour and sheer blond magnetism.

23 October 2007

There was a great fuss over the new European treaty. Gordon Brown had promised a referendum on a new constitution, but decided not to hold one, on the grounds that he might lose it. As old political hands will tell you, never hold a vote unless you know the result beforehand.

The prime minister had gone to sign the new treaty, but waited till all the other European leaders had gone before he showed up. Quite what this was intended to prove we never learned.

Gordon Brown returned from Lisbon to face his first big test over the non-existent referendum. He is agin one. I took a copy of the new treaty into the Chamber so that I could refer instantly to every topic that was raised. It includes 294 'articles', plus 63 pages of protocols, and it makes for a gripping read.

On page 26, for example, we find article 37 (b): 'In the first sub-paragraph, the words "without prejudice to paragraph 1 and Article 14 (3)" shall be replaced by "in accordance with Article 11 (3)" and "as well as the High Representative" shall be inserted, "keep the latter".'

And in the view of many Tories, you can certainly keep him, or her.

There are fascinating sections that tempt the reader onward, such as: 'The words "AND SPACE" shall be added to the heading of Title XVIII', which hints at the longest-ever series of sci-fi movies. Or new article 32 which reads in its entirety: 'The Union shall have legal personality.' Like Rumpole of the Bailey, perhaps.

David Cameron accused Gordon Brown of reneging on his promise to hold a referendum. Brown saw his opportunity. He leapt in with a stunning new piece of euro-jargon, the 'passerelle'.

Apparently it was Lady Thatcher who, unknown to the entire population, first legislated for passerelles.

I logged on to the EU website, hoping that a passerelle would be a delicious Belgian pastry, filled with cream and pralines. Instead it means, 'a footbridge, referring to the possibility of either moving a policy area from the intergovernmental third pillar to the supra-national pillar, or changing the voting rules in the council, or the extension of the article's scope of application.' No wonder we are not getting a referendum.

9 November 2007

A new star appeared in the Conservative galaxy.

The scene is Tory HQ. In a basement room, a team of people wearing security passes has been locked in. A middle-aged man in a lab coat steps onto the dais. 'Ladies and gentlemen,' he says, 'your requirements were specific. You wished my team to create a Tory MP who would refute the public's suspicion that your party consists entirely of wealthy, privileged people, who have no knowledge of, or connection with, the north of England.

'I am pleased to report that we have succeeded. In fact, we have done more. We have brought you today's version of

Alderman Foodbotham, the 25-stone, awesome-jowelled, iron-watch-chained, crag-visaged chairman of the Bradford City Tramways and Fine Arts committee, created by the columnist Peter Simple!'

As an excited buzz runs round the room, his voice drops.

'And I can inform you that this is the first time anyone, anywhere, has managed to clone a fictional character. In all modesty, I believe it is the greatest scientific achievement of the century!'

A curtain is pulled back. There stands a gigantic figure, with a great moon face, a rubicund complexion and an iron watch chain. The room erupts in a hubbub. Cries of 'The next election is won!' and 'Wozziz name?' ring out. The scientist looks slightly embarrassed. 'We gave him a joke name for our amusement, but of course you'll need something more serious. We called him "Eric Pickles".'

'But that's wonderful! I love it!' says the party leader. 'Eric Pickles he is, and Eric Pickles he shall be!' Yesterday we were privileged to watch the new creation in action. Mr Pickles, who like Alderman Foodbotham was leader of Bradford council, faced Hazel Blears, the tiny communities secretary whose poppy was level with the dispatch box. As always, she looked terrifically pleased with herself. If she had done a little jig, just to celebrate the sheer joy of being her, we would not have been surprised.

Mr Pickles rose, and the floor of the Chamber shook. He spoke with the air of one who would have been handing down the 10 Commandments if he hadn't mislaid his chisel. He told us that his great-grandfather had been chairman of Keighley Co-op. How utterly authentic!

How sad that the Speaker does not allow MPs to wear flat caps in the Chamber, or keep ferrets down their trousers. He quoted from Ms Blears's blog.

(The original Alderman Foodbotham would have imagined that a blog was a cheap substitute for cod for poorer people, to be served battered with chips.) 'Snap election,' he said, 'reet on!' (Only fictional northerners say 'reet' any more.)

He speeded up, but as he did so the microchip in his brain broadened and lengthened his words. 'Agency' became 'age-gunn-say'. The government had 'roared ruffshud' over local councils. 'I gre-e-ew up in a terruuss house. I kno-o-ow what it's like to be poo-wuh.' A fantastic tribute to British technology.

29 November 2007

One of the worst things that can happen to a politician is for someone to make a joke at his or her expense – a joke that sticks. It happened to Gordon Brown a few months after he became prime minister.

It was ghastly – the most horrible, tooth-rattling, goose-pimpling, stomach-heaving prime minister's questions since John Prescott stood in for Tony Blair. I was reminded of the only bullfight I ever saw: the great beast, tormented by the picadors, charging around the ring, lowering his head and bellowing with futile rage and pain.

Sheer pity made me want the bull to have a chance – not to kill the matador, but at least to toss him once, perhaps briefly to wipe the thin, satisfied smile from his face. I felt the same for Gordon Brown. It started when he got up to answer the first question, and Tories jeered at the near silence from Labour. David Cameron had darts to plunge into his hide, and he planted them with cruel care. The prime minister had promised to be open, trustworthy and competent. Could he stand there and make that claim again?

He asked about the cash for peerages inquiry. 'Does he expect us to believe that someone even Labour members believe is a control freak was preparing for an election, sorting out the finances with everyone involved in this scandal, yet did not have the first idea of what was going on?'

Mr Brown lowered his head and charged blindly. Wretchedly, he even raised Black Wednesday, which happened 15 years ago. The Tory leader delivered the *estocada*, the final sword-thrust: 'We have had 155 days of this government, with disaster after disaster. The prime minister's excuses go from incompetence to complacency and there are questions about his integrity. Are people not rightly asking, "Is this man simply not cut out for the job?"'

The attack was more lethal than it might have been. Mr Cameron could have gone over the top and raved about the worst government since George III. Saying, like Attlee, 'not up to the job', was far worse.

But far, far worse was yet to come. The agony was heightened. Vince Cable, the acting leader of the Liberal Democrats, said in his voice like a sheep with a tummy ache, 'The House has noticed the prime minister's remarkable transformation in the past few weeks – from Stalin to Mr Bean.'

A great howl of laughter seemed to fall from the ceiling. Even Labour MPs tried desperately to hide their laughter from the whips. Apparently many stab victims feel no pain at first, but are aware how much it will hurt later. This one will go on hurting.

The only relief came when Sir Patrick Cormack bizarrely asked Mr Brown what he would like for Christmas. Perhaps he expected a reply on the lines of 'an iPhone, or perhaps a giant bar of Toblerone'. Instead the prime minister said, from deep inside his pit of misery, 'I might have one day off.'

Mr Cable later revealed that he had thought the gag up in his bath. His wife had advised against using it, but he went ahead all the same.

13 March 2008

I fear that I misjudged Alistair Darling, who later turned out to be one of the most prescient chancellors we have ever had. Certainly he was wiser than his predecessor, Gordon Brown, who tried at one point to sack him.

Is Alistair Darling the most boring chancellor ever? Put it this way: he sent Geoffrey Howe to sleep. This is an epoch-making achievement, like beating Roger Federer at tennis – a sign that the torch has been passed to a new generation.

The former chancellor, now Lord Howe, was the proud holder of that ancient title, the ultimate mega-snooze, Denis Healey's 'dead sheep', a man whose first throat-clearing could empty a packed room.

Yesterday he took his place in the gallery across from the whipper-snapper bidding to depose him. Mr Darling had barely started talking in his soft Scottish monotone about 'stability', 'challenges of the future', 'flexibility and resilience' when Lord Howe's head slumped dramatically forward. For almost the entire speech, he slept in peace. Very occasionally he would wake with a start, look across the Chamber, and observe that Mr Darling was still speaking. Instantly his head dropped down again, and there it stayed.

It was a fine, touching tribute from the crasher's crasher, and Mr Darling must be very proud this morning. Indeed, so dull was his speech that for much of the time he heard the sound that other, lesser, public speakers dread – the audience talking among themselves.

Normally during a budget speech they'd be discussing new rules for mortgages; yesterday I suspect they were asking if their neighbour had caught Delia on TV, or how the kids were doing at school – anything to drown out the drone. But we know that Mr Darling regards being boring as a wise political strategy, so deep down he must have been delighted.

If you actually listened, your eyes propped up by match-sticks, a ballpoint pen lodged under your chin, it was eerily familiar. As Nick Clegg said later, 'I watched the prime minister very carefully and his lips scarcely moved while the chancellor was speaking.'

Finally it was over. Lord Howe, still asleep, was woken by the mass stampede of fellow peers pushing past him to seek gallon jugs of black coffee.

23 April 2008

Disasters continued to arrive on the government's doorstep.

Alistair Darling announced a £50 billion bailout for the banks.
But he did it all in that maddeningly calm way he has. If my
house was on fire, I hope the brigade wouldn't send him to
tackle the blaze. 'This is a serious situation. I intend soon to
make available a wide range of fire extinguishers. Asbestos
blankets will also be an important part of the rescue pack-
age...' A shower of sparks goes up from the roof with a great
swooshing noise. 'This house is better placed to withstand the
effects of fire than most others in the street,' he intones, with
the same infuriating placidity.

'But can't you hose it with water?' you ask desperately.

'We are conducting an urgent review of the use of water as
a fire retardant and I have tasked the committee to present its
conclusions within six months...'

In transport questions we might have heard about the
Terminal 5 fiasco, which left hundreds of passengers without
baggage, or indeed flights, and which has once again made Britain's reputation for incompetence a by-word round the world.
Or we could have heard about the crawling queues along
motorway roadworks in which no roads are being worked.

But that got only the odd glancing mention. What MPs
wanted to talk about was Mrs Gwyneth Dunwoody, the
Labour chairwoman of the transport select committee, who
has just died. She kept her position in spite of tireless efforts
by the government, who regarded her as a terrific nuisance.

I have to say that there was an ever so slightly sinister air
to yesterday's tributes, as if people could not quite believe she
was dead, and might one day return with her rasping tongue
and harsh, angry laugh. Ruth Kelly, transport secretary in the
government that did so much to get rid of her, called her 'a
truly outstanding parliamentarian and a great servant of the

people', but at least had the grace to add that she made 'pertinent, if sometimes mischievous contributions to debates'. This is obituary code for 'I personally found her as agreeable as a septic goitre'.

It was the Tories who went over the top, possibly because they could never hope to rival, and would love to copy, Mrs Dunwoody's ferocious disdain for the Labour government. Anne McIntosh even evoked Rupert Brooke: 'There will always be a corner of this Chamber that is forever Gwyneth,' she said.

It sounded like an MR James ghost story. A new member, arriving perhaps in 2010, insouciantly sits down in her old place and immediately feels a cold shiver down his spine.

Later he is found in his office, dead, a look of indescribable terror on his face. 'It looks as if he's been sat on, by a very large person, sir,' says the copper who finds the body. The Inspector shudders. He guesses what has happened. A black cat appears from nowhere and emits a terrible screech.

'It seems very strange to be here without her watchful eye,' said the Tories' Louise Ellman.

Without her watchful eye? I wouldn't be so sure. Did I detect in the distance a mirthless cackle of contempt? Or was it just an old rafter creaking?

17 June 2008

George W Bush paid his final visit to the UK.

Two of the least popular politicians in the world appeared together in London, propping each other up like drunks in need of a lamppost. People age in plateaux, looking much the same for much of the time, then suddenly appearing old. Bush looks thinner than before, more lined, more worn. It was as though he was physically disappearing. Brown, by contrast, looks like a poster boy for two hours' sleep a night.

The pair were speaking in the totally over-the-top Locarno room in the Foreign Office. It's like being inside a wedding cake. The prime minister spoke at length. The president favoured him with his 'I know I've seen this guy somewhere before, but I can't remember when' look.

Mr Brown's talk may have been long, but at least it was coherent. Bush sounded as if he were floating down his own stream of consciousness. 'Some are speculating that this is my last trip, well, let 'em speculate, who knows?' he said.

The language remains strange, random. He had no quarrel – pronounced 'kwarl' – with the Iranian people. He wanted free elections for the 'good folk' of Zimbabwe, which made them sound like the congregation at a Texan church supper.

Even after eight years of Bush, we still need to untangle much of what he says. 'Freezer eye-tie', for example, is 'free society'. Later he said that it wasn't 'only, you know, white gang Methodists who are capable of self-government'. Or it might have been 'white guy' or 'white goons' – hard to tell.

We pondered for a moment on all those Episcopalians and Catholics who are, apparently, incapable of self-government.

2 October 2008

David Cameron, in his party conference speech, showed a fondness for both the demotic and the erotic.

'I get the modern world!' declared David Cameron, and that was the message of his speech. It's not a claim that, say, Sir Alec Douglas-Home would ever have made, but then I don't recall him groping Lady Home after a conference speech either. Samantha Cameron was not so lucky. She was pulled on the stage looking nervous. Perhaps this was why she got several smackers on the lips, a definite snoggerama, plus innumerable strokes of the tummy, which presently, so far as we know, does not contain another little Cameron.

There was definitely something erotic in the air. The cry, 'Get a room!' hovered unspoken over the stage. 'I understand entrepreneurs,' he said, 'I go to bed with one every night.'

Presumably he meant Mrs Cameron, rather than, for example, Sir Alan Sugar. Samantha sells, among other things, upmarket notebooks. I was reminded of the old Donald McGill postcard that shows a man in the shop asking a pert young woman if she keeps stationery. 'Well, sometimes I wiggle about a bit,' she replies.

For the big speech, the conference had moved to the Birmingham Symphony Hall. Some people had been standing in line for three hours to make sure they got their place. They were seething with excitement. I thought some of them might pop. But at first he didn't give them many applause lines.

When he wanted a clap, he paused and scrunched his eyes up. The scrunch, visible on the big screen, was their cue.

Then they warmed up. They loved his line about experience. Experience was the excuse always used by failed incumbents through the ages. Jim Callaghan had had plenty of experience. 'But thank God we changed him for Margaret Thatcher!... If we listened to this argument about experience, we would have Gordon Brown as prime minister forever!'

There were tricky bits, such as the suggestion that prison doesn't always work. 'Come with me to Wandsworth prison and meet the inmates!' he said, and we had a vision of the entire Tory conference turning up at the famous gates and demanding admission.

Nor were they particularly happy about his 'aspiration for the poor and the disadvantaged'. Whoever joined the Tory party to fret about them?

Then another phrase that never dropped from the lips of Margaret Thatcher: 'We won't bottle it when things get tough!' But, being well brought up, he pronounced both t's.

Finally it was all over and he scuttled off with Samantha, possibly to the room they had already arranged.

17 October 2008

Peter Mandelson made his maiden speech in the Lords. Nominally he was moving the order that will allow government to take over HBOS. In reality, he was bailing out his own reputation.

It was a tricky moment. Normally peers are somewhat resentful of people injected into their House for political reasons, even though that's how most of them arrived in the first place, and if not them, their ancestors. So Mandelson found himself in the position of a used car dealer who has unaccountably been elected to White's Club and has to explain that he won't use his mobile phone on the premises and won't comb his hair in public.

He succeeded triumphantly. The Lords, always insecure in their constitutional role, love to be told what splendid folk they are, and he laid it on, not with a trowel but a steamroller.

He lathered them with a thick creamy lather made from the richest, thickest whale sputum. It was a great honour to speak there. What a wonderfully warm welcome he had received, and – here was the cunning part – 'also from the staff who work here and who add so much to the character of the House.

'It means a lot to me!' They adore people being nice about the staff – so much more rewarding than a tip!

The warm sticky foam was sprayed around. 'One of the great privileges of being a member of your lordships' House is the richness of the political experience gained from the decades, and available for our debates today.'

By this time, I thought that some older peers must be gasping for air through all the gunk. But he wasn't finished. He stuffed their mouths with molten marshmallows. 'There is not only a breadth but a depth in this House, which might be more generally acknowledged…' The message was, 'Nobody appreciates you. But I do.'

28 October 2008

One of the joys of covering the Commons is the occasional reminder of just how batty some MPs can be.

Sir Nicholas Winterton called for 'harsher' penalties against young hoodlums. Nothing unusual there, you might think. Sir Nicholas's mindset is, in Alexander McCall Smith's phrase, 'traditionally built'. He harks back to a time when Tory backbenchers used to call for the return of the birch and capital punishment, or possibly both. Miscreants could be thrashed to within an inch of their lives, and then hanged. Or, in less serious cases, the other way around.

But this is 2008, and Sir Nicholas seems to have softened over the years. What was his recipe for dealing with tearaways and scofflaws? 'They should be set to removing graffiti, removing chewing gum, and picking up litter!' he said.

You could almost hear the knights of the shires rolling in their mausoleums. What did their wraiths imagine that Sir Nicholas had in mind? 'Get those vandals out of bed before noon, and set 'em to scrubbing those walls!' Or, 'They don't like the taste of cold Brillo pads.'

Or, 'I don't think they'll be terrorising old ladies once they've tried lifting chewing gum with a garden scraper! A couple of hours of that and we might see a change of attitude! No, they won't be so keen to rip up train seats once they've picked up a few Coke cans and old burger boxes – and had to throw them in a black plastic bag! It's the only language these young thugs understand.'

So that was weird enough. Then things got stranger. Norman Baker, a Lib Dem, took up the cause of protesters at the Kingsnorth climate change camp in August. They had been the subject of over-zealous police action, he said. He had been told of officers confiscating items such as 'toilet rolls, board games and clown costumes'. He wanted an inquiry.

David Drew, a Labour MP, said that one of his constituents had been arrested at the camp for 'aggressively picking up litter'. I was reminded of the old Not the Nine O'Clock News sketch about Constable Savage, carpeted by his superior for arresting a man for 'loitering with intent to use a pedestrian crossing', 'smelling of foreign food', and 'wearing a loud shirt in the hours of darkness'.

One wonders how the police were debriefed after the ructions at Kingsnorth. 'Constable Savage, I see you have seized several dozen rolls of toilet paper. Might I inquire why?'

'Yuss, sir, I apprehended the toilet paper before it could be thrown, creating a potential hazard for my colleagues.'

'Did it not occur to you, Savage, that they might have needed the toilet paper to wipe their bottoms?'

'No sir, I assumed that with them being tree-hugging types, they would have utilised grass and leaves for that purpose, sir!'

'And why did you impound the board games?'

'Because they were in possession of metal irons, boots, a cannon and a warship, sir.'

'You blithering idiot, Savage. They were playing Monopoly. The only way anyone could have been injured was if they had stuck the pieces up their own noses! And what, in the name of all that's holy, is the penalty for "offensively picking up litter"?'

'Obviously, sir, picking up litter, like Sir Nicholas says.'

11 December 2008

Shortly before Christmas, Gordon Brown came out with a quote to stay with him until the end of his days.

It was a slip, but was it a Freudian slip? There is no way Gordon Brown would have announced during prime minister's questions yesterday that he had saved the world, if he'd been in full command of his brain.

But did it express some profound, half-secret feeling buried deep in his id, or ego, or wherever these things lurk? Did he really mean it, or did he just sort of mean it?

Other countries have congratulated him on the way he prevented British banks going bust. Some have followed his example. Possibly there is a small cluster of synapses that believes he really did save the world from sudden and total disaster. Perhaps the thought just popped out like champagne from a badly corked bottle. Or he could, like so many politicians, be in thrall to his own publicity. Here's what happened.

David Cameron was launching into his assault for the day. Putting money into the banks was all very well, but it hadn't worked. When was Gordon going to change his strategy?

He replied: 'The first point of recapitalisation was to save banks that would otherwise have collapsed.' So far, so predictable. He went on: 'We not only saved the world...'

There was a pause, in which MPs looked at each other and wondered whether they had heard what they had heard. In that moment, the prime minister had a chance to correct himself – 'saved the banks and led the way,' he said – but it was too late.

He was buried under a sudden, overwhelming, mountainous avalanche of laughter – laughter, hooting, derision, chortling, spluttering, screeching and general mayhem filled the Chamber like oil in a lava lamp, bubbling and swirling.

The Tories, of course, were the most affected. Genuine hilarity mixed with the joy of seeing the hated Brown discomfited. They slapped thighs, anybody's thighs, waved their order papers, rolled around, and allowed their faces to turn a deep red colour like a Christmas glass of port.

I was more fascinated by the Labour benches. Some MPs laughed openly, mainly those who thought the whips couldn't see or who didn't care what they thought. Some could be seen twitching horribly, trying to hold back their merriment.

Others, such as the chief whip, Nick Brown, glowered ahead, as if the Tory laughter was as grossly inappropriate as it would be at a funeral.

The laughter had gone on for 21 seconds (an age in parliament) when the Speaker first said 'Order!' When it showed no sign of dying down, he again said, 'Order!'

The prime minister tried to plough his way through. But he is hopeless at snappy comebacks; so, having repeated what he really meant to say, he decided to claim that the Conservative hilarity was in some way an affront. 'The opposition may not like the fact that we led the world in saving the banking system, but we did!'

But nothing would help. The laughter just kept bubbling up. When you thought it had finally died down, it erupted again.

Thus MPs were in the mood for more fun when Nick Clegg – often a figure of jest, I fear – rose to ask a sensible question about people who couldn't give back overpaid tax credits.

But all MPs remember his claim in an interview that, in his time, he had made love to 30 women. 'Recently,' he began, 'a single mother with two young children came to see me...' and he too was buried under a cloudburst of laughter, while one Labour MP shouted '31!'

11 February 2009

Public resentment against the bankers who got us into this mess remained high. The Commons Treasury committee hauled several of them in for questioning.

The disgraced former bankers appeared at the Commons yesterday. They were sorry. God, they were sorry. They didn't care who knew how sorry they were.

On the other hand, they weren't to blame. Not personally to blame, you understand. Nobody – nobody at all – had seen it coming. Everybody had got it wrong. So they apologised, but wanted to make it clear that it Wasn't Their Fault.

And they had lost money themselves. Oodles of money!

Andy Hornby, the former chief executive of HBOS, had taken his bonuses in the bank's shares, so he'd been cleaned out. Sir Fred Goodwin, who was CEO of RBS, said he had personally lost £5 million. Somehow, MPs avoided breaking down in wet, salty tears at this news. In fact, they got even angrier.

'You're in bloody denial,' cried George Mudie after hearing yet another explanation of how nobody had seen it coming, and suffering bursts of jargon such as 'increasing the longevity of wholesale funding', presumably lobbed out in the hope that nobody would know what it meant.

Viscount Thurso said that 99 per cent of his constituents felt that if a great big black hole opened and every banker fell into it, the world would be a better place. The four bankers in front of him grimaced, as if they felt it had already happened. Or wished that it would.

They had marched into the room so confidently – or at least as confidently as they could through the crowd that had gathered hoping for the modern equivalent of a public hanging. They sat down looking quite, but not very, nervous.

Sir Fred, sometimes described as 'the worst banker in the world', seemed almost relaxed and certainly measured, adopting the tone of a manager explaining to a customer why he is being charged 17.5 per cent on his overdraft, even though the bank rate is 1 per cent. The chairman, John McFall, asked them all if 'sorry' wasn't the hardest word.

It turned out to be the easiest word. They had indeed been sorry. Profoundly, unreservedly sorry, 'about the turn of events', one of them added, making it clear they meant 'sorry' in the sense of regret about something they could do nothing about ('sorry it rained at your picnic') rather than 'sorry' in the sense of 'I apologise.'

They didn't seem to feel any sorrow for the taxpayer. Sir Tom McKillop, past chairman of RBS, decided to come a bit cleaner. Why had they bought the Dutch bank ABN Ambro for €72 billion? Wasn't that much more than it was worth?

'Everything we paid for it was more than it was worth,' he said grimly. But look on the bright side – 94.5 per cent of their shareholders had supported the purchase.

Once again, their judgment was in error. But only because everyone else's was too. They blamed Alan Greenspan of the US Federal Reserve, who appeared to think that the good times would be rolling on forever. They were like people who believe that, since the average daytime temperature has dropped 20 degrees since July, we'll all need igloos next May.

Labour's John Mann asked whether they knew how much the JSA was currently. The jobseeker's allowance is actually £60.50 per week, but they didn't even know what JSA stood for.

After the session we learned that RBS was firing some 2,300 people, all of them paid far, far less than Sir Tom and his friends.

3 April 2009

A freshly inaugurated US president came for the summit. Politicians jostled to be near him and get some of that fairy stardust sprinkled over them. He gave a press conference with Gordon Brown.

Rather like Sarkozy, Obama loved Britain – just adored being among us. I will spare you the feast of platitudes. Next day we had to go to Docklands in London to be briefed on the summit itself.

The summit took place on the dark side of the moon. We left normal humanity behind us on the Tube – idealistic young folk with piercings to protect the planet – then were ushered into a series of buses, swept past driverless trains, deserted roundabouts, abandoned building sites and empty docks, with not a single human being in sight except for groups of police officers, holding back nobody.

You had to go through security in order to be admitted to security. At one point we had our ID checked at the entrance to a huge shed. It was completely empty. But at the other end we had our ID checked again. The buses swirled around in figures of eight, like the route taken by the Mafia to make sure blindfolded victims can't work out where they are.

Inside the hall, the size of the hangar in Seattle where they put together Boeing 747s, there were around 2,000 journalists.

It is amazing these days how, thanks to the miracle of modern communications, information of no use or value to anyone can be flashed instantly around the world. Hacks interviewed each other. Cameras filmed camera crews. The British had laid on free food – great dunes of sandwiches and salads for the most part. It must have cost enough to rescue a small Midlands auto parts maker. The soup was watercress – green shoots of recovery flavour, perhaps.

Now and again a world leader, or at least a world understudy, would appear and be fallen upon like a a wounded gnu spotted by a pride of lions. Peter Mandelson glided from table to table, briefing stealthily between the snacks.

A reporter from an American company was told to find out how the various world leaders felt about being 'at the fulcrum of history'. Lord Mandelson pondered the question for a moment, then said that the soup was nice.

There were two prayer rooms, for men and for women. The little image of a praying person was the same on both doors, which would have led to confusion if either of them had had any customers.

Then, finally, the talking was over and Gordon was among us. The summit had been a huge success. The global economy would be back on track faster than anyone could have imagined. He unreeled unreal figures, like a trader in an Arab souk unrolling an overpriced carpet. There would be $5 trillion to rescue the global economy. 'A new world order is emerging, and a new era of co-operation!' He was full of the fulcrum.

Two British TV reporters asked, in effect, the same question: what's in all this for your voters? What they wanted was a soundbite for the news, something like, 'safer homes, safer jobs, and a quicker end to the crisis,' perhaps.

But Gordon Brown does not do soundbites. Instead he does bread and butter puddings, great bowls full of stodge, lumpy with facts, judgments and declarations. You could almost sense the despair back at TV centre as his reply went on and on. I must confess that over the past few days I have got slightly tired of the sound of Gordon Brown's voice, but since that has never troubled him, it doesn't matter.

Around the centre, national leaders were all recounting how it was their personal efforts that had made the summit such a success. Only a curtain separated the leaders from each other, so we could hear Gordo and Sarko explaining, in stereo, how it was all to their own personal credit.

23 April 2009

It was in this summer that the great expenses scandal broke out. MPs were caught out in all manner of dodgy practices, such as charging for maintenance that including moat-cleaning, for floating duck-houses, for their husband's porn films, and for interest on mortgages that had long been paid off. Some went to jail. Oddly enough it was often the smaller amounts that enraged the public most. The home secretary charged 18p for a bath plug. Jeremy Browne MP spent half an hour on Radio 5 Live being quizzed aggressively about a Kit-Kat he had claimed from the public purse.

Oddly enough little of this was debated in the Chamber, not least because all sides knew there were enough skeletons in each party's closet to keep a Bart's anatomy class going for a year. Instead we heard the sound of the stable door being clanged shut time and again. Take Gordon Brown's appearance on the internet, shortly after the scandal broke.

The prime minister announced the swingeing cuts in MPs' allowances yesterday – on video. In the old days, premiers spoke to the Commons. But that has one huge disadvantage – MPs can answer back. Viewers of YouTube can't. (But they can show their interest in other ways: for instance, 'Gordon Brown picking his nose' has had 376,000 hits and counting.)

Anyhow, there is his latest policy pronouncement on number10.gov.uk. What was most amazing was not the content of his statement, but the brand new smile. This smile has clearly been worked on for a long time, possibly by a professional smile consultant. ('Now, Gordon, darling, lift the corners of your mouth. Let's see those incisors! No dribbling, mind.')

It cannot have been tried on a focus group, since it is quite terrifying. Think of the Joker in the Batman films. Imagine Munch's *The Scream* only upside-down. Then again it is the kind of smile you might deploy on a first date with someone you'd found on an internet site. ('Hmm, it says "good sense of humour essential". Maybe if I smile a lot, she'll think I have one.') It's the smile a 50-year-old man might deploy on the parents of the 23-year-old girl he is dating in a doomed attempt to reassure them. It's a doctor saying, 'Now this is going to hurt just a teeny bit, but if you're a brave little soldier, the nurse might give you a biscuit.'

It is certainly meant to be friendly, even though it is scarier than anything Hannibal Lecter might have come up with. I thought of a supply teacher with the worst class in the school, desperately hoping to win them over by sheer niceness. It's a smile a terrified kidnap victim might use on his captors: 'I must say, I think you chaps have got an awfully good case.'

But what makes it truly scary is that the smile is deployed entirely at random. 'Going round the country, I have been struck by the comments of young people.' Big cheesy smile. 'A detailed written statement setting out our plans will be made by Harriet Harman.' Again, the manic grin. Does the very thought of Harriet Harman cause him to smile uncontrollably?

'Those ministers who live in official residences would not be entitled to this allowance.' Again, the smile leaps from the screen for no discernible reason. I began to wonder if he was wired up to something, possibly operated by a nine-year-old boy who is having a lot of fun.

'While the committee on standards in public life looks at the issue...' Smile! Now he is almost at the end, and able to visit his plastic surgeon for a face-drop, or whatever is the opposite of a nip and tuck – a slice and stuff, perhaps.

11 May 2009

The principal victim of the expenses brouhaha – apart from the MPs who later went to jail – was the Speaker, Michael Martin, whose handling of the whole affair made matters horribly worse.

The Speaker stood up to make his statement about the scandal. The House was far from full; no doubt many members were saving money by hitch-hiking to London.

Michael Martin began: 'We face a catastrophic loss of public confidence in the entire democratic process. The public are enraged. At a time when millions are facing financial hardship, they see us sucking up their money like thirsty camels at an oasis. As the man who presided complacently over this mounting chaos, while claiming extremely generous expenses myself, it is clear that my continued presence can only delay the crucial task of cleaning out the stables. I hereby tender my resignation.'

Did he say that? Of course he didn't! Instead he gave a performance that, to use today's fashionable word, was truly lamentable. Oh, he did say that things would have to change and that MPs should stick to the spirit as well as the letter of the rules. But then he got on to what really bothered them: their (or rather, our) money. The police had been called in. The person who had leaked the details of the expenses to the Daily Telegraph was clearly capable of selling MPs' account numbers, signatures and passwords. The Commons commission would look into the whole subject, that very night. In other words, the crime was the leak, not the pilfering.

Great. The whole statement lasted about three minutes. But as soon as he left his script things started to go the shape of an over-ripe pear. Kate Hoey, for one, wanted to know why the Met had been called in when they had a huge job to do in London. As it happened, the Telegraph had been very discreet with members' bank details.

You would have thought from his rage that she had questioned the Speaker's parentage. 'Might not this be seen as a way of hiding...' she started to say, but he shut her up. 'I listen to the honourable lady often, when I turn on the TV at midnight, I hear her public utterances and pearls of wisdom on Sky News ... it's easy to say to the press, this shouldn't happen, it's a wee bit more difficult when you don't have to give quotes to the Express – to the press, not the Express – and do nothing else. Some of us in this House have other responsibilities, not just talking to the press!'

This sort of semi-coherent abuse is not what Speakers are supposed to do. Norman Baker, a Lib Dem, was next in the line of fire. He wanted the expenses claims to be published more quickly. 'Another member keen to say to the press what the press wants to hear!' barked Mr Martin. He was losing it.

You knew his head was somewhere distant when he referred to Ann Widdecombe as 'the right honourable gentleman'.

15 May 2009

At the time it seemed that Michael Martin might even survive this appalling display. Gordon Brown, a fellow Scot, seemed ready to defend him, and Tories were not keen to have a new Speaker chosen before they had a majority. But it turned out that Mr Martin's petulance – he had admitted being 'in a bit of a bad mood' – was the beginning of the end for him.

You cannot overestimate the mood of paranoia, hilarity and madness that pervades Westminster. Normal-looking MPs seem to have messages branded on their heads, reading 'tennis court repairs', 'wife's tampons', or 'moat cleaning', like Hawthorne's scarlet letter.

In the Chamber, members were still doing the bowing and scraping bit – 'with your permission, Mr Speaker – as if he were someone who still mattered. I haven't met an MP yet who doesn't think Michael Martin should go, even if they doubt that he will.

News broke that Andrew MacKay had been obliged to resign as an aide to David Cameron, who has been trying to win the 'holier than thou' vote all week. MacKay and his wife, Julie Kirkbride, had been 'double dipping', each one claiming the second-home allowance on one of their two houses, while the other claimed the moolah for the other house, if you follow me. Since 2001 they cleared £282,731. (In a magnificent irony, Ms Kirkbride last claimed expenses when she was a political correspondent for the Daily Telegraph – the paper that has brought us all this information.)

MacKay made his way down the latter-day Via Dolorosa that leads to the Millbank studios of the 24-hour news services. With his weird complexion and bulging eyes, MacKay looks like a kipper that has been smoked before it's dead.

'I was advised to do it [by the fees office],' he said plaintively. The fees office seems to have been run on the lines of a dodgy car dealership. 'If you got cash, I can knock the VAT off, mate… don't worry about those bloodstains on the back seat, I can clean that off for you…'

MacKay's interviewer seemed puzzled. 'You said that you had a friendly conversation with David Cameron,' he said. 'But he has told the media that he is angry.'

MacKay: 'Well, it was friendly within limits.' Friendly within limits! What a wonderful euphemism for sheer, gibbering rage!

19 May 2009

Things swiftly got worse for the Speaker.

It was gruesome, pathetic and miserable. You had to watch it through your fingers, with teeth clenched and stomach knotted. It wasn't even tragic, if tragedy means a great man brought down by his own weakness. Michael Martin is a weak man brought down by his own weakness. He resembled a boxer totally outfought, tottering numbly around the ring, barely aware of what was happening, staggering into his opponents' fists, somehow staying upright amid the swaying. In any more humane arena the referee would have stopped the fight ages ago. But he is the referee, and he's not stopping anything!

One felt one should feel sorry for him. But it is hard to feel pity for someone who has blundered into a situation and shows no awareness that he needs to blunder right out again.

He not only failed to announce that he would resign, he didn't even mention the possibility. Instead, he intends to hold a 'top-level meeting'. Faced with the Great Fire of London, he would have told the fire brigade to stay where they were and announce a commission, to report in the autumn. He just doesn't get it.

One MP after another rose to tell him to resign. To his credit, he did call the ones most likely to attack him, though of course if he hadn't, the subsequent furore would have blown him away like a dandelion seed in a hurricane.

He did give a sort of apology. 'To the extent that I have contributed to the situation, I am profoundly sorry.' It was, everyone kept saying, a historic day for parliament. Or at least a hysteric day.

The only good news for the Speaker was bad news. He was supported by Bob Spink, a former Tory MP turned UKIP member, and so largely despised by all sides. It was like being praised for your banking skills by Fred Goodwin. The end must be very near.

Mr Martin finally took the hint and retired as Speaker, only to be swiftly promoted to glory, or at least the House of Lords.

3 July 2009

One of the more depressing monthly occasions in the Commons is the question session on the environment.

I don't suppose that the countryside was ever really idyllic, but it must once have been a more agreeable place than it is now. Every month, agriculture questions in the Commons opens a window on a world of misery, in which farmers battle with falling prices, rising costs, EU bureaucracy, rapacious supermarkets, bizarre diseases of livestock, and to cap it all, Defra.

I wondered vaguely how a memoir of a country childhood, written perhaps in 2050 but recalling the present day might go. All the jargon could be heard in yesterday's exchanges.

'It was the year of our Lord 2009, and my carefree days seemed to be filled with endless sunshine. I was a merry young lad, working on a train-to-gain apprenticeship at the old call centre in Farmer Pettigrew's converted barn. Kelly Braithwaite was my girl, and at weekends she and I would roam over the hill sheep farming sector, seeking out nitrate vulnerable zones, for with all our kissing and canoodling we were generally too late for the day-rate vulnerable zones.

'Sometimes we would take a can of extra-strength Irish cider and sit under a black plastic-covered hayrick as the sun went down. Afterwards I would throw the empty can into a copse, and Kelly would give me a tongue-lashing to remember. "Do not be a silly ha'poth, my girl," I would tell her. "I am merely participating in the 'recycling on the go infrastructure', as outlined by the new under-secretary of state, Dan Norris!"

'Soon we were on our way back home, and paused by Farmer Catchpole's set-aside. We would play a simple game, spotting indicator species – birds, insects and invertebrates. As country folk said round our way: "Find a ladybird afore your tea / You'll have a viable measure of increased biodiversity."

'One night Kelly and I were walking hand-in-hand through the gathering dusk. I nipped off to empty my bladder of the recycled cider and to light a fag, boldly defying the government's stated opposition to "slash and burn" policies. Then, out of the darkness we saw an eerie figure clad all in white. Kelly grabbed my arm. "It must be the ghost of old Ned Sowerbutts, who was ruined by the collapse of the Dairy Farmers of Britain, with the consequent reduction of milk prices to 10p a litre, and who fell in his drunken state into a vat full of slurry, forgetting that the new regulations on slurry storage do not apply until 2012!" she gasped.

'"No, that is no ghost!" I cried. "That is old Amos Flowerdew, the government trial badger culler," I told her. "He means no harm, except to badgers, though if he offers you a whiff of what he has in that spray can, you would be wise to refuse."'

22 September 2009

The party conference season began with the Liberal Democrats. Vince Cable, still at the height of his popularity, made a controversial speech.

The Lib Dem deputy leader described a new tax, on people whose houses are worth more than £1 million. For every pound their house is worth over the million mark, they'd have to fork out half a penny, averaging £4,000 a year.

This mansion tax would certainly make life difficult for estate agents, who would need to execute a swift U-turn and start telling people how awful the properties they're selling are. 'Some restoration required' would turn into 'serious deterioration needed'.

Instead of just saying 'with many original features', they would have to add, 'which can easily be ripped out'. 'Set in 10 acres of rolling parkland' will become 'hideous prospect of bombsite covered in toxic waste'. 'Two hundred yards of excellent fly fishing' would appear as 'serious flooding danger'.

Potential buyers will be shown the original Adam fireplace and told, 'But you can easily replace it with a coal-effect Cosyglow with Formica surround.' Dinner party conversations will swivel too: 'The people two doors away paid one and a quarter mil last year, but they demolished the conservatory, painted the outside puce, and they've managed to get it down to 900K!'

'That's marvellous. Our friends have a lovely Queen Anne house, but they dumped a rusty old Volvo in the front garden, and it took nearly a hundred grand off. We're planning a colony of bats in the guest room.'

11 November 2009

During the 2009 Labour conference, the Sun came out in favour of the Tories, for the first time in four elections. Desperate to justify its position, the paper kept dredging up fresh anti-Brown stories. They were not hard to find.

It was excruciating. You would have needed a heart of Kevlar not to sympathise with Gordon Brown yesterday as he used his prime ministerial press conference to try to portray himself as warm, caring, capable of grief and fully hooked up to a human nervous system.

The prime minister has been caught in a ghastly trap by the Sun, which on Monday printed a letter he had written to the mother of a soldier killed in Afghanistan. It was full of spelling mistakes, apparently including her name – though this was difficult to tell since he has handwriting like a spider suffering from existential angst.

On Sunday night he had phoned the woman, Jacqui Janes, and contrived to use a call meant to express sympathy and regret to embroil himself in an argument. Mrs Janes told the newspaper: 'It sounded like he was trying to put me right, instead of making me feel better.'

Those of us who have followed Brown over the past two years know how she felt. But why do we connive to inflict such torment on our leaders? Watching him twist and turn in the gales of artificial rage from newspapers was awful. He is no good at soft, empathic, emotional. At least not in public.

You sensed that some awful consultant had been drafted in and had told him to let it all hang out, Gordie baby. Let them see the real you, the egg inside the sausage meat!

So he did, or at least tried to do. 'I feel for a mother's grief. I understand the pain of her sadness. I understand very well the sadness that she feels, and the way she has expressed her grief is something I can clearly understand.'

He apologised for his handwriting, not just to Mrs Janes, but to anyone who had had to read it.

But how many ways are there of saying the same thing? 'I wanted to say, but couldn't because I did not know her, that when there is a personal loss it takes time to recover, that loss can never be replaced. You've got to take every day at a time,' he added. What he wanted to say, I assume, is that he had known similar grief when his infant daughter Jennifer died. But he could not say that, because more ordure would have been dumped on him.

There is no comparison, they would have said. No one is blaming you for her death. She didn't die because you declined to pay for that piece of equipment that might have saved her life.

Every answer came back to the same answer, the one he had to give, time and again. Had it anything to do, he was asked, with the general view the country held of him? Was it his unpopularity, the questioner meant but did not say, that was making people so cynical about the war in Afghanistan?

'I am a shy person,' he said – news to us – 'but I try to go round the country and debate about Afghanistan issues.' Then back to the leitmotiv: 'But I also do feel the pain of people who are grieving. I understand the sadness and anger sometimes of people who have lost loved ones...'

The whole thing was awful. He's not good at doing it, and we shouldn't make him do it.

9 April 2010

The election was finally upon us. Gordon Brown demonstrated why he was, perhaps, not the most engaging candidate ever to mount a platform.

It was the crucial press conference for Gordon Brown. The Tories were making the running with their claim that national insurance increases would lead to lost jobs. Things were this bad: the prime minister told us that he loved his wife. It took some doing. In fact it had to be dragged out of him like a recalcitrant tapeworm. So at least there is one vote in Downing Street that's in the bag.

We assembled under Labour's new poster. This shows the sun coming up over a flat field of wheat. It is no doubt meant to symbolise warmth and lush prosperity, though it reminded me of the field in North By Northwest, where Cary Grant is strafed by a crop duster.

Gordon Brown arrived. He was smiling that terrible smile, the one that says: 'This is going to hurt me more than it hurts you, and you're not going to like it either.'

He was introduced by Lord Mandelson, who was on chirpy form. The Tories claimed they could cut £12 billion in public spending, 'just like that!' It was the old Tommy Cooper line. 'I can't recall your name, but the fez is familiar.'

Alistair Darling, the chancellor, hurled statistics at us. I felt like Cary Grant as the figures flew past. One of them was 10.5 billion. Another was 381,000. There was a slight air of desperation about them. Somehow they hope against hope, if they can hit us with enough facts and figures, we will work it out for ourselves. They handed out a leaflet. It was full of statistics and graphs that candidates will be encouraged to use on the doorsteps. Thus: 'DCFS, DECC and FCO are all saving millions by outsourcing back office services. And MoJ is introducing a new shared service centre for HR, finance and procurement transactions. Think on't before you vote.'

'You can't spend money twice,' the chancellor intoned. Why not? Gordon Brown did it for more than 10 years.

The recovery, Brown said, was 'robust but fragile'. What, like a plastic Ming vase? Or a filigree breezeblock? How could it possibly be both?

Then came the question that almost stumped him. Why was his wife playing almost as much part in the campaign as he was? He hadn't expected that. 'My, my, my wife Sarah and I are travelling round the country together. I made a statement to that effect.'

'A statement to that effect.' Not since Prince Charles asked if he was in love and replied 'whatever love is' has anyone sounded less romantic in public. The prime minister realised that something was missing. 'I really enjoy the fact that Sarah is with me. She is the one who warns me not to smile at people.' No, of course he didn't say the last bit! I made that up, but it would be very helpful if it were true.

The hacks were determined to get some kind of confession out of Mr Brown. David Cameron had called Samantha 'my secret weapon'. Was Sarah his? Finally we extracted it. 'She is the love of my life,' he said. But immediately he must have felt that he had gone too far. He started to row back. 'We work well together. And we are enjoying the campaign.'

Before it could get any worse, Peter Mandelson interrupted. 'There you are,' he said, 'isn't that nice?'

14 April 2010

The Tories launched their manifesto in the now semi-derelict Battersea power station, site of the Pink Floyd album cover with the flying pig. They have put a glass-topped atrium inside the old building. You look out on a desolate scene, the crumbling structure held up by props and girders, looking as if one of the great chimneys might collapse at any moment, killing off half the party. It has a melancholy grandeur, as if someone had put a conservatory inside Tintern Abbey. Pigeons dive-bombed us, narrowly missing the glass.

The Conservatives had assembled dozens of ordinary people on stage and sprinkled members of the shadow cabinet among them, so that a member of the public might find him or herself sitting next to a household name, such as Theresa Villiers, or Owen Paterson, or Jeremy Hunt, or that other bloke. How thrilling to be able to go home and say: 'I was chatting away only this morning to – Grant Shapps!' and get the delighted reply, 'Who?'

There was a video. Julie from Llandudno was depicted making her breakfast, just like David Cameron in his first Webcameron broadcast. They even had a close-up of her dashboard as she drove her children to school, to prove she was inside the speed limit. Former Labour voters for safer roads!

What is this patronising nonsense? Are we supposed to say, 'Gosh, she's just like us – a housewife, mum, charity volunteer and careful driver. It's the Tories for me this time!'

George Osborne spoke. I have finally worked out who he sounds like. Close your eyes next time you hear him speak, and it's Ann Widdecombe. Try it next time he's on TV.

Finally David Cameron introduced the Conservative manifesto, which is a dark blue hardback and looks like a tombstone. The theme is that the next government can save money by getting people to do the work themselves, whether it's taking planning decisions, holding elected representatives to account, saving local pubs and post offices, appointing the chief constable, checking wasteful public expenditure online or founding new schools. This is to be known as the Big Society.

'It's about we, the people!' said Mr Cameron, with great conviction but terrible grammar.

Gosh, life is certainly going to be busy if the Conservatives win the election. Luckily their campaign against waste means that there will be mass sackings. Otherwise nobody would have time to do everything the Big Society demands of us.

8.00am Get up, discover that transport department has spent £40 on 'consultancy'. Write furious letter.

9.30am Support Mr Patel at post office by buying premium bonds and Romanian wine, two for £3.99.

11.30am Picket police station, demanding resignation of chief constable.

1.00pm Lunch. Help keep local pub open by eating Ginster's microwaved steak pie washed down with five pints.

2.30pm Smash Mr Patel's windows as warning to him not to serve booze to under-16s.

3.30pm Establish new school.

4.30pm Veto council tax rise online.

6.00pm Break to watch Eggheads.

7.30pm Sack local MP, just for the hell of it.

8.30pm Stand for mayor.

10.00pm Have second thoughts about local MP. Unsack him.

10.30pm Bed.

The scariest moment came when Andrew Lansley, the shadow health minister, said: 'You want to be your own boss, and you can with us.'

What does this mean? Do-it-yourself operations? 'The procedure you need at the time you want it. All you require is a sharp knife and a mirror...'

16 April 2010

This election was the first in which the party leaders debated with each other on television. The first debate, held in Manchester, was the start of that brief phenomenon, Cleggmania.

In the end, the debate was livelier than any of us had the right to expect. After a start as stiff as a starched dress shirt, the three men got stuck into each other, talking over each other, chipping in and barracking, so that the poor moderator, Alastair Stewart, trying and usually failing to shut them up, sounded like a racing commentator: 'Mr Brown, Mr Cameron, Mr Brown now, Mr Nick Clegg! Briefly, Mr Brown!'

All three were wearing dark suits with the appropriately coloured ties. They looked like the villains in a Quentin Tarantino film, lined up in the bar after the heist.

The first historic question was asked by Mr Gerald Oliver, a retired toxicologist. I hoped it would be 'what's your poison?' but instead it was about immigration.

Delicate stuff, but Gordon Brown moved in confidently. He talked about a chef he had met somewhere or other, the first of dozens of people they've encountered in the campaign who, wonderfully, reflect their policies. 'Let's be honest with each other,' he said, which is politician-talk for 'Let's all agree with me.'

Nick Clegg's strategy was to make the two big parties sound drearily identical. 'The more they attack each other, the more they sound the same!' he remarked in a pre-digested and regurgitated soundbite.

But he was the one who spent most time gazing straight at the viewers rather than the audience in the hall. He looked mournful, as if appealing for news about his children's missing puppy.

He said that immigrants should be allowed only if they worked in regions where they were needed, and didn't move elsewhere. David Cameron riposted with the historic first joke.

'Will they have border posts on the M62?' he asked.

At this point the audience, expressly forbidden to cheer, jeer, clap or even laugh, was looking somewhat stunned. Viewers at home could switch off or over. Or even go to the loo. But this lot had spent hours queuing to get in, and now they were stuck.

Then law and order. Clegg said that short sentences turned prisons into colleges of crime. Cameron said that his mother had been a magistrate and had dished out loads of short sentences. So Clegg was attacking his dear old mum! Things were turning nasty, which was hopeful.

At this point, Brown deployed a battery of soundbites, each of which had the smell of a spin doctor sprayed all over it.

'David, I'm grateful to you for putting up all those big posters because they show me smiling. So I'm very grateful to you – and Lord Ashcroft.'

Cameron shot back with a question. 'This is not question time, it's answer time, David,' said Brown. 'You can airbrush your answers but you can't airbrush your politics,' another line that might have sounded better if it hadn't been so obviously microwaved.

By now they were getting tired, as if they had all switched onto autopilot. In the media room, the spin doctors were at the back, telling us how dazzling their man had been before he had even finished being dazzling. Brown tried another little joke: 'At least, we weren't up against The X Factor or Britain's Got Talent!' Of course they weren't; they're on ITV too.

We clustered round the television to discover the result of the instant poll. 'Gassy material being ejected high into the atmosphere – and it could go on for days!' said an expert. It turned out to be the Icelandic volcano.

Then the result: Clegg was the clear winner with the public.

But still no news of that missing puppy.

7 May 2010

Election night, and the main broadcasters held parties. The BBC's was on a boat moored on the south bank of the Thames.

The mood was set by Andrew Neil, addressing the revellers on the BBC boat, or 'ship of fools' as someone called it quite early on. 'The Dow has fallen by 1,000 points, and the gilts market is opening early,' he announced. 'Enjoy yourselves!'

ITV was in the less exciting surroundings of the old County Hall, home of the Greater London Council. Whispering Geoffrey Howe arrived, relishing the fact that soon after Margaret Thatcher had tried to abolish democracy in the capital, large parts of the vast hall had been converted to a luxury hotel.

ITV had the politicians – Roy Hattersley, plus Geoff Hoon, the former defence secretary who was caught in the cash for consultation scam. I thought it took some top brass neck for him to turn up at all. They also had union grandees, such as Bob Crow, Britain's best-loved hate figure, and Charlie Whelan of Unite. Bob can stop the tubes more or less by snapping his fingers, so you're too late for your plane, but that doesn't matter because Charlie has got British Airways cabin crew out on strike. It's a full service arrangement!

Bob Marshall-Andrews, who has stood down as an MP, said sarcastically at midnight, 'Look, we've won three, and they haven't won any! We're unstoppable!'

Over at the BBC it was celebrity heaven. Slebs love being with other slebs, and lost no opportunities to schmooze with each other. The celebrated psephologist Bruce Forsyth was there. He was the first person to be interviewed about how the election was going.

Arguments broke out. Was Martin Amis the most famous person there, or was that Piers Morgan? Stars of stage, screen and BBC 24-hour news kept bouncing down the gangplank.

Britain's top atheist, Richard Dawkins! Maureen Lipman! Joan Collins! Christopher Meyer, the former ambassador to Washington, who first told the world about Tony Blair's 'ball-crushing trousers'. Top historians such as David Starkey and Simon Schama, Ben Kingsley, Nicholas Parsons, presenter of the in-depth current affairs programme Just a Minute, Jeanette Winterson, Mariella Frostrup, John Sergeant, and Alistair McGowan, who could be any one of those if you asked him.

Every now and again, three of the celebrities would be seized by one of Andrew Neil's satraps and hurled into the bilges, where they would be punished by having to sit on comfy sofas and to stop drinking for five minutes. And say how they thought things were going, as if they had any idea, since nobody was paying attention to anything that was going on in the election. The exit poll came at 10.01pm, and hardly anyone bothered to look up.

David Cameron

8 May 2010

The election gave no party an overall majority. The Tories had failed to get anywhere near the huge number of seats that had seemed likely a year before, and even though the Lib Dems had lost several constituencies, they did hold the balance of power. Labour seemed certain to be thrown out of office, but the results had been far from the 1997-style landslide they had feared.

A frantic few days of horse-trading, wheeler-dealing and negotiation began. Smoke-filled rooms of legend had become rooms equipped with bottled water and nutritious organic snacks.

It was the craziest day in British politics for some time, perhaps ever. It began with news of the voters who had stormed the polling stations, trying to get in before voting ended. It was becoming third world. The prime minister announced that it was his 'duty' to provide Britain with strong, stable government. He was firmly lodged at Number 10, probably not tying coloured labels on the furniture for the removal men.

You can imagine how it would be reported abroad. 'General Brown declared that the so-called popular vote had been "an error". He would remain in office as head of a national government of unity and reconstruction. To inspire confidence, opposition leaders would be jailed.'

So the man who had lost the election was staying put, but for his own good. He was trying to put together a government of losers.

News came that Nick Clegg had arrived in the capital from his power base in the northlands. TV cameras got a lock on his car and followed it from St Pancras to Westminster, like OJ Simpson being pursued across Los Angeles, though Mrs Clegg was, we were told, still alive.

He arrived at Lib Dem headquarters, where he was cheered as if he were someone who had actually won more seats than his predecessor. Clegg was in the ghastly position of being both the wallflower at the ball and Cinderella, forced to choose between the two ugly sisters.

I counted 13 camera crews, a heaving, pullulating, media mass – what American reporters sometimes call a 'goat-fuck'. A security helicopter thrashed overhead, so it was almost impossible to make out more than the occasional word:

'Disappointing... more votes than ever before... real change...' Somehow we got the impression that he would be seeing the Tories first.

On the foreign exchanges, the pound spiked upwards. Traders are like nervous grannies trying to sleep. They hear a noise and assume it's burglars. Then a voice says, 'It's all right, Nan, I kicked the cat,' and they go back to sleep. Until a floorboard creaks.

So the graph on the screen looked as jagged as the iceberg that sank the Titanic. Exit polls suggest a hung parliament, and it crashes down. Nick Clegg has warm words for the Tories and it leaps up again. Esther Rantzen loses humiliatingly in Luton – actually that didn't have any effect, but it's worth celebrating just the same.

The whole of Westminster was a fevered manic mass. TV satellite vans zoomed around the streets looking for any politician, or failing that, any hack. College Green, the patch of grass in front of parliament, was covered in tents and tall wooden platforms for the TV crews and presenters. It was Glastonbury for political anoraks, without the mud. Gangs of tourists wandered round, gazing up at people who must, to them, have been as unfamiliar as the Belgian foreign minister's press secretary might be to us.

Gordon Brown came out of Number 10. He had his sombre face on, the one that looks as if he has just been wrestling with the Giant Serpent of History. There was an economic menace. Alistair Darling was attending to it, somewhere in Europe. The implication was clear. How could we protect jobs and sterling without Alistair in charge? This was the man he had been trying to sack a few months before.

It was right, he said, for Clegg to speak to Cameron first. But he had something more to offer – economic stability, far-reaching political reforms. It was like the old Shirley Bassey hit, I Who Have Nothing. I might not be able to offer you riches, or even sufficient seats to form a stable government, but I LURVVV you!

Finally we heard from David Cameron. His equivalent to Brown's sombre face is the tilted head. The greater the angle of tilt, the greater the sincerity. This was no time for party political bickering, grandstanding or cheap point-scoring. He outlined the many wonderful policies he and the Lib Dems had in common.

I realised what this reminded me of. Brown and Cameron were too embarrassed to talk to Clegg. They were like a teenage girl getting a friend to tell that fit boy that if he asked her to the school dance, she might think about it. We, the media, were meant to pass the message on: 'He really, really likes you!'

13 May 2010

The coalition was consummated in a short but moving ceremony in the garden at the back of 10 Downing Street.

'This is what the new politics looks like,' said Nick Clegg, as he stood in the sun-drenched garden. It looked more like a civil marriage. This is a press conference that would have been illegal in 45 American states.

There were trees in the bright green colours of early summer, a trimmed lawn, the happy couple in their smartest clothes. All it needed was a band, a marquee and a table for the presents.

All the guests marvelled at how delighted they looked. And they have so much in common. The groom is from Eton and Oxford, whereas the groom is from Westminster and Cambridge. They handed out copies of the pre-nup, or 'coalition agreements reached document' as they call it.

Earlier they had posed on the steps of Number 10. They might have been conjoined twins. You had the feeling that if they ever fell out, they would have to go to Great Ormond

Street hospital to be surgically separated. The man who had told us we had to vote Conservative to avoid the horrors of a hung parliament, was full of the joys of a hung parliament.

It was going to usher in the new politics, in which the national interest was more important than party. It was a historic, seismic shift! By contrast, St Paul might have spent years changing his mind.

Apparently it had nothing to do with electoral arithmetic. It was all inspiration. 'We did both have a choice,' said the new prime minister. 'We looked at minority government, and we thought, "This is so uninspiring."'

He was asked how he felt the morning after the night before, hooked up with someone he barely knew and had hardly spoken to. 'I woke up thinking, "This is so much better than the alternative!" I had a great sense of inspiration and excitement!'

It turns out that Clegg will take prime minister's questions when Cameron is away. It will give him something to do during those long, lonely days when Cameron is in Washington, or Brussels, or Witney. 'I'm looking forward to a lot of travel!' said Cameron, while Clegg smiled happily.

They'll be sharing accommodation, of course. 'There's a corridor connecting Number 10 with where I am, but I don't yet know where I am,' said the deputy prime minister, with an air of the existential angst that must come to anybody who doesn't yet know where he is.

Things got more metaphysical. 'This will succeed through its success,' said Cameron. Suck on that one.

Inevitably there was a bad fairy at the wedding, who pointed out, 'When you were asked what your favourite joke was, you said "Nick Clegg".'

'Did you?' asked Clegg.

'I'm afraid I did,' the prime minister replied.

'Well, I'm off!' said his deputy, again with a merry smile. All the happiest partners recall the time when they couldn't stand each other. It's utterly romantic, like The Taming of the Shrew.

All too soon it was over. 'Bye, and thanks for all your lovely gifts, especially the fondue set and the hostess trolley!' No, of course not, but they did look awfully happy.

11 June 2010

New ministers began to appear at the dispatch box.

Eric Pickles yesterday answered his first questions as secretary of state for communities and local government. What a tale lies behind that simple fact, a story worthy of JB Priestley, Roy Hattersley or even Jeffrey Archer.

Come back with me to Bradford in 1887, when young Obadiah Pickles – bored by the bland food of the day – began to marinade baby cucumbers in vinegar and spices, cooking his recipes in an abandoned pigeon loft.

At first he gave them to friends and family, who were delighted by the crisp crunch of the vegetables, and the fragrant tang of the flavourings. Obadiah then hit on the idea of sending his son Zebedee to stand outside fish and chip shops, offering slices of the delicacy to customers as they left the shop.

Before long, the public was clamouring for the Co-op to stock the treat, and soon Pickles was doing a roaring trade in what he called 'Pickles' Exotic Vegetable Condiment'. Like the relish itself, the title was a mouthful, and soon happy Bradfordians were referring to the savoury morsels simply as 'pickles'.

Within 10 years, a turnover of a few pounds had become a vast half-million pound business. A local advertising agency, Saatchi and Entwhistle, was engaged and they came up with a snappy slogan: 'Plump for Pickles' pickles, the pickles picky people pick.'

Jars were even found in wealthy London homes, introduced by servants who discovered that their aristocratic masters also loved the tasty tracklement. One cunning poster showed a cheeky urchin dressed in Eton clothes, saying: 'Me mam says that foie gras tastes like nowt wi'out Pickles' pickles!'

Within a few years Obadiah had built an 18-room mansion in an unusual Gothic-Palladian style, on the hills overlooking Bradford. 'It's the bits they leave behind on t'plate that paid for this!' he would tell awestruck visitors. When the old man finally died, still in harness, Zebedee took over and brought new ideas with new products. 'Pickles' Piccalilli, the piquant palate-pleaser' was an early success.

But his son, Eric, was a disappointment. He tried a new relish involving sun-dried tomatoes and Bacardi vinegar, but his heart was not in the business, which was taken over by Cadbury, then in turn by Kraft. Pickles' pickles – 'the original and only' are now made in Poland.

Meanwhile, Eric went into politics, becoming leader of Bradford's Conservative group. Unable to find a Tory seat in the city of his birth, he moved to what his grandfather would have called 'the soft south'. In 2006, the party's new leader, David Cameron, tried a pastrami on rye sandwich garnished with Pickles' pickles, and was so delighted by the fact that

Eric came from the family that he promoted him to the party's highest levels.

Not that Mr Pickles had much to say yesterday. He cuts a mighty figure at the dispatch box, being the shape of a gigantic gherkin, but he left nearly all his answers to his understrappers, most of whom would not know the difference between balsamic vinegar and non-brewed condiment.

16 June 2010

After 12 years, the Saville inquiry reported on Bloody Sunday, the day in 1972 in which 13 civilians were killed by British forces in Derry. David Cameron's speech on the day the report was published, including the frank admission that the army had got things dreadfully wrong, was regarded as one of his finest.

At 3.29pm the news had been leaked in Derry, and the cheers of the crowd burst from every TV set in the Commons as we dashed to hear Cameron's statement. He, by contrast, was received in a sombre, almost fearful silence. MPs might not have been surprised, but they were certainly stunned.

The prime minister could hardly have done better. For someone who was aged five at the time of Bloody Sunday, it was a poised and almost perfectly judged performance.

And all the more difficult for someone who has had to spend years paying tribute to the British army, to their courage and patriotism. When it comes to our lads in uniform, no politician wants to say anything that is not cut from a template of praise.

'I never want to say anything bad about our country,' he said. He never wanted to call our soldiers into question. They were, he believed, the finest in the world. Clearly an enormous 'but' was on its way.

'But,' he said, 'the conclusions of this report are absolutely clear. There is no doubt. There is nothing equivocal. There are no ambiguities. What happened on Bloody Sunday was both unjustified and unjustifiable. It was wrong.'

The Commons was, if anything, even quieter when he went through the most startling and shattering conclusions. No warning before the soldiers opened fire, which they did before anyone shot at them. Soldiers had lied to protect themselves. Some of the dead had been fleeing, or going to the aid of the wounded. Every sentence slashed through the silence.

'The report refers to one person who was shot while "crawling away from the soldiers". The father who was hit and injured while going to the aid of his wounded son.'

I doubt if the Commons has ever heard a statement so raw, etching with acid into the polished veneer of our nation's image of itself.

For someone of his generation, he said, Bloody Sunday was something learned rather than lived through. 'But what happened should never, ever have happened, and for that, on behalf of the government – and indeed our country – I am deeply sorry.'

He also set the day in context, reminding us of the scores of soldiers – for the most part as innocent as any civilian – shot dead because they were wearing a politically inconvenient uniform. The IRA would never be put on an even footing with democrats. 'But neither will we hide from the truth that confronts us today.'

As Lord Saville had said, Bloody Sunday came as a tremendous boon to the IRA, and made the continuing conflict far,

far worse. (Of the 3,500-odd people killed in the 40 years of the Troubles, around one-seventh died in the year following the massacre.)

Various Unionists, such as Ian Paisley Jr, watched from the gallery by his father, pointed out the suffering of many Protestants in Northern Ireland. But this was not their day.

22 September 2010

We went along to the first Liberal Democrat conference since their return to power, albeit as a minority party, for the first time in more than 60 years. As always they had their own pressing concerns.

Liberal Democrats discussed intimate same-sex relations, and for once it wasn't about Cameron and Clegg.

Evan Harris, the former MP, said he had been listed as the party's only 'out' gay member. 'And I'm not even gay!' he said.

This proved, once again, how eager the party was to demonstrate diversity.

The motion was to let same-sex couples have proper marriages, in church if they wished, instead of mere civil partnerships. Fred Dunsford, a wheelchair user, was against the idea because most voters wouldn't like it. Facing one member of an oppressed and ignored minority opposing the wishes of another oppressed and ignored minority, the conference didn't know which way to turn. So they compromised and gave him a light sprinkling of applause anyway.

Liz Williams talked about 'all my lesbian, gay, bisexual and transsexual friends' in all of whom she 'sees the same grace'. Blimey, I thought, she must have some terrific parties.

Sara Bedford was not gay, but was treated with the same reverence as if she were. She described her typically Lib Dem wedding anniversary, which she had spent at a Lib Dem meeting while her husband did the ironing at home. She recalled taking her daughter to a Gay Pride march and telling her that some people didn't approve of gay relationships.

'Mummy,' the little girl replied, 'surely love is a good thing? People should be allowed as many hugs and kisses as they want!' This heart-warming tale brought loud applause.

A former prison chaplain described how he had 'happily made friends of murderers, rapists and paedophiles, and you can't get more inclusive than that!' Well, you could always support the rights of paedophiles to marry underage children in church, I thought (but would not have dreamed of saying).

Ed Fordham of north London had been asked by a woman what his 'dear wife' thought of politics. 'I said, "My dear wife – he's over there." She replied, "In Hampstead, as long as it's not animals, we don't mind."'

Things were getting more surreal. Jenny Barnes announced: 'Liberal Democrats are different, and as a transsexual I welcome that. There is obviously a huge impact on a transsexual's partner when they realise that their partner is not of the gender they were assigned at birth.

'I have a friend who is fully transitioned, and wants to stay in her relationship, so it's very confusing for her and her wife.'

She went on to explain that she couldn't marry in a church because she wasn't recognised as a woman, and she couldn't marry a woman, because that would be a same-sex partnership. But help was at hand. 'Luckily I'm an atheist, so I'm not bothered.'

You can be sure nothing as interesting as all this will crop up at either the Labour or Conservative conferences. Brian Paddick, the former policeman who ran as the Lib Dem candidate for mayor of London, described his fully legal wedding to a 'gorgeous' Norwegian man in Oslo. He had been deeply moved, as we all were. 'We really feel, my husband and I – that's husband and husband – really equal.' The conference passed the motion by a huge majority, as if you needed to ask.

27 September 2010

In September, against most expectations, Ed Miliband was elected leader of the Labour party. It had been widely assumed that the mantle would fall on his brother David, who lost by a very narrow margin.

Ed Miliband faced his first rite of passage yesterday, being interviewed by Andrew Marr. He looked as nervous as a young man at his first job interview. You could imagine his mum brushing the dandruff from his shoulders and straightening his tie. His legs were apart, and his hands were clasped between them.

In short, he looked like a geek. He did have some good news for the middle classes, but they will probably beware of geeks bearing gifts.

Ed had a tough task ahead. He had to spend an hour talking about absolutely nothing and giving nothing away. Except how much he loved his brother. 'He has shown the most extraordinary generosity to me,' he said, several times. 'He is a fantastic person.'

Almost everything he said was in accordance with the law of the nonsensical reverse. For example, Ed said that he was 'passionate about Britain'. Had he said he was passionate about Bolivia, we might have paid attention. He felt we should have great respect for nurses. ('I despise nurses with every fibre of my being.') He thought strikes should always be used as a last resort. ('Get the lads out, and only then talk to management – that's my plan.')

He was, he assured us, his own man. ('I am a puppet, ready to be manipulated by whoever can grab my strings.') He represented the change that Labour needed. ('No real problems in our party. I plan to put my feet up and leave well alone.') Unity would be his watchword. ('Let's keep fighting each other – it's always fun!')

Their new leader might be embracing change, but the Labour conference continues as it always has for more than 100 years. The event is actually run by the Conference Arrangements Committee, a terrifying backroom body that resembles the old Soviet Politburo trying to rewrite the Talmud.

At the start of business, Margaret Wheeler, a handsome woman with a flat but mellifluous voice, recited the latest bureaucratic horrors that the CAC has devised.

She describes, in a tone that might be apt for thanking Mrs Prendergast for the loan of the tea urn, details that only someone with a feel for four-dimensional mathematics could understand. 'We have adopted the contemporary issues process to enable supporting statements to be treated as motions. These appear in CIC1 and will be composited this evening... your submission is not accepted as contemporary,' she told some poor bastard who had challenged an unimaginably obscure ruling.

Compositing is an ancient Labour tradition which has nothing to do with enriching garden soil. It means, roughly, combining several motions as one, usually neutered so that the leadership isn't put to any trouble. A man with so much hair above and below his face that you could scarcely make out his nose came to the podium and raised a point even more arcane than the earlier arcane points.

He got a crisp elucidation from Ms Wheeler. 'The constitutional amendment is laid before you as an appendix, closed after other rule amendments had been finalised, and the NEC is not subject to the three-year rule.' Touché!

I don't suppose more than 2 per cent of the people in the hall understood a single word. But they understood one thing – you don't mess with the CAC.

7 October 2010

The Tory conference platform was dominated by a large cut-out of the party's logo, which was meant to represent a tree. My colleague the cartoonist Steve Bell decided that it more closely resembled an elephant peeing. Confusingly, the tree was painted with the Union flag.

David Cameron used his speech to flesh out some of his vision of the Big Society. It is going to be even more hectic than we thought. Yesterday the prime minister told us we were going to have to start a great project in our neighbourhood, launch a business, demand a new school, patrol the streets against crime, and root out waste in government.

There won't be a spare moment in the day. At 6am, we'll

be up, tramping the streets, marching drunken revellers off home. By 8am we'll be working on a spanking new community project, possibly building a life-size model of Percy the Pissing Pachyderm for the park. By 9am we'll be founding a new business, possibly cold-calling people in India and asking if they have all their insurance needs. This will leave a few minutes to eradicate waste in local government, by Tazering a minority self-esteem co-ordinator, grade II. Then we will demand a new school. The prime minister wasn't clear how we might do that. Perhaps we'll stand outside Michael Gove's house bellowing 'We demand a new school!' until a patrol of local vigilantes bundles us into the back of a van and makes us paint old folk's homes for 180 hours.

This, we were told, was 'the Big Society – blasting through!' It demanded 'big citizens'. So amid all those foot patrols there will be huge people, blasting through. What happens if they meet? Won't there be a fight?

So life is going to be very hectic. And the same is true of all of us, apparently. 'The British people are not passengers – they are drivers.' Back-seat drivers for the most part. 'Look out, there's a giant micturating elephant straight ahead!'

18 January 2011

Much of the time Cameron speaks in grandiose sentences which mean less than appears at first. 'Teachers nurture the human capital that will create enterprise,' he said about this time, and I found myself thinking of some poor sod levering himself out of a staffroom armchair, saying, 'I suppose I'd better go and nurture the human capital that is Year 9.'

He also became celebrated for changing his mind. One of the earlier flip-flops came with the plan to privatise the nation's forests.

I've worked out what it's like – the government resembles the dodgems at a funfair. Ministers all sit in their own cars, driving in a random direction. They press the accelerator: sometimes the car moves forward, but often it goes back or nowhere at all. Swing the wheel to the left, and the car goes right. Or vice versa. Drivers crash into each other, and sparks fall from the roof. The difference is that the spectators are having fun while the drivers are close to despair.

Yesterday's fender-bender, or bumper-thumper, was the plan to sell off forests. Caroline Spelman, the environment secretary, whose bill it was to be, had to announce its demise in the Commons. She had already been royally shafted by David Cameron, who had killed it off in question time. Mr Cameron is a PR man, and he can spot a disaster looming. Privatising trees was the equivalent of trying to sell 'Mr Snotty' brand toothpaste, or calling a rock band the Kiddy-Fiddlers.

So it was a humiliation for the government, which makes it a normal day. Mrs Spelman had decided that her best defence was frankness. She took complete responsibility. She had boobed. Got it all wrong. And she admitted it, at enormous length.

It might have been slightly more convincing if she had spent a little less time proclaiming her own shining virtue. She averred, not once but twice, that she always told her own children that honesty was the best policy. I wondered what teatime might be like in the Spelman household.

'Mummy, I have done a bad thing.'

'I am so glad you want to tell me about it. Now, get it off your chest, darling, and let Mummy know what happened.'

'I promulgated a policy that would have raised consider-able sums, but which failed to take into account the strength of public feeling, Mummy.'

'Why, you little bastard! Take that!'

She told us about her own great integrity in the tone of voice you might use for saying that, if the weather were inclement, the fete would take place in the village hall. It made life slightly difficult for Mary Creagh, her Labour opposite number, who might have expected some credit for the debacle. She had to acknowledge Mrs Spelman's apology. But she had a swingeing attack all ready, and didn't want to waste it. Given that it was like taking candy from a fish, or shooting a baby in a barrel, it wasn't very good, partly because she had to cope with contin-uous barracking from Tory MPs trying to cover Mrs Spelman's embarrassment, partly because she ended by announcing, 'If they won't stand up for the countryside, we will!'

The notion that Labour was more friendly to people who live in the country delighted the Tories, who shouted 'More!' in a mocking sort of way.

Mrs Spelman continued to praise her own candour, relent-lessly. 'It is a good example of how humility is a valuable quality in a politician,' she mused.

'Even if I say so myself!' yelled Labour's Kevin Brennan, so puncturing the most truthful politician since George Washing-ton also chopped down a tree.

27 January 2011

One of the new intake best-loved by the opposition is the Honour-able Jacob Rees-Mogg, the son of Lord Rees-Mogg, famed as the least reliable prognosticator since the pre-war astrologist who called Hitler 'a man of peace'.

His son, by his accent, bearing, background and lack of self-awareness, is a gift for Labour since he is a perfect reminder of the old class war which nurtured and delighted so many of them. The night after this session, Rees-Mogg Jr appeared in a BBC documentary about class in Britain, and declared himself 'a man of the people'.

Prime minister's questions were about the economy. Later there stood up the Honourable Jacob Rees-Mogg. A great cheer rose from the Labour benches. They love him. Like Cameron, he went to Eton and Oxford. He was conceived in privilege, and nine months later born in privilege. No doubt he wore a three-piece romper suit in Harris Tweed, obtained by his parents from Toffs 'R' Us. Over his head there hovers a phantom top hat, and behind his back you can almost hear the tailcoat flapping. You sense the presence of Nanny in the public gallery, leaning over to make sure he has wiped his nose.

If the middle-class Andy Coulson exists to make the prime minister conscious of the people he needed to reach, then Rees-Mogg is there to remind him of the folk whence he came.

The Speaker silenced the Labour oiks. Rees-Mogg thanked him, in the manner in which he might thank his gamekeeper. 'Is not the lesson from the noble Baroness Thatcher that, once you have set an economic course, you should stick to it?' He sat down triumphantly while, no doubt, David Cameron inwardly groaned. Labour MPs cried, 'More, more!'

4 February 2011

Environment questions are rarely fascinating events, though they do throw up some jargon you will never hear on The Archers or read in Cider with Rosie.

They were discussing the EU's appalling Common Fisheries Policy. My mind drifted to Hemingway's novel, The Old Man and the Sea, and how it might have turned out if Hemingway had needed to take account of the new rules. All jargon is from the session.

'The old man's forehead crinkled and above him the sun flamed in the pewter sky like the eyes of a Parisian *putain*. *Madre de Dios*, he had had bad luck. His mind returned to his youth, when his skin was smooth and the women thought him beautiful, to the lost days before the CFP's broken regulations, based on a centralised, top-down system, had come into force under directive number 687 (B,i[d]). "Local and regional sea-based management," he muttered with his sour breath, before spitting on the stones that lay beneath his feet.

'"Get in the boat!" he said to the boy. "Today we will catch us a marlin, a marlin great as any whale, with skin like a baby's skin, and this we shall sell in the market for many, many pesos."

'"But old man," said the boy, "the market is closed. The government now tells us that it is 'supermarkets who are key in driving forward the fisheries agenda'."

'The old man spat again. "Boy, hear me. None of this will change until the coalition wins the support of the radical end of the EU reform spectrum!"'

(This goes on, in Hemingway's bloated prose, till the old man finally hooks his marlin and spends two days pulling it in.)

'"Fish, you were a fine and noble opponent," said the old man. "And now I shall return you to your ancestors and to your offspring."

'"You cannot do that," cried the boy, "for you will contravene ministerial policy on driving down discard levels!"

'"Imbecile child! I shall do as I please!" And the old man spat once more.

'"But, old man, following the latest catch quota trials, investment incentives and selective netting, we now have statutory on-ship CCTV, which will observe all that you do with an eye as all-seeing as the all-seeing eye of God himself!"

'"Bugger," said the old man.'

2 March 2011

As deputy prime minister, Nick Clegg had his own question time. Following the great decline in his popularity, these events could be embarrassing as Labour spotted a victim.

Question time with Nick Clegg was unremittingly awful, grim, nerve-shreddingly ghastly. You yearned for him to wake up, sweat soaking his pillow, realising that it had all been a terrible dream, a mother's soothing hand on his brow.

I wondered if the bullies felt some remorse. Did they ask themselves what it must be like for an innocent, vulnerable man to face such torment? Was there the teeniest twinge of conscience that they had made life hellish for someone so unable to cope with their abuse?

At the same time, do we not suspect that the victim covertly accepts, even welcomes, his fate? On the surface, Mr Clegg seemed quite unprepared for what was coming his way, like someone walking down a railway track who is astonished to hear the 10.40 from Euston approach.

It started fairly quietly. Roberta Blackman-Woods wanted to know about the plan for MPs to be recalled by their voters if they had broken the rules, and if so, how many of them would be Liberal Democrats. The rest of her words were lost in a delighted roar. Mr Clegg said that the bill would deal only with serious wrongdoing. 'Exactly!' yelled a dozen or more Labour MPs.

Chris Bryant joined in the monstering. Who decided who had broken the rules? What about a party that promised 3,000 more police officers, then cut the number by 10,000? Mr Clegg responded with nervous hand signals, the left making a cowpat, the right hand a spider dancing on a hot plate. At one point he called for MPs who could 'speak out, and, er, er, you know, articulate…' Send for Lionel Logue!

A Conservative, Andrea Leadsom, tried to help him. Big mistake. What was he doing to restore the public's faith in politics and in MPs? This time the Labour roar was mixed with shrieking and cackling, as if we were watching a convention of drunken witches. Mob hysteria was taking hold. The Clegg reply, 'Our programme is directed to restore public faith in MPs,' only raised the noise level.

Harriet Harman cruelly pointed out that the word 'Clegged' now meant 'completely betrayed'. And John Mann asked brutally, 'What is the point of Nick Clegg?'

There are many answers to that. He could have said something like, 'The point is fighting for a country that pays its debts, but is fair, just and open. I'd like to know what the point of the honourable member is.' Almost anything would have sufficed, except for the answer he got, which was: 'Err.'

Gleeful Labour MPs must have been tightening their body parts to prevent nasty accidents on the benches. But Mr Clegg continued. He chuntered about how a chief executive is still a chief executive, even when he's abroad, a football-manager is still in charge of his team even at an away game. I wanted to lean over and shout, 'Stop digging!'

A Labour voice shouted, 'Only two minutes left!' and bang on the hour, the Speaker ended the misery.

16 March 2011

William Hague, the foreign secretary, seemed puzzled, discombobu-lated. It had been revealed that he had shared a hotel room with an aide, and he felt obliged to explain why he and his wife Ffion had not had children. She had had, he said, several miscarriages. The press were merciless, as usual. I felt obliged to call in the services of our most famous detective.

To Foreign Office questions, to answer the conundrum asked by all the British people, or at least the media: has William Hague lost his mojo? This was not a question ever asked of Lord Palmerston.

I wondered how Sherlock Holmes would have tackled the problem.

'Mrs Hudson knocked on our door. "Mr Holmes, there is a most distinguished gentleman to see you!"

'Moments later, there walked into our rooms one of the best-known men in all of England, a man whose face would have been instantly recognised by an earl or a chimney sweep.

David Cameron

It was none other than Sir Peter Tapsell, one of the most celebrated politicians of our age.

'"I perceive," said Holmes, "that you have walked here from parliament on a matter of the highest importance."

'"You astound me," said our visitor. "I had heard of your powers, Mr Holmes, but…"

'"A simple matter. It is raining heavily, and you are soaked to the skin. Clearly you walked since if even a cabbie had known you were consulting me, the news would cause the greatest alarm and agitation in the chancelleries of Europe. Now, let us hear of your difficulty."

'Sir Peter groaned. "I will be blunt," he said. "It is the foreign secretary. He has lost his mojo. His mojo! I need hardly tell you, Mr Holmes, that if the news were to leak out it would bring comfort to our enemies and the most terrible anxiety to our allies. The mojo must be returned, and forthwith! I implore you to assist us in this most urgent enterprise!"

'"Pray tell me under what circumstances it was lost."

'"It appears to have gone missing last year, after he shared quarters with another man."

'"And this is now a crime?" asked Holmes, airily waving at our shared bachelor quarters.

'"Enough of one," said the unhappy legislator, "but the mojo was only discovered to be missing when the matter of Libya came to the forefront of our concerns. A number of horrifying misjudgments occurred. And when we searched for the mojo, it was missing!" He buried his head in his hands.

'"A simple matter, but not devoid of interest," said Holmes after our visitor had left. "Clearly the mojo was lost when the foreign secretary was in the midst of one of his notorious 17-pint drinking sessions.

295

'"I suspect it will be easily traced in the members' smoking room, possibly in the bottom of a beer crate, where it may have been carelessly thrown by the inebriated minister."

'And so it proved to be. The mojo was swiftly restored, and the greatest in the land were able once more to sleep soundly in their beds.

'A few days later, on 15 March 2011, Holmes and I took our places in the Commons gallery. Our client, Sir Peter, rose. "I have never known a foreign secretary surrounded simultaneously by so many difficult problems. I want to say how much I admire the cool efficiency with which he is dealing with them."

'"A most satisfactory ending," said Holmes. "And now I suggest we return and set about some of Mrs Hudson's excellent devilled kidneys!"'

24 May 2011

For a short while, the media became obsessed with 'super-injunctions', court orders which not only prevent someone from being named, but make it illegal even to convey the fact that the injunction itself has been granted. One of these had been obtained by Ryan Giggs, the footballer, even though his name was so well known that it was chanted from the terraces.

An MP yesterday named Ryan Giggs as the prominent footballer who had obtained an injunction to prevent the media from reporting his affair with a former Big Brother contestant.

The MP cannot be identified, by me at least, since he is, prima facie, guilty of a breach of parliamentary convention, if not the law. (Also he is so hungry for publicity that he would willingly have gone to court to demand that the media did report his affairs.)

So my ruling is that it would not be in the public interest, or his family's interest, for me to name him.

The MP stood up during a brief session devoted to injunctions and privacy law. The attorney general, Dominic Grieve, had already announced that there would be a committee of both houses devoted to the matter. This is the government's way of saying, 'Shut up, will you, while we try to work something out.' John Prescott – now M'lord Prescott – sat in the public gallery, alternately laughing and scowling.

John Whittingdale, who chairs the culture committee, said you would need to be living in an igloo not to know the name of the footballer. There was a danger of making the law an ass. (A bit late to worry about that, I thought.)

Mr Grieve made it clear that nothing would affect parliamentary privilege. But he didn't promise that the media could necessarily report what was being said in parliament. This would truly be a politician's worst nightmare – they could beaver away to expose wrongdoing but nobody could know about their zealous work. Unless they used Twitter.

Then came the moment. I was slightly surprised that the Speaker called the MP, who I can reveal sits for a Midlands constituency and isn't exactly the hunkiest he-man in the House, not that that narrows the field much, frankly. The MP has form, and has tried to break injunctions before. But if he had not been called, he would have barged in on a point of order later, so perhaps Mr Bercow had no choice.

The MP rose to say that about 75,000 people had named Ryan Giggs on Twitter. 'It is obviously impractical to imprison them all, and with reports that Giles Coren faces imprisonment…'

The Speaker leapt up. The thought of Giles Coren's Prison Feasts, a 13-part series on BBC 1, was too much. He slapped the MP down, saying that these occasions were for discussing principles, 'not seeking to flout, for whatever purpose'. We were in a state of shock. Mr Bercow had used a transitive verb without an object. Can parliament sink any lower?

We were left to ponder the meaning of these events. Rich footballer has an affair: two days' wonder in the tabloids. Rich footballer tries to hush up affair: this one will run for months if not years.

The MP in question was John Hemming, a Liberal Democrat.

26 September 2011

The Labour party continued with the long and painful process of resurrection.

It must be baffling to be a Labour supporter these days. Looking at the line-up on the platform they may feel like residents of the old Soviet Union seeing absolutely no one they recognised take the salute at the May Day parade.

Murphy, Flint, McKechin, Creagh, Lewis, Khan – these are the great new stars in Labour's Milky Way. Admittedly, the massed workers and peasants might recognise Balls and Cooper, and a few obsessives might even be able to name the present leader.

(At one point Ed Miliband tried to start a standing ovation for the new general secretary. Some of the conference followed his example, but very slowly, and in the grumpy manner of a schoolboy told to get up and tidy his room. This is known as 'amsirac', which is 'charisma' spelled backwards, almost.)

But one thing that always remains the same is the Conference Arrangements Committee. Since the days of Keir Hardie, the CAC has been the real power during this week of the year. Its words are law, its diktats dreaded. This year it had decided that there would be only a two-hour debate on a document called Refounding Labour to Win. There would then be one vote on a take-it-or-leave-it basis.

The new chair of the CAC is a misleadingly diffident fellow called Harry Donaldson. He told us about the arcane and archaic relationship between contemporary motions, the priorities ballot and the compositing meetings, which have everything to do with making the conference debate topics which won't cause embarrassment to the chaps in fur hats watching the missiles trundle past.

Mr Donaldson was introduced by the conference chairwoman, Norma Stephenson, a spunky old duck of the kind I recognise from my northern childhood. I'd love to eavesdrop on a conversation in the snug between her and Gillian Duffy of Rochdale. Or a cage fight. At one point, when she thanked her union, Unison, for their support, she teared up and wiped her nose with her right hand. On the giant screen it was a commanding image, and one which no Soviet leader would have allowed. (He'd have used his fur hat.)

Anyhow, a series of delegates went up on stage to complain about the short debate and the lack of votes. They got, if not short shrift, then sawn-off shrift. One elderly fellow, Ted Masters, perhaps outstayed his welcome slightly. When he said, 'There's a famous Frank Sinatra song...' someone turned his microphone off, then back on, so he resumed '... this is no way to run a democratic party,' and you could see the puzzled audience thinking, 'oh yes, I remember it, "This is no way to run a democratic party, doo-be-do-be-do".'

The time came for a vote on whether there would be more votes. Ms Stephenson called for a show of hands. Quite a lot of people raised their arms in favour of the CAC decision. Then a similar number raised their arms against it. 'That is carried,' declared Ms Stephenson. There was a rustling in the ranks. 'Card vote!' said one brave soul, who may have been taken away and shot, his body buried underneath the conference centre even before you read this.

6 October 2011

David Cameron had to cope with the fact that the economy was stubbornly failing to improve.

It was the Always Look on the Bright Side of Life speech. The economy may be crucified, choking to death in the burning heat, but David Cameron has a message for us: 'When you're chewing on life's gristle, don't grumble, give a whistle!' (Not the words he used, but what he meant.) We know that all politicians believe you have to be an optimist to win votes, but this was crazy. The worse things were, the more hopeful we should be. He for one was fed up with 'can't-do sogginess'. It was time for us all to stop sitting down and to start standing up.

As well as standing up, we have to be marching forward. We face a time of challenge, but that only makes it a time of opportunity! We should dry ourselves off, get on our feet and stride forward. (Have you ever tried striding backwards? It's impossible. You'll be arse over tit in moments.)

He marched forward on to the lectern with the possessive insouciance of a hoodie swaggering on to his sink estate. He's stopped doing the speech without notes, and had it up on two tele-prompters, one left and one right, so it looked as if he was umpiring a match at Wimbledon. (I can't have been the only member of the audience tempted to walk up – sorry, stride – and yell: 'You cannot be serious!')

It was rough luck that the latest figures showed the economy was in an even worse state than we thought. How did he deal with it? He completely ignored it. ('If life seems jolly rotten, there's something you've forgotten.')

Behind him, the Tory logo, instead of being covered in the union flag, was decorated with the blue skies of our future, dotted with only light, fluffy clouds. It was Percy, the Panglossian Pissing Pachyderm! 'Let's reject the pessimism. Let's bring on the can-do optimism!' What was his leadership all about? 'It's about unleashing your leadership!' We'll all be leaders, leaving the logistical problem of who'll be left to be a follower.

Like so many politicians, he is morphing into Tony Blair. There is the same smooth, deliberately hazy confusion between ambition and achievement, between what he would like to do and what he has actually done. The result is a feelgood aura, a mood as dreamy and undemanding as a toilet paper commercial on television.

There were people who thought that the government's plan for the economy was wrong. They were wrong. 'Our plan is right. Our plan will work,' even if you couldn't see it working. It was like the foundations of a house, invisible but essential. This was out of Economics for Dummies. Why don't they take these images further? 'Our economic plan is like a Teasmade. While you sleep you can't see it working, but when you wake up there's a lovely cup of tea.'

Mind you, he did add the odd barb. Ministers had been asked to read out books for blind people. Ken Clarke should read Crime and Punishment, twice. And for Boris Johnson, who broke the omerta rule on Tuesday night and said he wants to be prime minister: 'The Joy of… [long pause] …Cycling!' A little warning there, I thought.

Then the little crazed bits. Early one morning, he'd been reading an EU directive about whether people with diabetes should be allowed to drive. 'What's that got to do with the single market?' So we were away with a traffic report: 'There are reports of long holdups on the M40 due to diabetic drivers…'

And a final exhortation to 'show the world some fight! Let's pull together, work together!' And 'see an optimistic future!' Or as Eric Idle put it: 'When you're feeling in the dumps, don't be silly chumps! And always look…'

20 October 2011

October saw the resignation of the defence secretary Liam Fox, after it became clear that he had breached the ministerial code. In fact you could say that he seemed to be running the defence department as a subsidiary of a company owned by him and his close friend Adam Werritty.

Some resignation speeches change history: Geoffrey Howe with his broken cricket bats, for example. Some create an ineradicable image in the public mind, such as Norman

Lamont's revenge on John Major's government: 'They are in office but not in power.' Some are little better than self-justifying whinges: Ron Davies after his ill-advised walk on Clapham Common.

And then there is Liam Fox, who spoke to the Commons on Wednesday. What a farrago of self-regarding, self-congratulatory self-exculpation it was! He even contrived to tiptoe round the notion that he had done anything wrong. 'The ministerial code has been found to be breached,' he said, as if it were like a hurricane battering a levee, a force of nature for which nobody is to blame.

And why had he come under attack? Because for more than a year, he had bent the rules, constantly and persistently, in the face of warnings from his most senior civil servants? Hardly. His fall was, in part, the result of machinations by unnamed enemies. It was the result of 'personal vindictiveness and even hatred. That should worry all of us.'

Time and again he implied he was the victim. But all had not been lost. There had been a tidal wave of support and encouragement from everyone: fellow MPs and cabinet members, constituents, family and friends, and most of all from his wife, who had offered 'grace, dignity and unstinting support'.

You would imagine that he had, through no fault of his own, contracted a life-threatening illness, his fear and pain swept aside by the kindness of everyone around him. 'I may have done wrong, or possibly not,' he was saying. 'That doesn't matter because everybody loves me.'

He rose to cheers from Tory backbenchers. They accept a myth that he was one of the finest of all defence secretaries. He certainly gave us an aircraft carrier without aircraft, and arranged for armed forces members to be sacked while at war.

He began with what sounded like faux modesty. He had been in Libya where he met a man who showed him photos of his dead children. 'A few days later I resigned. One was an unbearable human tragedy, the other a deep personal disappointment.' So his own peccadillo was as nothing within the greater realm of human unhappiness.

'I accept that it was a mistake to allow distinctions to be blurred between my professional responsibilities and my personal loyalty to a friend.' But that too didn't matter, because he had been cleared of the serious charges against him. The cabinet secretary's report cleared him of receiving money or endangering classified material. That had been implied. It was 'deeply hurtful'. But he accepted it was not only substance that mattered but perception, which is why he resigned. In other words, I didn't do wrong, but people may have got hold of the idea – heaven knows how – that I did.

Every bit of information, no matter how irrelevant or immaterial, is sensationalised, where opinions and even accusations are treated as fact.

3 November 2011

The state of the economy led to increasingly testy, even bad-tempered, scenes in the Commons as the testosterone-charged Ed Balls clashed with the more languid public school types, George Osborne and David Cameron.

The world economy may be about to collapse into the sea, so naturally the Commons discussed the urgent question of Ed Balls' hand movements. These are more or less continuous, along with his barracking, which is conducted at too low a level for those of us in the galleries to hear, but is a constant distraction for Tory ministers. It's what cricketers call sledging, as in the fielder shouting to a plump batsman: 'Why are you so fat?', to which the reply is: 'Because every time I [short word meaning 'make love to'] your wife, she gives me a biscuit.'

I doubt if Mr Balls says anything on those lines. What seems to rile the Tories most are his gestures. He never stops. It's like watching one of the signers at a conference, although instead of communicating sign language, he is signalling 'Balls'. His current favourite involves holding one hand level, palm down, waved gently from side to side. This is meant to imply that the economy is flatlining. David Cameron barked at Balls: 'You can go on making your rather questionable salutes...'

The implication was clear: it was a Nazi salute. This seems a little unfair. It looks more like a gesture from a covert German liberal who wanted to get it half right, so placating any passing stormtroopers while signalling to his friends that he didn't really mean it.

The session was maniacal. The prime minister did make a reference to the perilous state we're in, saying: 'There is a global storm in the world economy, and it is in our interest to help others to confront that storm.' And keep our heads held high, while not being afraid of the dark, and waiting for the golden sky and the sweet silver song of the lark, as I have helpfully added for him. Ed Miliband – to encapsulate his reply – said the dreams of the British people had been tossed and blown, and there was precious little hope in anyone's heart.

As tempers rose, the Speaker intervened. 'Some people are so excited, they are going to burst, which would be a bit of a problem,' he reflected. Suddenly we were back with Monty Python's Mr Creosote, the grotesquely fat diner who is tempted by maitre d' John Cleese to finish with 'jus' one little wafer-thin mint'. This causes him to explode, scattering blood and intestines all over the restaurant.

What a magical day that will be in the Commons! Especially if it's Eric Pickles.

24 November 2011

Balls tried to show off a more tender side to his nature when he gave an interview to a political magazine in which he said that one of his favourite programmes was The Antique's Roadshow, which sometimes made him cry.

'Someone comes in with some family heirloom … and the expert says: "Do you know how much this is worth? It's valued at X thousand pounds." And they say, "It means much more to me than money." Incredibly emotional!'

On Wednesday, the prime minister was taunting Ed Miliband about the way he wants the government to tax bankers' bonuses and use the money to create jobs for young people. He listed everything that the Labour leader has wanted the bonus tax to be spent on: nine different items and counting.

'This is the bank tax that likes to say "yes"!' he exclaimed. 'No wonder the shadow chancellor has stopped saluting and started crying.'

This was a reference to Mr Balls's 'flatlining economy' gesture, which involves his holding his hand horizontally and which Cameron affects to believe is a Nazi-style salute.

But I sympathise with the lachrymose Mr Balls. Some things carry emotional freight and are immensely hard to let go.

'Now what have we got here?' 'It's a very old Labour party. It's been cherished in my family for generations.' 'Marvellous! Look at the craftsmanship on that constitution. You don't see that kind of work any more. And some of those MPs are gorgeously detailed. Just have a close look – they might almost be human! I don't quite recognise the leader here, but I'm sure he was very well known in his day. Now I have to say it is a bit worse for wear. Perhaps it's not been looked after as carefully as it might?' 'Well, I'm afraid it has been knocked about a bit over the years.' 'Yurrrs, it does look pretty rough. And there's not much demand now for these old-style political parties. So, if you can get a fiver and a few Tesco discount coupons you'll be doing very well.' (Balls breaks down in great, racking sobs.)

9 February 2012

Prime minister's questions sometimes puts one in a philosophical mood.

Some pages from Dr Rhetoric's casebook:

People often ask me: 'Do politicians lie?' My answer is no, in the same way ladies do not sweat. Instead they perspire.

So no politician ever lies. But he is sometimes guilty of a falsehood. We rhetoricians divide these into several recognised categories.

For example, there is the 'Falsehood Optimistic'. This is something the politician believes to be true at the time that he says it. For instance, George Osborne in 2010 said the economy would grow steadily throughout 2011. He hoped this was true. He probably thought it was true at the time. By sheer misfortune it turned out to be completely untrue.

Then there is the 'Falsehood Unintended'. A good example of this comes in the 2010 Tory manifesto when the party promised no 'top-down reorganisation' of the health service. They just changed their minds. If you said, 'I'll go to Tesco' and instead you went to Asda, would you have lied? No.

The most common form is the 'Falsehood Evasive'. Take prime minister's question time on Wednesday. Ed Miliband pointed out, again, that every health service professional was opposed to the NHS reforms – including the very GPs who are supposed to benefit most from the changes.

The prime minister replied: 'Ninety-five per cent of the country is covered by GPs who are not actually supporting our reforms, but are implementing our reforms!' So why does the Royal College of General Practitioners say that the changes would 'cause irreparable damage to patient care'? All the prime minister was saying in effect was, 'doctors are doing what they are told and not breaking the law'.

Labour was especially keen to exploit this – ahem – somewhat misleading suggestion, since a Number 10 source was recently quoted in another newspaper (The Times) as saying that Andrew Lansley, the health secretary, should be 'taken outside and shot', for incompetence.

The prime minister riposted with the 'Falsehood Improbable', and said Lansley was more likely to hold on to his job than Miliband was. The two leaders then exchanged various 'Falsehoods Statistical', in which carefully selected numbers are used to imply whatever nonsense the speaker wishes to convey.

Most unusually there is the 'Falsehood Blatant'. At the end of questions Mr Peter Bone (who reminds me of the TS Eliot couplet, 'Webster was much possessed by death / And saw the skull beneath the skin') raised the question of Sarah Teather, a Lib Dem MP who is an education minister.

She has refused to vote for and spoken against the government's welfare reform bill. 'Why', the sub-cutaneous skull inquired, 'is she still a government minister?'

Mr Cameron replied: 'The honourable lady is a government minister and supports government policy, as all ministers do.'

This is plainly not the case. Thus it is what we scholars called the 'Pants On Fire Falsehood'.

2 March 2012

Environment question time is often the most depressing session of the month. Our once green and pleasant land is covered with a horrid mixture of disease and bureaucracy, to say nothing of useless wind farms. As I listened, I imagined how it might appear on the TV show Escape to the Country. All references are to Thursday's grim proceedings.

'Terri and Jason are desperate to get away from life in the busy city! They want to wake up to birdsong instead of sirens, and gaze out at meadows not building sites. And we think we've found the perfect property! It's a four-bedroom thatched cottage, covered in roses, with a lovely secluded garden, fully modernised inside. The price? A very affordable £325,000. Well, Terri, waddya think?' 'I think I'd like it a lot better if the fields weren't covered in stillborn lambs, with stunted legs twisted under their tiny, woolly bodies.' 'Sure you would, Terri, but that's the Schmallenberg virus for you! It's spread from the continent, and it's heading west across England, leaving a trail of dead sheep. But the good news is, it's not a notifiable disease yet. Jason, what say you?' 'I have to admit I was wondering about those big men in black suits with earpieces, standing at the farm gate.' 'Yup, they're the bouncers, enforcing the electronic identification scheme for sheep, recently negotiated with the European commission! Waste of time if you ask me, as this new virus means that very few sheep are going to reach drinking age anyway.' 'Why, look, there's a sheep dog! Like Lassie! Isn't he lovely? Why is he staggering round like that?' 'There you are, Terri, he's a victim of compulsory microchipping for the central register of non-prohibited dogs. I'll bet he'd rather be rounding up sheep, but he can't, because they're all dead!' 'But there are so many dead animals here. It's, it's, just so awful!' 'Oh, you'll get used to it. Most of the dead badgers culled in the new anti-bovine-TB programme will be hauled away to the incinerator. But it's a bit like empty burger boxes – there's always a few get left behind!

'And those dead hares – well, they were chewed up by grey-hounds, after the coalition government got round to repealing the Hunting with Dogs Act. Still, seen one hare, you've seen the lot, eh, Jason?' 'We thought we'd like to go for a walk in the woods there, but they seem to be surrounded by a high wire fence.' 'Ah, you see, when the government backed down on sales of public forest land, as the minister said, they "never did involve total disposal of… the forestry portfolio". So the copse is now owned by MagnaCo Inc, and I'm afraid you can't go in. Not without risking electrocution!' 'Oh dear. Perhaps at least we could visit a lovely country church?' ''Fraid not, the bats

sites, beer cost a shilling a pint, few people had television and needed to draw the curtains to watch it; when every film ended with the national anthem and she was even made to watch the cup final.

So we were in Flummeryworld, that theme park where the British are so happy and at ease. Attending such an event is like being wrapped in velvet and tucked into a presentation box. Westminster Hall is the oldest public building in Britain, and probably Europe. It was packed. I spotted several left-wing Labour MPs, for even in parliament if you scratch a republican you will often find a quivering royalist.

Trumpeters of the Household Cavalry were lined up under the great stained-glass window to the south of the hall, like the world's poshest window cleaners. The band of the Scots Guards played Fantasia on Greensleeves.

Various processions arrived, swirling about, including doorkeepers, serjeants at arms (actual and deputy), the clerk of the crown in chancery (Sir Suma Chakrabarti KCB), train-bearers, chaplains, the gentleman usher of the black rod, plus the lord speaker, an ancient title that goes back all of six years. In Flummeryworld there must be constant renewal, like the rides at Disneyland.

Beefeaters, or 'the Queen's body guard of the yeomen of the guard' – for the most part elderly grizzled men – arrived in their Tudor costumes, with their pikes. It was like being inside a Ladybird book on the glorious pageant of our island history.

Then we heard the traditional sound of walkie-talkies squawking outside the door, as anxious officials awaited the presence. The royal couple walked in a few feet from the media seats. We could have shouted 'break a leg, your majesty!' but happily no one did.

Next the speeches. The lord speaker from the House of Lords – in Flummeryworld, the peers are still the more important House – used the language unrolled for such occasions. Lady D'Souza praised her 'stewardship'. She was grateful because parliament had been 'granted the privilege' of being 'the first of Your people formally to honour Your jubilee'. In the text of her speech, even the royal pronoun had a capital letter, and somehow the baroness managed to pronounce it.

She mentioned the new stained-glass window, which was a present paid for by MPs and lords (will any of them try to get their contribution on expenses?). 'Your Coat of Arms and Royal Cypher will bathe the Hall in colour.'

She ended with a flourish, which might have been trumpeted rather than merely spoken. 'Your Majesty, the lords spiritual and temporal in parliament assembled give thanks for this, your diamond jubilee. We look forward to the years to come and we pray that you and your realms may enjoy the peace, plenty and prosperity that have so distinguished your reign!'

John Bercow, the Commons speaker, was slightly lighter (the Queen had been on the throne for almost 11 years before he was born). But he recalled rationing when it meant more than just waiting for the latest iPad. He praised the way she had helped hold the nation together when it 'could have been torn asunder' – asunder being one of those flummery words never used in real life.

Then he said, slightly alarmingly, that she was a 'kaleidoscope Queen'. What did this mean? That if you picked her up and shook her, she'd look different? It turned out to be something to do with change and variety.

He slipped into a cascade of the letter S. The jubilee would be full of moments 'striking for the sincerity expressed as much for the scenery encountered. Sixty years of stability, 60 years of security, 60 years of sacrifice, 60 years of service.' The applause was long and, I think, genuine.

Then it was her (sorry, Her) turn to reply, in that voice as familiar to us as our own childhood. She was 'reassured' that she was only the second British monarch even to have had a diamond jubilee. 'I have had the pleasurable duty of treating with 12 prime ministers' and there was laughter, as there always is at royal humour – though perhaps tinged with relief that she didn't add: 'Mind you, there wasn't much pleasurable about treating with Ted Heath. Or Gordon Brown.'

Over such a period, she thought, 'one can observe that venerable old age can be a guide but not a prerequisite for success in public office' – another slight ripple of amusement. And there was praise for Prince Philip, 'who is well-known for declining compliments of any kind'.

Then, after barely 20 minutes, it was over. The royal party and the costumed characters from Flummeryworld went off together for drinks and nibbles, and the rest of us emerged blinking into the real, workaday world, which just happened to be washed in bright sunlight.

1 May 2012

The next great scandal involved Jeremy Hunt, the culture secretary, who appeared to have done all he could to facilitate the Murdoch family's attempt to take full control of the satellite broadcaster, BSkyB. One of his aides had even sent News International the content of a statement Hunt was not due to make to the Commons for another two days. David Cameron's bad temper was let out of its box once again.

The prime minister went green with rage after being called from election trip to face questions he thought he'd already answered

The prime minister was angry. Very angry. Incredible Hulk angry. He'd been dragged back from an election trip by the Speaker, who is loathed by most Tories anyway, to answer questions which he thought had been answered last week. He arrived in serious mouth-frothing mode.

You can always tell when he's getting ratty. The answers descend to personal abuse, and the bald patch grows. On Monday afternoon it had shifted down towards the bottom of his scalp. And a new element appeared: he goes red. Not just pillar-box red, or even silk-clad film star on the red carpet red, but a deep, lustrous Nicholas Soames crimson.

He started by shouting and yelling, and worked himself up from there. The line was: Leveson would decide. This was a side issue to make people forget the real story, which was, as usual, the state in which Labour had left the country.

Ed Miliband was, again, pretty good, and for once knew when to shut up. If Jeremy Hunt was using the News of the World defence – one rogue political adviser – then he should be fired for being clueless. But the special adviser had to go to protect the culture secretary. And the culture secretary had to stay to protect the prime minister.

It was at this point that the Cameron face began to change colour, like a chameleon hiding on House of Lords wallpaper. Marlon Brando as the Godfather might have murmured 'he has displeased me. Take care of it', and minions would know what he meant. But the prime minister takes the opposite approach. 'Weak and wrong!' he yelled at Miliband. Secret Labour meetings with Murdoch! Pyjama parties! 'Get your facts right! Bad judgment, rotten politics, plain wrong!'

There comes a point when surfing on sheer rage is enough to carry a man, more effective than logic, judgment or facts could ever be. Margaret Hodge, the public accounts chairwoman, pointed out that Jeremy Hunt's permanent secretary had refused 10 times to confirm that he had authorised the rogue special adviser, Adam Smith.

The din, already massive, continued to grow. Everyone was on edge. The Speaker accused MPs of 'baying noiselessly' before correcting himself. David Cameron sneered that Hodge liked to let her committee 'drift into these areas', a pettish remark greeted with a great, camp 'Whoo!' from Labour.

Chris Bryant asked how the Murdochs knew government policy, word for word, two days before parliament and the world were told. Cameron didn't try to answer; he merely abused him. Dennis Skinner said Jeremy Hunt was keeping his job when thousands around the country were losing theirs. Why? To take a bullet for the PM.

The PM, now floating on a magic carpet of his own fury, told Skinner he had a right to take his pension, and advised him to do exactly that. There has been some Twitter activity about this insult to a harmless old gent. But Skinner has been dishing it out for 42 years now, and is quite capable of taking it back. He has his fans, but he is not yet a national treasure.

17 May 2012

'Calm down, calm down!' said Ed Balls to David Cameron as he was banging on about police budgets at prime minister's questions. Labour has decided it has found Cameron's weak spot – his temper. I assume they hope to goad him into losing it again. With any luck, they might get a real spittle-filled, face-purpling outburst, which would get a million hits on YouTube.

'I am extremely calm,' the PM replied, but he said it like Herbert Lom as Inspector Clouseau's boss. You may recall the scene in which, very calmly, he slices off his finger with a cigar-cutter.

Ed Miliband spotted the incipient rage. 'I know you are going to have extensive training before you go before Leveson. I have a suggestion – it should include anger management.'

There is nothing more infuriating than being told you are in a temper when you are not actually in a temper. Cameron made a tremendous effort to rein himself in. 'Leave him, he's not worth it,' he must have told himself, metaphorically grabbing himself by the lapels and pushing himself back on to his stool.

And the session had started so amicably. Miliband welcomed the fall in unemployment. Then he asked what discussions the prime minister had had with the new French president about growth.

This was a trap, since Cameron treated Monsieur Hollande with a complete ignoral when he visited London, as Miliband reminded him.

'But,' Miliband continued, 'I am sure that a text message and "LOL" will go down very well.'

The reference to Cameron's cosy text messages to Rebekah Brooks was also a trap. LOL can mean so many things. 'Leave it Out, Loser' perhaps. Or 'Loss Of Liberty'. We shall see.

The PM was prepared. 'Perhaps I have been overusing my mobile phone. But at least I know how to use it, rather than just throw it at the people who work for me! You can still see the dents!'

Did he mean that Gordon Brown had scarred his Myrmidon Miliband for life? He did not explain.

The Labour leader got on to the police, who were 'absolutely furious' about Cameron's broken promise to protect the front line. The prime minister's reply was: 'Oh dear, he is having a bad day.'

Nobody knew what that meant. But he finished with his usual pub car park abuse: 'I often wonder whether your problem is that you are weak, or that you are left-wing – your problem is that you are both.'

But the high point of the session came when Sir Peter Tapsell arose. We could almost hear the flapping of wings as the Recording Angel himself arrived to take down Sir Peter's every word, written in flame on tablets of gold. Did Chancellor Merkel regret not having taken our prime minister's advice last October about 'the big bazooka'?

That sounded more like Silvio Berlusconi than David Cameron, who crisply – even calmly – said that the euro might be close to collapse. When history is on the march, Sir Peter is always in the vanguard.

24 May 2012

Once again the prime minister lost it. He called Ed Balls a 'muttering idiot' and, as his face went brick red again, was obliged to withdraw the word.

It must be rough on the Speaker. He's like a rugby referee trying to police a game where thumping and grabbing are not only part of the fun, but the main reason spectators go. How do you decide that the thumping and grabbing – or in this case the insults – have stepped over some imaginary line? In rugby that line is drawn somewhere south of eye-gouging; in parliament it's not so easy.

Admittedly the PM had been driven to the edge of his reason by the shadow chancellor. It's just that the edge of his reason seems to creep closer every week. Balls had been winding him up for the entire session, saying over and over again – 'tell us about the recession, tell us about plan B, have another glass of wine!'

This is a reference to a recent book that says Cameron likes to have four glasses of wine with his Sunday lunch. In the new, puritan booze dispensation, this is thought to be rather a lot, though I don't imagine a minimum price would make much difference to Chateau Margaux or whatever he drinks with the roast beef and yorkshire. He also likes to 'chillax' and admits spending too much time playing a game called Fruit Ninja. Either way, he spent much of Wednesday angrily lobbing fruit over at the Labour benches. As the Australians say of someone they don't like, 'You know what he can do with the rough end of a pineapple.'

My theory is that the Tories are far more worried about the Labour frontbench's recent successes than they will ever let on. All polls have the Labour party ahead of the Tories, but for the first time some put Ed Miliband himself ahead of Cameron. For nearly two years now, the Tories have said, 'Well, the economy might be a basket case, but at least we know the voters will never pick a Wallace lookalike to run the country.' Now even that comfort blanket has been whisked away. The Conservative party resembles the survivors on the Raft of the Medusa, dying of starvation and thirst, waving desperately at an invisible sail, hearing that someone has just kicked over the last bucket of fresh water.

It all began fairly well. The prime ministerial bald patch was smaller than usual. He merely called Ed Miliband 'incompetent' – poleaxing rather than chillaxing – and declined to answer a question about the 'fire at will' policy recommended by a Tory donor and condemned by the Lib Dems as 'bonkers'. Various oleaginous backbenchers rose to grease about the government's astounding success. Tories cheered him dementedly. Labour MPs cheered Miliband, not least because, for the time being, he looks as if he could one day win an election.

19 June 2012

One of the ministers who most enraged the opposition was Michael Gove, the education secretary, partly because of his radical policies, partly because he seems rather smug, partly because he is cleverer than most of them.

Another lunatic day in British politics. In Europe, the economy was imploding, again. In New York, Boris Johnson was admitting that he yearns for 'supreme power', adding an aside to his interviewer, 'Don't print that', which, of course, is his way of saying, 'Make sure you include that in your article.' As always with Boris, you never quite know if it's just a joke, or if he means it, or somewhere in between.

He spoke about the special appeal of the city of which he is mayor: 'You can't get famous in the fucking village,' adding, 'There is a greater range of girls at the bar, of reproductive choice.'

Sounds like every hour is happy hour at Boris's favourite watering holes. They probably have blackboards outside: '1 main course, 1 drink, choice of reproduction, £9.99. Why not hold your office party in our private womb?'

In London, another possible Tory leader was taking education questions. Kevin Brennan, a Labour spokesman, wanted to know why Michael Gove was having a 'chilling effect' on teacher morale. (This was a reference to Gove saying that Lord Leveson was having a 'chilling effect' on press freedom, a remark that seems to have angered the judge.)

The education secretary replied, 'Facts are chiels that winna ding.' When Labour members laughed at this impenetrable quote from Burns, Mr Gove denounced their party for their failure to increase foreign language skills. I don't imagine that Gove, who is Scottish by upbringing, actually means that 18th century Scots dialect should be taught in English schools, so I suppose he was joking, too. But these days, who can tell? Apparently what it means is 'facts are fellows that cannot be overturned', not a view held by most politicians, who regard facts as chunks of Plasticine, to be moulded into whatever shape suits them best.

There was a brief discussion of sex education in schools. According to Nick Gibb, the minister, there is talk of sending children's sex education DVDs to the British Board of Film Censors. This is extremely bonkers. 'This film is rated suitable for age 15 only. When a man and a lady love each other very much, they look under the gooseberry bush…'

But the finest mad moment came when Steve Pound MP raised the question of schoolchildren's food – not the stuff served in school dinners, but the vile rubbish sold outside schools, such as one in his constituency which is surrounded by 'a cordon of fast-food outlets selling congealed, deep-fried lumps of mechanically extruded neo-chicken sludge.

These foul [or fowl] premises are undermining any attempt at healthy eating!'

Mr Gove heartily agreed. His message was, he said: 'KFC UFO.' There was a pause, then it suddenly occurred to many members of the House that the three initials concealed a rude word, and it had nothing to do with unidentified flying objects. The education secretary may deny that he was hiding an obscenity. But I should warn him that any attempt to wriggle out of it winna ding wi' me, nor wi' Mr Pound, who confirmed that's what was meant.

20 June 2012

The government announced plans to reform the civil service on Tuesday. The scheme boils down to, 'There'll be fewer of you, you'll have to work harder, and if you don't you'll be fired.'

Naturally they can't put it like that. Instead the whole thing was floated on a great flotilla of jargon. Francis Maude, the minister, used enough jargon to stuff a dead grizzly. But he has a diffident, nervous manner, so he sounded more like a vicar in a new parish, listing plans for the coming months.

'We must embrace new ways of delivering services, and need to be digital by default!' he said. 'Digital by default' does not mean you're so angry you can't even talk, so you flip a V-sign instead. Mr Maude presented this wheeze – everything has to be done online, so it will be like trying to book a flight on Ryanair without forking out £100 for 'optional' extras – rather as if he was announcing the date of the harvest festival.

He described the faults in the present civil service. These include 'focus on process rather than on outcomes, a risk-averse culture, and rampant gradism', whatever that might be. ('I regret to say there has been a regrettable level of absenteeism at choir practice.')

The civil service had to be 'smaller, pacier, flatter and more digital'. Like a pancake-throwing contest, I suppose.

The hesitancy grew worse. 'Er, um, transaction and operational,' he intoned. ('In future floral arrangements, instead of being the responsibility of Mrs Bigsby, who we thank for her splendid work in the past, is to be outsourced.')

What was astonishing was that apart from a handful of Labour MPs who jeered at the more egregious neologisms, everyone seemed to know what the minister was talking about. Some of them even nodded wisely when he talked about 'sharpening accountability', 'digital project management capabilities' and 'delivery through the cadre of permanent secretaries'.

Once he had stopped reading out the statement, which was written, I hope, by one of the 10 per cent of civil servants who'll soon be sacked, Mr Maude relapsed into perfectly coherent English, though he did get a little confused at times. 'We do need to say that,' he said at one point, 'because it goes without saying.'

After the discussion, I went digital by default and pulled up the plan on my interweb computer screen. Here the language is even more impenetrable. 'Rigorous daily collective self-evaluation,' is recommended, presumably instead of morning coffee and a biscuit. We need 'lean continuing improvement' and 'demanding methodology'. There is to be something known as 'the delivery landscape'. Sir Bob Kerslake, who is head of the civil service, claims that he is 'passionate... that we must build on what is good'.

'Passionate' is one of those newly neutered words. Once it was about ending world poverty, or loving a good woman. Now sandwich chains claim to be 'passionate about food'.

And it is these people who bang on about 'openness', 'transparency' and 'interfacing with the public' even though the public can barely understand a word they say.

5 July 2012

It turned out that Barclays, and possibly other big banks, had been fiddling Libor, the rate at which banks lend to each other. It is a difficult and complicated matter, but what it boils down to is that bankers were once again enriching themselves at our expense.

Shambles upon shambles! The omnishambles is now a megashambles, a shambles in Europe, a shambles in the banks and of course let's not forget the great ongoing, rolling permashambles of the government.

David Cameron appeared in the Commons to report on the latest EU summit, which as normal appears to have been pretty well useless. Mind you, instead of feebly kicking the can down the road, this time they gave it a slightly harder kick down the road. But, as John Redwood – who always regarded the euro much as Billy Bunter might regard a light lettuce salad – pointed out, there is almost no money left in the existing bailout fund, and the amount proposed in the new bailout fund wouldn't even cover Spain.

As Cameron said, trying to demand a larger fund, but sounding more like the editor of the Sun, 'It's important that the bazookas are big enough.' Supershambles!

Cameron came under huge pressure from the Tory Euro-sceptics, who now think they have a very good chance of getting the 'in/out' referendum on Europe that they have always craved. Ed Miliband, who really is becoming more impressive, accused him of 'weekend hokey-cokey'. On Friday he had ruled out a referendum, hours later 100 Tories had demanded one, so on Sunday he said there might be one after all, at some time or other, and then William Hague had said, 'We are not changing our position!' Aaargh! Hypershambles ahoy!

Miliband pointed out that politicians investigating bankers 'would not command the respect of the British people'. You can say that again. You might as well have an inquiry into used-car dealers by estate agents. The prime minister defended the idea of MPs looking into the bank scandal, rather than a lawyers' inquiry. 'As for the shadow chancellor, no one would like to see him in the dock of a courtroom more than me!'

At this Ed Balls smiled one of the biggest smiles I have ever seen. Forget the Mona Lisa, forget the Cheshire Cat and the Joker – this was a slip fielder whose sledging has just caused the other side's star batsman to hit his own wicket. It was a smile that might have met at the back of his head.

Sir Peter Tapsell arose and pointed out that he had opposed the old regulatory arrangements 'in a speech I made in 1997'. Instantly scores of archivists scurried to the cellars of the Palace of Westminster, where Sir Peter's speeches are all stored on bronze tablets, so that they may be preserved for humanity in the event of a direct bomb hit or, come to that, the heat death of the universe.

5 July 2012

The head of Barclays was obliged to come to the Commons and explain himself to a select committee. He failed.

Barclays' Bob Diamond was on the receiving end of a tidal wave of cynicism, scepticism and sheer disbelief from MPs on Wednesday. Not that you'd have told from looking at his face. It was all so painful for him. He loved Barclays. It was run by 140,000 of the most wonderful people in the world. He made it sound like a cross between the royal family and a charity. They were the most honest people you could ever meet, except when they weren't.

Was he contrite? You might have expected a tiny bit of contrition, like a dob of jam in a cheap doughnut. In fact it was as hard to find as a Higgs boson in the Grand Canyon. You could whirl Mr Diamond round in the Hadron collider without getting a single cheep of remorse.

His technique was to stonewall. He agreed that what had happened was wrong. We know he thought this, because he never tired of telling us. And it wasn't only wrong; it was bad, abhorrent, reprehensible, appalling, inexcusable and improper. It made him angry, really angry. It had made him physically sick! And yes, he was in charge. But he wasn't to blame. Or, as he put it, 'I don't feel personally culpable, but I do feel a sense of responsibility.' Pat McFadden asked if he thought that he symbolised a culture that needed changing. 'I don't think so at all,' he said.

(I wondered where we had heard this before. Why, from other bankers, of course, and indeed from Mr Diamond, who said last year that the time for bankers' remorse was over!)

He didn't know anything. To reverse the saying, it was all below his pay grade. Traders were shouting their mad crooked wheezes across the trading floor, but nobody had told him. It had happened seven years ago, but he only learned this month! Presumably because he loved Barclays so much, he couldn't imagine that anyone who worked for it could do anything bad, wrong, reprehensible, sick-making, etc. Indeed, the problem might have been that some of his employees were too honest. Barclays' Libor rate was too high, which implied that it was having trouble raising funds. So it was in everyone's interests for the rates to be fiddled down! No wonder Andrea Leadsom (Con) inquired whether bankers lived in a parallel universe.

John Mann (Lab), never knowingly underbellowed, told him he'd seen nothing, he'd heard nothing, and he knew nothing. 'Either you were complicit, or you were negligent, or you were grossly incompetent... at this rotten, thieving bank!'

Andrew Tyrie, the chairman, who normally looks like a public school headmaster chastising the boy who threw a stink bomb in the organ loft ('This will hurt you more than it will hurt me'), permitted himself a slight smile at this assault, like the glimpses of sunlight we've had in this miserable summer.

Mr Diamond had clearly been told to keep his cool whatever was thrown at him. He even called the MPs by their first names, as if they were among his oldest friends. They replied with a chilly 'Mr Diamond'.

Near the end, he protested his own decency, honesty, personal freshness, and so on. 'Citizenship is one of my four planks,' he declared. So, as we suspected, he really is a planker.

Now, I have to confess that my seat was opposite Mr Diamond's back, and I could only see the incredulous look on the faces of the MPs. Those who watched on the live feed thought he kept his dignity. It is the first rule of political reporting: being there is a poor substitute for watching it on TV.

10 July 2012

The Liberal Democrats insisted that House of Lords reform had to be tackled in the current parliament. Many Tory MPs disagreed with this, and specifically disliked the plans made for the Lords' replacement – later 91 of them voted against the 'guillotine' that would have pushed the bill through the Commons without filibustering.

The debate on the House of Lords was perfectly bonkers. It began with Jacob Rees-Mogg, the boy who was raised in Harris Tweed nappies, declaring that 'because of the bishops, this is a hybrid bill'. Hybrid is a technical term, but the exciting notion of hybrid bishops could solve all that unpleasant argument in the Church of England. Dioceses that didn't want a woman bishop could have a hybrid one instead. Just don't look under their cassocks.

Nick Clegg rose to a barrage of noise. He revealed that the Queen had already agreed to the bill in advance. She had just rolled over and accepted it, even if it takes away her right to appoint peers, something her forefathers have had for centuries and was especially useful when they were short of money. Or needed a few hundred pikemen.

He declared that there was only one other country in the world that had an unelected second chamber. It was Lesotho. We were supposed to be shocked. I'll bet they're pretty horrified in Lesotho too, realising they're being compared to a gimcrack, dysfunctional parliament like ours.

The noise level grew. Every time Clegg paused two dozen MPs stood up, all quivering to fell him with an unanswerable argument. The deputy prime minister often gives the impression of a supply teacher out of his depth in a sink school. Almost everything he said was greeted by cacophony from the horrid boys at the back of the class. The Speaker had to intervene. Clegg quoted Churchill in his support.

As the Tories cheered, Churchill's grandson, Nicholas Soames, rose majestically to reprove him. His grandpapa had come, over the years, to have a 'great deal of respect' for the Lords. It is apocryphally said of Mr Soames that when he makes love to a woman, she feels as if a wardrobe has fallen on her with the key sticking out. Clegg must have felt a Stanley knife sticking out.

He pleaded. He plucked. He begged. The reform bill was the result of 'sincere' endeavour. As Charlie Brown asked in Peanuts, 'How can we lose when we're so sincere?' Answer: very easily.

At one point he said the bill would pave the way to 'a different kind of politician'. MPs were outraged. Who needs a different kind of politician when you've got us? The noise level rose from 'ear-bleeding' to 'making your eyes wobble dangerously in their sockets'. They jeered like a football crowd, pointing and yelling in effect: 'You're basing your argument on an untenable premise and you know you are!'

The interventions kept coming. Why no referendum? Why a 15-year term of office? Why PR so that the Lib Dems would have a permanent veto? They hated the bill. Almost nobody rose to support poor Clegg, and finally, mercifully, he was able to sit down.

17 July 2012

Next we learned that the 'security' firm, G4S, in spite of winning a £300 million contract to provide guards for the Olympic Games, had admitted – roughly a fortnight before the Games began – that it would only be able to provide a fraction of that number. Their managing director was hauled before an incredulous select committee.

It was horrible, painful, almost bestial. I have never seen anyone get such a monstering at a select committee. If Nick Buckles weren't a multimillionaire who got rich by paying peanuts to people who can't get any other work, you might begin to feel sorry for him.

Almost. As it is, we found it hard to believe not only that he is still in his job as chief executive of G4S, but that he was ever appointed in the first place.

He came across as someone who couldn't organise a tea party at Twinings, or a pig-out in a pie shop. If I saw him searching bags and patting down pockets outside the beach volleyball venue, I'd run a medal-winning mile to reach safety.

Like Manuel, he knew nothing. It had all come as a terrible surprise, mere years after the contract had been signed.

This is how miraculously incompetent he seemed to be: 'My first priority is to make sure that my company comes out with its reputation intact,' he said, in the first few minutes.

Reputation intact? What distant planet does he come from? Its reputation has been shredded across the front pages of the world. They can restore shattered Ming vases these days. But the reputation of G4S is in tiny, irreparable shards, a global joke, a source of multinational mirth.

It didn't help that Mr Buckles wears a silly mullet hairdo, and has a tan that is the result of a recent holiday, somewhere hot, that contrasted with the pallor of most MPs.

But you've never heard of anyone being brown-faced with shame. And he had no more contrition than, say, Bob Diamond. He hadn't known. He hadn't even bothered to find out before coming to the select committee. And he plans to keep the £57 million management fee, on the grounds that they will be delivering some of the promised security guards! This is the equivalent of a plumber bursting a pipe, flooding your house, then demanding his call-out fee because he'd already put a lot of work in.

Here are just some of the words MPs used to describe him and the continuing disaster: 'fiasco', 'shambles', 'humiliating', 'inexcusable', 'astonishing', 'amazing', 'unacceptable', 'amateurish'. And that was just throat-clearing.

Nicola Blackwood told the wretched Buckles: 'Your performance today will lead quite a lot of people to despair.'

Before the meeting she had had little confidence in G4S. 'Now we don't have any at all.'

When the home affairs committee have found a victim they grab him like a pride of lions and chew off as much as they can. When Buckles said that he was 'disappointed' the chairman, Keith Vaz, the Mighty Vaz of Vaz, said that he was disappointed when his football team didn't win. 'Isn't there a better word?' he asked, his voice dripping with sarcasm like juice from a very sour lemon.

Buckles might not have been contrite, but he knew how to do rueful.

David Winnick told him his company's reputation was 'in tatters'. 'At this moment I would have to agree,' he admitted. He revealed that he hadn't known about the crisis until 3 July

– less than four weeks before the Games begin. And three days later his sidekick, the majestically monickered Ian Horseman-Sewell, was boasting they could not only cover the Olympics here, but another one simultaneously in Australia! Wired to the moon, as the Irish say.

Disaster followed disaster. It turns out that too few G4S staff turned up at a cycling event in Surrey. When would Mr Buckles know how few people would show? At 9 o'clock, he said. That's 9pm *after* the understaffed event.

Mr Horseman-Sewell chipped in. There was a difference between people not showing up having been accepted, he said, and a shortfall. We were in the realm of the higher metaphysics. I understood this to mean there was a difference between the no-shows who exist in the form of real human beings, though absent, and shortfall, who don't exist at all.

MPs came up with a stream of horror stories, of constituents who had been accepted and vetted, and had then heard nothing at all. Those who had paid for training then not received contracts. A woman who had spent 84 minutes on the hotline to find out if her son was required, and no one could tell her.

By this time Mr Buckles was looking like a stunned fish – floppy mullet front and back. He was asked if G4S would pay for the accommodation for the police who would need to be drafted in. Long pause. '… Er, yes,' he finally said, making Mr Vaz believe he was making policy on the hoof. By this time, though, I suspected that if the committee had demanded a suite at the Ritz for every copper, he'd have promised it. With no charge for the minibar.

After nearly two hours the horror was over. With a hardly disguised demand from Vaz for his resignation fresh in his ears, Buckles somehow dragged himself away.

Index

Index

335

and Obama's UK visit 250–2
as PM 143
as 'PM for ever' 241
as 'prudent' chancellor 143, 144
Radio 2 appearance of 221–2
'saved the world' speech of 245–7
Smith quoted by 116
as 'Stepfather of the Nation' 219
tackles 'Ecclestone fib' 116
temper of 319
TV debate involving 268–70
and 2000 petrol crisis 116
and 2007 floods 228–9
verb-free sentences of 220
waving inability of 225
Brown, Jennifer 263
Brown, Nick 127–9, 247
Brown, Sarah 116, 265
Brown, William 189
Browne, Jeremy 252
Browne Wilkinson, Lord 70
Bruno, Frank 9
Bryant, Chris 293, 317
BSkyB 315
Buckles, Nick 331–3
Budgen, Nicholas ('Nick') 40
Bumper Boy's Book of Wartime Speeches 146
Bunter, Billy 325
Burns, Robert 72
Burrows, Geoff 128
Burton, John 216, 217
Bush, George HW 38
Bush, George W 239–40
Buster (dog) 170

Cable, Vince 235, 236
conference speech of, 2009 260–1
Callaghan, James ('Jim') 69, 241
Camelot 224

Cameron, David 190–2, 200, 203, 231, 232, 235, 246, 275, 279, 315, 325
ageist insult of 317
Always Look On the Bright Side of Life speech of 300–2
Balls goads 317, 319–21
becomes Tory leader 204
Big Society idea of 267, 286–7
as Blair's heir 204
and Blair's resignation 224, 225
'Bloody Sunday' speech of 280–1
and BSkyB bid 315–17
cartoon character of 18
children of 205, 207
'civil partnership' label of 276, 282
conference speech of, 2008 240–2
and economy 304–5
general election campaign, 2010 265–7
grandiose sentences of 287–8
Incredible Hulk anger of 319
and MPs expenses 256–7
paternity leave of 206–7
at PMQs 204–6, 224, 277, 307–9
and polls 320
temper of 315–21
tipped as Tory leader 191, 193
TV debate involving 268–70
u-turns of 288–9
Webcameron broadcast of 266
Cameron, Samantha 205, 241, 242, 265
Campbell, Alistair 103, 113, 156, 157, 163–4, 181
Channel 5 signs 178–80
diaries of 167, 168
and Iraq War 167–8
Campbell, Ann 30
Campbell, Sir Menzies ('Ming') 187, 224
Cannabis Tree, The 120

Capitalist Realism 73–4
Carlton Club 88
Casablanca 166
Castle, Barbara 69
Castro, Fidel 93
Catchpole, Farmer 259
Catherine the Great 207
Chakrabarti KCB, Sir Suma 313
Chamberlain, Neville 111
Chandler, Raymond 160
Chaney Jr, Yvonne 65
Channel 4 48
Channel 5 178
Channel 7 91
Chapman, Dinos 171–2
Chapman, Jake 171–2
Charles, HRH Prince 265
Hoggart's meetings with 30
Chaytor, David 107
Chelmsford, Bishop of 63
Chesterton, GK 161
Chiltern Railways 74
China Syndrome, The 118
Chirac, Franc 52
Christ, Andy 151
Christie, Agatha 13
Christmas:
cards 76–7, 142
renaming of 101
Church of England 63, 94, 329
Church, Judith 50
Churchill, Sir Winston 146, 156, 158, 330
Cider with Rosie (Lee) 291
Circle of Time 61
Clapham Common 303
Clark, Alan 56, 86
Clark, Greg 227
Clarke, Kenneth ('Ken') 31, 87, 88, 129, 135–6, 302
Clause Four 94
end of 27
Cleese, John 306
Clegg, Mrs 274
Clegg, Nick 237, 247, 274
'civil partnership' label of 276, 282
as DPM 277, 292–4
lack of support for 330

Index

Index

Fordham, Ed 283
forest privatisation 288–9
Forster, EM 139
Forsyth, Bruce 271
Forsyth, Michael 71
Foster, Michael 96
Foulkes, George 62
Fowler, Sir Norman 39
fox-hunting 96–7, 100, 183
Fox, Liam 171
  resignation of 302–4
Freud, Lucian 135
Frinton-on-Sea tennis
  club 3
Frostrup, Mariella 271
Fuck Face 172

G4S 331–3
Gaitskell, Hugh 27, 198
Galloway, George 72
Gardner, Lady 143
Gardner, Lady (Trixie) 143
Garnett, Alf 126
gay age of consent 20
gay marriage 284
gay pride 283
general elections:
and 24-hour news 271
  1992 137
  1997 78–80, 273
  2001 122–7
  2005 187
  2010 263
  celebrities wheeled out
    for 271
  and Cleggmania 268
  exit polls 271
  and hung parliament
    277
  party leaders' TV
    debates, 2010 268–70
  polls 321
  Thatcher wheeled out
    for 78
George III 235
George V 142
Gibb, Nick 322
Giggs, Ryan 296, 297
Gilchrist, Andy 151
Giles Coren's Prison
  Feasts 298
Gilligan, Andrew 162–4,
  166, 167, 169
Gisborough, Lord 70

Give Us a Clue 169
Glad the Impaler 65
Glaisdale, Lord Simon
  of 21
Glastonbury 45, 275
Glorious Future 75
Glossop, Baron Howard
  of 21
Glover, Julian 10
Gnasher 125
goat-fuck 45, 130–1, 274
Goodwin, Archie 111–12
Goodwin, Sir Fred 248–9,
  258
Gordonland 145
Gorman, Teresa 45
Gove, Michael 287, 321–3
Graham, Tommy 72
Granita 23
Grant, Cary 264
Grant, Hugh 196
Gray, James 172
Great Fire of London 258
Great Leap Forward 75
Great Ormond Street
  Children's Hospital
  276–7
Great Scottish Whinge 70
Great White Corona 230
Gree, Ian 33
Greenham Common 52
Greenpeace 104
Greenspan, Alan 249
Greer, Germaine 33
Grieve, Dominic 297
Grossman, Loyd 47
Guardian 1, 2, 18, 50, 107,
  186
  libel cases against 60
Guernica 170
Gyratory Gynaecologists'
  Gulch 27

Habitats Directive 311
Hadron Collider 327
Hague, William 88, 105,
  107, 111–12, 326
  aide shares hotel room
    with 294
  conference speech of,
    1977 47
  as Foreign Secretary
    294–6
  mojo of 294–6

  at PMQs 139
  as Tory deputy leader
    206–7
  as Tory leader 122–4
Hamilton, Neil 60, 80
Hammer 64
Hansard 149–50, 151
Hardie, Keir 198, 299
Harman, Harriet 254, 293
Harris, Dr Evan 282
Harris, Rolf 170
Harrods 32
Harvard 224
Hattersley, Roy (later
  Lord) 50, 170, 270, 278
Hayward, Hattie 7
HBOS 242, 248
Healey, Denis 236
Healey, John 227
Hear'Say 124
Heart of Darkness 152
Heath, Edward 229, 315
Heath, Sir Edward 86
  Thatcher feud with 104
  Thatcher shares
    conference platform
    with 104–6
Heathrow Terminal 5
  fiasco 238
Hegel, Georg 214
Hemingway, Ernest 291
Hemming, John 298
Henry V 158
Heseltine, the Unbalanced
  61
Heseltine, Michael
  ('Hezza') 20, 48, 63,
  96–7, 230
  as Board of Trade
    president 54
  as Lord of Time 61
Hewitt, James 26
Higgs boson 327
Hill, Harry 89
Hilton, Lady 143
Hindenburg 45
Hirst, Damien 171
Hitler, Adolf 98, 167, 290
Hodge, Margaret 317
Hoey, Kate 255
Hoffman, Abbie 12
Hogg, Douglas 48
Hoggart, Simon:
  early career of 1–2

Index

Index